DECOLONISATION AND LEGAL KNOWLEDGE

Reflections on Power and Possibility

Folúkẹ́ Adébísí

First published in Great Britain in 2024 by

Bristol University Press
University of Bristol
1-9 Old Park Hill
Bristol
BS2 8BB
UK
t: +44 (0)117 374 6645
e: bup-info@bristol.ac.uk

Details of international sales and distribution partners are available at bristoluniversitypress.co.uk

© Bristol University Press 2024

British Library Cataloguing in Publication Data
A catalogue record for this book is available from the British Library

ISBN 978-1-5292-1937-1 hardcover
ISBN 978-1-5292-1938-8 paperback
ISBN 978-1-5292-1939-5 ePub
ISBN 978-1-5292-1940-1 ePdf

The right of Folúkẹ́ Adébísí to be identified as author of this work has been asserted by her in accordance with the Copyright, Designs and Patents Act 1988.

All rights reserved: no part of this publication may be reproduced, stored in a retrieval system, or transmitted in any form or by any means, electronic, mechanical, photocopying, recording, or otherwise without the prior permission of Bristol University Press.

Every reasonable effort has been made to obtain permission to reproduce copyrighted material. If, however, anyone knows of an oversight, please contact the publisher.

The statements and opinions contained within this publication are solely those of the author and not of the University of Bristol or Bristol University Press. The University of Bristol and Bristol University Press disclaim responsibility for any injury to persons or property resulting from any material published in this publication.

Bristol University Press works to counter discrimination on grounds of gender, race, disability, age and sexuality.

Cover design: Nicky Borowiec
Front cover image: Adobe Stock/ Tatiana

Contents

Acknowledgements iv
Preface v

Introduction: Setting the Scene of the Law School and the Discipline 1

1 Theories of Decolonisation; or, to Break All the Tables and Create the World Necessary for Us All to Survive 14
2 What Have You Done, Where Have You Been, Euro-Modern Legal Academe? Uncovering the Bones of Law's Colonial Ontology 38
3 Defining the Law's Subject I: (Un)Making the Wretched of the Earth 65
4 Defining the Law's Subject II: Law and Creating the Sacrifice Zones of Colonialism 92
5 Defining the Law's Subject III: Law, Time, and Colonialism's Slow Violence 108
6 The Law School: Colonial Ground Zero – a Colonial Convergence in the Human and Space–Time 128

Conclusion: Another University Is Necessary to Take Us towards Pluriversal Worlds 148

References 158
Cases Cited 190
Index 191

Acknowledgements

To those who have loved me, to those who gave me my name, to those who stand with me, to those who stand against me, to those who see me, to those who do not, to those who gave me words, to those who have questioned me, to those who have inspired me, to those who encourage me, to the things that failed to destroy, to those who will read these words, to those who will not, to the earth we walk on – the earth that will swallow us, to the air we breathe, to those with whom we share this planet, to those we will dream with, to those we dream of, to those we dream without, to the sky we exist under, to the waters we need to live, to those who have gone ahead, to those who will come after us, to the better world we may never live to see, to its dreamers, its architects and builders … I give thanks, I acknowledge you, and to you I dedicate these words.

Preface

I wrote this book because the ideas in it would not let me rest. They would wake me up at night, interrupt my work, and disorder my reflections. I got into the habit of writing these ideas in short notes on random pieces of paper and on my phone, just to get away from them. As academia in the Global North began to be more interested in 'decolonisation' as a term of art, I wrote about these ideas in my blog, in book chapters, and academic articles. None of these formats seemed to properly encompass the broad scope of how I wanted to explore the ways in which decolonisation relates to academic knowledge in law. And even here in this book, there is still more that I want to say.

I came to decolonisation, as a topic of study, before and within my study of law. As a cosmopolitan child of the '80s, I witnessed the global anti-apartheid movement. I read books written by writer–scholar–politicians who were pillars of the anticolonial and decolonisation movements across Africa from the '50s to the '80s. Some who trained as lawyers. So, from quite early on, the study and practice of law pointed me to its liberatory potential for ending continuing colonial logics as well as other global harms and injustices. So, I, like many others before and after me, came to the law school, because I heard freedom and justice and peace in its name. However, in time we all learn, though often not so explicitly, that the coloniser's justice is not justice for the colonised. We learn that 'the claim of the universal translatability of the English word "justice" ... is an extraordinarily presumptive one' (Gordon 2013: 70). We all learn that peace is not equally distributed. We all learn, eventually, that freedom for those racialised below the abyssal line is not the same for those racialised above it. We could suggest that legal education opens students' eyes to the true nature of the law, especially when the focus of legal education is on black letter or doctrinal law. As Justice Oliver Wendell Holmes tells us, 'The common law is not a brooding omnipresence in the sky, but the articulate voice of some sovereign' (in *Southern Pacific Co v Jenson* 1916: 222). Student disillusion it could be suggested then, is caused by false expectation. However, this statement by Holmes not only tells us what is, but also invites us to consider what is possible within legal knowledge. Where does power reside? Whose voice articulates it? What is sovereign in this world?

However, this book is not a how-to on 'decolonising the curriculum'. *This is not even a book about decolonising the curriculum.* I feel that this phrasing (that is, 'decolonising the curriculum') misuses the specific register and nature of colonisation/decolonisation and does not convey precise meaning. 'Decolonising the curriculum' is a phrase that without engaging with the specificity of the political and anticolonial origins of the praxes and logics of decolonisation, operates as a mismatched action and object. In that sense, it is akin to phrases like 'measuring the yellow' or 'climbing the fragrance'. This book is also not an argument for decolonisation. The argument for decolonisation lies in the structures of our world – structures that continue to reproduce racial injustice, extreme poverty, and inequality, as well as environmental devastation. It is evident that at each turning point in history – the end of racialised enslavement, flag independence for colonised nations, the worsening climate emergency, and the necropolitical management of pandemic realities – we continue to miss opportunities to prioritise life – all life – over risky economic largesse for some ... we miss every chance to save from perdition, ourselves, and the earth upon which we currently precariously survive. We miss the chance to fashion a compassionate global and legal system, preferring a dispassionate one that is unable to properly read and protect all life and space–time.

Ultimately, this book is about power and possibility, because through it I am urging us (mainly legal scholars, but also nonlegal scholars and non-scholars) in our use of decolonisation as praxis, to pay closer attention to how power is transmitted through legal knowledge in the university ... through teaching, research, and other related activity. I also want us to be very creative with the idea of possibility. We should be able to push very strongly against the boundaries of what we consider to be possible and settled. So, we can save from perdition, ourselves, and the earth upon which we currently precariously survive. Therefore, my approach to possibility is not just acceptance that the current world's structure cannot bring forth liberation for all, but also the realisation that this is not the only structure that is possible.

This book is meant to open a conversation, not to close it. Thus, understanding the impossibility of tertiary education confining and defining decolonisation, this book focuses on curating, from many schools of decolonisation, some fundamentals of decolonial work that can be done within universities, with specific reference to legal education. I engage with epistemic injustice as a product of colonialism and trace its footprints within legal knowledge. Writing this book comes from the concern that we do not yet have fully developed epistemic tools to imagine and build new, just, flourishing, and inclusive worlds. Consequently, it aims to contribute to thinking through new pathways to lead us to new questions that help us drag ourselves out of the night of human suffering into the light of new worlds. This book is a reminder that despite the inequalities produced by coercive power, the law school and the university still remain fields of possibility.

Introduction: Setting the Scene of the Law School and the Discipline

> What a flimsy thing the law was, so dependent on contingencies, a system of so little comfort, of so little use to those who needed its protections the most.
>
> Hanya Yanagihara (2016: 356)

> The law is the shadow toward which every gesture necessarily advances; it is itself the shadow of the advancing gesture.
>
> Michel Foucault (1987: 35)

Law: the state of play in a field of promise and disappointment

As Yanagihara and Foucault note, law is a powerful and sometimes discomfiting feature of planetary life. These characteristics, especially law's globalising display of power, can be related to the pervasive effect of the colonial project and its exports around the world. One of the oft-cited benefits of colonialism, is the dubious gift to the colonised world of the 'rule of law'. With this 'Law' comes the 'Law School' as an intellectual vanguard. Scattered across the world, these schools are often centres for incubation of new legal minds, but also crucibles of research, revolving around new strands of legal knowledge and thought. This introduction places law schools in a global context, reflecting on the current state of the law school in the UK. This includes a picture of the diversity (a word with fungible and varied meanings) within law schools in the UK, as well as the experiences of marginalised students and staff.

Across my time learning, practising, researching, and teaching law, I have witnessed and experienced the disorientation that comes with the field – punctured illusions and dashed expectations. Our students often arrive at university, full of ideas of what the world is, and the great things they would like to do within it ... and yet the teaching of law can sometimes crush their spirits. We claim to teach them about *the* world, but sometimes we have no idea of what *their* world is. For some, their reality says: '[l]aw is not fair, it does not treat people equally, and its violence is lethal and routine' (Akbar 2015: 355). Without acknowledging the truth of these experiences, the knowledge we transmit about the world proceeds from within the limited and a selective perspective of a discipline implicated in producing unequal social realities. In holding so tightly to the theories, concepts, and principles that we ourselves were taught are sacrosanct, we may lose sight of the potential we have, from within the field, to change those sacrosanct theories, concepts, and principles. Disrupting the production of global and local social injustices and inequalities, means reconsidering the supposed neutrality of our knowledge processes – both in teaching and research. We can re-envision the cultivation of legal knowledge as, '"the practice of freedom," the means by which men and women deal critically and creatively with reality and discover how to participate in the transformation of their world' (Shaull 2018: 34).

Currently, we teach our students a particular vision of a particular world. A world that has been derived from a limited way of thinking about the relationship between humanity and the earth. A world designed by the law as we teach it. (In this book, this version of law is distinguished from pre-existing and still existing indigenous jurisprudence systems.] It can sometimes feel as if Euro-modern legal knowledge is hermetically sealed from the world (Davies 1994: 5). Admittedly, where clinical education and socio-legal pedagogy are offered, there has been and continues to be room to break these seals. Nevertheless, as a discipline and a profession, the field retains immense untapped potential to contemplate the transformation of this current world, marked as it is by massive inequality, political instability, large-scale poverty, and impending environmental collapse. So, the law school stands at the centrepiece of time and space, connecting the past and the future, always questioning possibility ... always promising more.

Most attendees of law schools in the UK (and across the common law world) are undergraduate students studying for a qualifying law degree (QLD). Historically, the QLD was officially recognised by solicitors' and barristers' professional bodies as the first stage in qualifying to practise in either of those branches of the legal profession. The number of jurisdictions requiring a QLD for legal practice is on the wane, however. In the UK for example, the Solicitors Qualifying Examination (SQE) has replaced the QLD requirement from 2021. However, the Bar Standards Board (BSB) still requires the QLD for qualification as barrister. In the UK, this undergraduate degree is completed in a minimum of three years of full-time study. Across the world, wherever law is done as an undergraduate degree, a similar degree would be completed in three to five years. In a

UK-wide historical context, law schools in universities are a relatively recent introduction in the academic and legal landscape, even though both separate spheres of activity – law and academia – have existed for a significantly long time. Yet the endeavour to combine the two, in the UK especially, could only be described as successful after the end of the Second World War (Twining 1994: 25–6). In contrast, in Western Europe, legal education has long been embedded in universities (Stolker 2015: 20). In most countries across the world, the default milieu for the training of each new cohort of legal practitioners is the law school (either as a postgraduate or undergraduate degree), within a university. This predisposition for most of what is designated the Global South, was imported from Europe. Thus, the legal systems in postcolonial/settler states, for which these law schools serve as feeder systems, are usually either common law, civil law, or a hybrid of the two.

In determining the curricular content and research aims of law schools, the emphasis tends to be quite narrowly defined by supposed national needs. This focus often ignores the international origins of national challenges, as well as the origins of borders and of the state itself. It also ignores the fact that human relations on this planet have always been and will almost always be inevitably highly globalised. Human activity is necessarily, and has always been necessarily, simultaneously global and local in nature, and thus inevitably always has had global and local consequence. Thus, one could argue, that the current focus on the state as the predominant organiser of juridical life will be short-lived and has merely interrupted longer periods of more globalised activity on either side of this state-focused era.

These curricular and research aims imbue law schools with varying individual characters, yet this does not completely disrupt their similarities. The canon, the core offering of law schools, around the world almost universally includes private law subjects (for example, tort, contract, land, equity), administrative law (constitutional law, public law) and criminal law. In the UK, the subjects mandated by the QLD are (naming conventions may differ): Criminal Law, Law of Torts, The Law of Contract, Land Law, Trusts, Public Law, and European Union Law. Further to this, it is usual for most law school curricula in the UK to additionally include either as options or core subjects, Jurisprudence, Legal System/Methods, Employment Law, Company Law, International Law, Human Rights, Family Law, Law of Evidence, Banking Law, and Commercial Law. Some of these subjects are part of the core curriculum in countries where the law degree is completed in more than three years. For example, in Kenya, where the minimum length of a law degree is four years, Family Law, Evidence, and Jurisprudence are included in the QLD-equivalent. In Singapore, law students are mandated to study Evidence during their three-year degree.

Research in law schools is also varied and similar, as well as linked to curricular offering. The original impetus of academic legal research in the UK was merely to elucidate legal rules for the benefit of lawyers. However, legal research currently delves into, among other things, the nature of the law itself, its relationship with society, as well as interdisciplinary and empirical research. Some law schools are very research-focused, others vocational, while quite a number sit somewhere in the middle of this spectrum, with staff being involved in teaching, research, and administration in different proportions.

The increasing consumerisation of higher education in the UK has contributed to questioning the value of law schools and the law degree to society. This consumerisation is also implicated in the introduction of the SQE. The growing cost of a university education, as well as the increasing disconnect between the content of law school activity and the society which it serves (local and global), raises questions about the future of the law school in the UK, and around the world. This calling into question is further troubled by the growing diversity of law schools. Diversity brings a multiplicity of knowledge into the law school, challenging the orthodoxy of Euro-modern law's universality, neutrality, and objectivity. Yet, law attempts and has attempted to achieve its pretensions to universalism by synecdochical equivalence between a particularised–sanitised vision of Europe and the world. The law school within a university is home to many universes – a pluriversal space. Yet the untranslatability of these universes inherently woven into Euro-modern law means that only one of these universes is made dominant and universal. What happens to the silenced verses at, and of, the university? Can they ever be put in true equal conversation with Euro-modernity? Can we acknowledge that, 'there is no universal legal code and no such thing as pure legal objectivity, but rather a complex overlapping plurality of legal systems and legal meanings?' (Darian-Smith 2015: 649). Can a diverse law school, without more, cultivate pluriversal legal knowledge?

Diversity is not pluriversity in the university

Law schools in the UK are of various sizes, from over 200 undergraduates per cohort, to over 600.[1] This increase in school size is fuelled inter alia by an increase in numbers of people with 'protected characteristics'. This increase is not replicated in the same numbers across postgraduate degrees and members of academic staff. Consequently, this surge in diversity has

---

[1] UCAS Undergraduate Sector-Level End of Cycle Data Resources 2020 https://www.ucas.com/data-and-analysis/undergraduate-statistics-and-reports/ucas-undergraduate-sector-level-end-cycle-data-resources-2020

not entirely mitigated claims of elitism within law schools. There have been various academics specifically critical of the hierarchical nature of legal study in the UK (Stanley 1988: 78–86; Lacey 2014: 596–600). They contend that the nature of learning in law schools predisposes them to suppress critical reasoning or dissent and reinforce sociopolitical hierarchies, entrenching law schools in an ideology of superiority (Kennedy 1976: 1685; Thomson 1987: 183–97). Thomson particularly suggests that in law schools 'the truth claims of legal knowledge are not only treated as unproblematic but are rarely raised in education at all,' and that there is a certain preoccupation in the foundational subjects with use and content of law that turns legal education into a study of 'rich people's law' (1987:184–5). Stanley argues that the predominance of private law in the 'core' curriculum, 'spurns the practical and the theoretical, and automatically operates to preclude all but the most basic of academic aspirations, as the ideological framework of the hierarchy requires it to do' (1988: 83).

Because law schools are housed within universities, structural inequalities produced by long-standing universities' processes also compound the hierarchisation of knowledge. This is more marked when we consider the multifaceted vulnerabilities unveiled at the intersection of what is simultaneously uncovered and hidden by 'protected characteristics'. For example, non-white students are underrepresented at top-ranked universities and are over-represented at the lower-ranked universities.[2] There is a massive awarding gap between white and Black students;[3] Black students drop out of their degrees at a higher rate, with lower levels of employability; non-white students record lower levels of satisfaction with their degrees, are more likely to be subject to racism or racialised microaggressions that universities seem reticent to investigate or punish (NUS 2012; Neves and Hillman 2016: 10; Mirza 2018: 6–14; Sian 2019: 21–65). Black female students generally indicate much higher levels of anxiety or pressure, aggravated by the foregoing (Aronin 2016: webpage). Non-white students report racial bias from staff and other students, which include low expectations, representations as disruptive, unintelligent, troublesome, and insolent; they feel erased from the content of their study, they feel targeted, and are thus more likely to be isolated (hooks 2003: 48; Warmington 2015: 270). The university and the

---

[2] Between 2007 and 2008, 107th ranked London Metropolitan University had almost as many Black students as all 20 Russell Group Universities. (NUS 2012: 20).

[3] In this monograph, I have chosen to capitalise 'Black' and not 'white'. This choice reflects the central argument in the book. In other words, 'Black' and 'Indigenous' have become ethnicities due to the systemic and historical erasure of 'Black' and 'Indigenous' groups. This use is therefore contextual to the argument of the text itself. This approach has been followed by many institutions, including Associated Press: https://apnews.com/article/archive-race-and-ethnicity-9105661462

law school reflect the society in which they operate; the society which has been produced by a particular history with negative ideas about particular groups of people (Shilliam 2018: 5).

This picture is compounded by Euro-modern law's pretensions to objectivity, neutrality, and universality, which ignore historically contingent contemporary entanglements between power and possibility. Burridge and Webb posit that by adopting neutrality and eschewing any emphasis on values within legal knowledge in law schools, the pursuit of neutrality operates to the detriment of the pursuit of good (2008: 266). Haraway also disputes the disembodied nature of academic objectivity which asserts 'the power to see and not be seen, to represent while escaping representation ... [arguing] this gaze signifies the unmarked positions of Man and White' (1988: 581). For Haraway, all knowledge is subjectively situated and embodied. Thus, the type of objectivity often pushed forward in law schools is a denial of the body and a denial of space–time (Foucault 2021: 139–64). It is a distortion of reality. What Crenshaw calls 'perspectivelessness' – the idea that to know and apply the law is to stand outside of life (1988: 1–14). Law has a certain origin, trajectory, and history; it has alliances with different manifestations of coercive power, embedding within it the interests and desires of the powerful. In this sense, law is not just an abstract tool for regulation, but it also carries within it, its own directions. It is: 'a form of power/knowledge that actively constructs [political] desire and regulates the modes of its insertion into executive policy-making, legislative schemes and judicial processes' (Modiri 2015: 248).

Consequently, claims to academic objectivity deny the enfolded truth of the world in which its legal knowledge has been and is being produced and transmitted. A claim to all-seeing objectivity, neutrality, and universality refuses to engage with the workings of power, the restriction of possibility in legal meanings, as well as the universalised 'particular' that is Western masculinist law. This position, therefore, ignores the not-so-hidden covenant between Euro-modern legal knowledge and many forms of power – including racial, class and patriarchal power. Such legal knowledge (in this book described as Euro-modern legal knowledge) reflects 'the cultural values associated with whiteness' (Davies 1994: 314). Whiteness, here, represents a power structure that does not always correlate with skin colour racialised as white. Whiteness as a legal and global power structure,

> institutionalizes the enduring asymmetries of power between the global South and global North and pervasively fashions and legitimates certain legal practices, meanings, and imaginations that have their origins in the global North [and thus] remains to this day intrinsically and pervasively cultural and racially biased. (Darian-Smith 2015: 649–50)

Such law, 'is the creation of a particular set of historical and political realities and of a particular mind-set or world-view' (Nunn 1997: 325). This worldview sharply contrasts with jurisprudence from within indigenous knowledge systems (in this book, this includes not just indigenous knowledge from the Americas and Oceania but also from Africa and Asia). Therefore, the question that confronts us is not just the problematic of a body of law that universalises the powerful–provincial and erases the abyssal–peripheral, but how that universalising conceptually and persistently renders certain bodies and space–times untranslatable and illegible through Euro-modern law. In other words, the pact between law and power manifests itself in legal meanings that impose hierarchical boundaries between what should be similar bodies and spaces and temporalities (Pirie 2013: 52–72). Thus, 'historical injustices' of indigenous dispossession can often be considered moral or temporally defunct questions beyond the purview of contemporary legal knowledge. Similar boundaries could also be drawn in discussions of current police brutality, selectively hard borders, domestic violence, homelessness, climate change, and so on. In drawing these illusory boundaries erasing embodied and situated knowledges, Euro-modern law presents itself as a legal fiction that creates legal fictions of life (Williams 1988: 13). This tendency is (re)produced both in research agenda as well as the assemblage of curricular content. Thus, the legal curriculum also reveals itself as 'part of a selective tradition, someone's selection, some group's vision of legitimate knowledge' (Apple 1993: 1).

Legal knowledge in law schools, in this guise, not only denies bodies and space–time, but fundamentally denies its own ontology. By being silent on these erasures and epistemic 'borderisations', Euro-modern legal knowledge can shroud in mystery its own complicity in (re)producing inequalities in the world and so present itself innocent of the violent societal abstractions committed in its name. Therefore, Cohen's discussion of law as a social process bears detailed reproduction:

> the notion of law as something that exists completely and systematically at any given moment in time is false. Law is a social process, a complex of human activities, and an adequate legal science must deal with human activity, with cause and effect, with the past and the future. Legal science, as traditionally conceived, attempts to give an instantaneous snapshot of an existing and completed system of rights and duties. Within that system there are no temporal processes, no cause and no effect, no past and no future. A legal decision is thus conceived as a logical deduction from fixed principles. Its meaning is expressed only in terms of its logical consequences. A legal system, thus viewed, is as far removed from temporal activity as a system of pure geometry. In fact, jurisprudence is as much a part of pure mathematics as is algebra,

unless it be conceived as a study of human behavior – human behavior as it molds and is molded by judicial decisions. Legal systems, principles, rules, institutions, concepts, and decisions can be understood only as functions of human behavior. (1935: 844–5)

Thus, Cohen reminds us that the social process of law makes those processes contingent upon human structures of coercive and authoritative power. A corpus of legal knowledge that is silent on this, cannot honestly produce and transmit true knowledge. This is important as people often look to law to provide solutions to local and global problems. However, borderisation within the study and practice of law distances itself from originating the world's challenges … this self-imposed distance from reality makes the law immaterial (Grabham 2016: 13). Therefore, the field has been criticised for holding itself forward as being able to resolve challenges manufactured by itself … a dishonest field that perpetuates itself by creating problems and providing ineffectual solutions – creating a never-ending need for itself (Thomas 1973: 295). By denying its own ontology, Euro-modern legal knowledge forecloses the possibilities of transformation that it promises to many who enter into its field and many more outside of it who look into it for hope.

In response, critical legal studies and its offshoots lean heavily on the boundaries that law places between itself and social realities. In a broad sense, critical legal studies, as a field, by dwelling on the entanglements between being and knowledge, questions and critiques how orthodoxy in law, legal research, and legal education avoids drawing necessary links between law and the sociopolitical/socioeconomic realities they produce (Davies 1994: 191). This area of study seeks to trouble the presumed objectivity, positivity, neutrality, and transparency of Euro-modern law. However, despite the ambitions of critical legal studies, I suggest that the field does not go far enough in those ambitions. It often takes an atomised approach to confronting power, either conceptually (law and economic theory; law and gender; law and race) or jurisdictionally. In other words, restricting their analyses by space–time. Conceptual restrictions often take the concept's boundaries as fixed, while the borders of jurisdictions place spatial limits on such confrontations. This is not to dismiss critical legal studies to the advantage of decolonising theories. They are both options to which we can turn, which we can read together (as is done in this book) to offer us an after-world, beyond this apocalypse, rather than mere evaluation.

Apart from offering hope for transformation, unsettling law's assumptions of objectivity is also of specific pedagogic merit to help *all* learners of law understand the truth about the structure of the world – how it is produced and maintained. The current silences about Euro-modern law's ontology also operate as a specific form of violent, and sometimes traumatic, epistemic 'gaslighting' to students and staff whose embodied and situated knowledges reject the hagiographies of Euro-modern legal knowledge. Law students and staff who have constantly lived their lives on the other side of the power of these processes – those for whom the intersection of embodied-situated knowledges of law is particular – are not easily appeased by law universalist affects. Therefore, demands for change, such as for 'decolonisation' and 'antiracist pedagogy', are often heard most stringently from these bodies of bodies. Such university citizens recognise that Euro-modern objectivity masquerades its violence by maintaining the status quo as norm. This status quo normalises structures in which people with 'protected' characteristics, within the institutions of the law school and the university, to receive any protection, must persistently narrate themselves as harmed, as damaged, as broken … to a supposedly objective, but actually disbelieving audience (Tuck 2009: 409–28). An audience unwilling to see them, unwilling to disrupt their own comfort by an inch and so unwilling to change the system from which they benefit. Diversity is offered as a panacea to this harm. Yet without acknowledging the pact between power and Euro-modern legal knowledge, diversity merely diversifies the face of power, is based on deficit logics and so problematises the very people it claims to protect (Adebisi 2021: 429–39). This form of objectivity also lends itself to the continued disappearance of knowledges and bodies, either through epistemic violence or state violence that disappears bodies into prisons, beneath waters, under unmarked graves, and even into thin air. Refusing this violence means recognising all lives are precious … including the lives of agents of structural violence. They too do not have to live this way. None of us do. This is the unfulfilled promise of the law school – that we may within it cultivate the knowledge to produce flourishing, new worlds.

Beyond diversity: liberation, justice, and the promise of decolonisation

The continued dominance of doctrinal law, as Thornton argues, arises from law's propensity to reflect the interests of the powerful (1998: 370–72). Consequently, capital interests and power direct the ontology of law and therefore, Euro-modern legal knowledge, causing a seeming commitment of doctrinal law to 'rules rationality' and protection of capital. Darian-Smith, who describes the ontology of modern law as 'Euro-American', echoes and complements Thornton's argument, by tracing law's current origins to the economic power dictates of the colonial project (2015: 647–51; 2013: 247–64). Thus, Euro-American law, according to Darian-Smith, is law which began in Europe, but also arose out of colonial activities in the Americas, Africa, Asia and Oceania, and whose ontology places Euro-America at the centre of the world. This designation intimately ties

Euro-modern law to colonialism's interests, origins and uses. Further to this is the fact that the outcome of colonisation for most of what is now designated the Global South, was the transplantation of this ontology of law across the world, in tandem with the erasure and/or demotion of indigenous jurisprudences. Thus, this globalisation of a particular vision of law (and humanity) is implicated in the definition of colonialism used here – an ontological condition of modernity which outlives administrative and territorial colonisation and describes 'long-standing patterns of power that emerged ... that define culture, labor, intersubjective relations, and knowledge production' (Maldonado-Torres 2007: 243). It is these long-standing patterns of power, the mechanisms for reproducing them, and their outcomes, that are of concern to this book. Colonialism as a mechanism of material accumulation and dispossession, of necessity produces specific inequalities that cannot be repaired solely by diversification. Decolonisation within Euro-modern legal knowledge requires us to interrogate its role in producing these inequalities through the persisting, mutating, and interweaving scarlet thread of colonialism, and to unceasingly and effectively, act in response. This action comes with no guarantees, despite requests for assurances of success. Nevertheless, humanity faces increasing dangers from global injustice, massive inequality, and environmental devastation – dangers which find some of their originating and/or crystallising logics in the capitalist-colonial-enslavement project (by which I mean the continuous entangled hierarchisation of humanity and space–time that mainly serve the accumulation of capital).

What could it mean to 'decolonise the Law School'?

'Decolonising the curriculum/law school' has become a term of art, whose activity, especially within higher education in the Global North, often does not involve decolonisation at all and whose proposed area of influence should extend well beyond the curriculum. Therefore, in this book, I am more interested in exploring what decolonisation is, broadly, than in adopting this misused term of art. At the outset, it must be accepted that for the discipline to embrace decolonisation as praxis, academics must very deliberately acknowledge and oppose the problematic premises upon which the discipline has been advanced. Consequently, Chapters 1 through 5 invite an unsettling of some specific premises, especially the ways in which uses of body-politics have facilitated the granting of unequal transactional value and power to the human and to space–time. So, we must recognise that the very onto-epistemology of Euro-modern law, by regulating and reproducing Eurocentrism, has placed primary value in property and property-fication as well as its relationship to capital accumulation. It has through these processes made itself a shape and container for Euro-modernity and the resulting law/legal knowledge is therefore not an 'empty vessel' into which we can pour our boundless hopes for new worlds. In response, according to Baars, '[o]ur resistance must turn against the concept of private property, against capitalism and against law: away from legal emancipation and toward human emancipation. Our imagination and our organising must turn towards the creation of alternative forms of relating, producing, and distributing' (Baars 2019: 379).

In line with Baars, this book is not prescriptive about the ways in which this turning away must proceed but, sets up and ultimately suggests entry points into varied individual and communal action that engages with the praxis of being in a law school for the purpose of flourishing worlds beyond it. This includes looking further than our very narrow definitions of law and our restricted understanding of the world, to include indigenous jurisprudences and other ways of knowing, being and thinking in the world. Thus, it is important to decentre Europe in our understanding of law – including the spaces and times in which both intersect. Decentring Europe means dismantling its unchallenged epistemological position as the self-justified standard of humanity, legal epistemologies, political structures, and legal conceptualisations (Gordon 2014: 88–9). This decentring allows us to see the past, present, and future in ways that engage with new possibilities for 'relating, producing, and distributing'. It should be noted that an admonition to decentre Europe is not an embargo on studying the space, men, and times of Europe and Euro-modernity, but a request to stop studying these as if they are unquestionably superior and universal stories of the world.

It is important to note, that as a theory and practice within legal knowledge, decolonisation cannot be its own goal. In other words, a critical adoption of decolonisation should be done for the purpose of the world it may produce, and not just for a department to identify itself as 'decolonised'. Decolonisation as a political project responds to specific untenable conditions of global life. The aim of decolonisation anywhere is that decolonisation should no longer be the aim everywhere. There is a difference, therefore, between 'decolonisation' (within and outside of academia) that merely *acknowledges* the colonial nature of a discipline and decolonisation that seeks to *disrupt* and *dismantle* the colonial nature of the world. There must be an honest recognition that within higher education, the workings of institutional power mean that the most radical instances of 'decolonisation' only begin to hope to do the former, and the space to do the latter often exists outside of academia. These structural and epistemological limitations should not lead to an abandonment of decolonisation as praxis but, may help us not to over-exaggerate the impact of our activity within it, in the spaces we teach, research, work and live. In other words, we need to work within the limits of what is achievable inside law schools within neoliberal universities, embedded in capitalist structures, while we simultaneously create new worlds beyond them. Thus, our work will accept that units and degrees cannot really be 'decolonised' when they are subordinated to institutions, professional standards, nation states, and global orders that rely on colonial logics and praxis. However, we can, within these structures, reimagine the world we want our epistemologies to produce. Thus, we must have as our guiding star, decolonisation as an immediate, continuing, and stubborn refusal of colonial conditions of domination, dispossession, and dehumanisation, as well as of the epistemologies that keeps coloniality eternally reemergent. Consequently, for our purposes, *decolonisation is not curricula/research redesign or innovation*, though these may help us achieve our goals. Decolonisation's strategies present to us, as Icaza suggests, a decolonial 'option' or toolbox (not a grand theory), to reimagine the world (2017: 27). In other words, for those of us within academia, who wish to adopt its logics and praxis in our work, decolonisation (as a collection of theories and praxes) is one means to redesign our work, so that it redesigns the world. While simultaneously being alert to the ways the long-entrenched structures of the world (including Euro-modern law and the logics of the capitalist-colonial-enslavement project) are constantly acting back on us and redesigning us (Willis 2006: 70).

Nevertheless, and consequently, in our consideration of what is required to radically redesign the world, we must be able to distinguish between what can be reformed and what must be abolished. In making this distinction we need to be alert to the dangers of re-narrating institutions and structures of physical and epistemic violence as sites of liberation. Decolonisation demands that some structures be dismantled. We must also understand the temporal space between reform and abolition, into which we need to invent praxes and theories that will fill the gap left by what has been dismantled, lest it resurrect, vampire-like. Furthermore, marrying decolonisation with legal knowledge necessitates an appreciation of the context-based and multifaceted approaches within theories and praxes of decolonisation. Effective utilisation of decolonisation in legal education requires us to engage with how law's complicity with slow violence shows up in macro and micro ways in legal education.

Therefore, one of the reasons I suggest it is impossible to effectively 'decolonise our teaching/research', is that this ambition fails to acknowledge how colonial logics have ordered the university sector and the world in which we live. The standards to which we teach, research, and work within academia are continually subjugated to logics of (dis)possession introduced and intensified during the colonial-enslavement project and globalised under the auspices of capitalism. In other words, the university and its history have been complicit in colonialism, in patriarchy and in capital accumulation, and those logics have shaped the world, the university, and the law school in very fundamental ways. Unsurprisingly, due to pressures from within and without, the space of the university remains hostile to knowledge cultivation that seeks to change the outcomes of this complicity. It is naïve to suggest, therefore, that a curriculum, or research project or university department is decolonised when it sits within a neoliberal university and is enmeshed in a world driven by racialised capital. What this book strives for, is a way to engage with those tensions, while still remaining true to the radical vision of decolonisation.

Outline

The book is ostensibly divided into three sections. The first section, which includes this introduction and the first two chapters, sets the scene, and spatial–temporally locates the law school within colonial and decolonial knowledge structures. This section contextualises the relationship of decolonisation with legal knowledge within the Euro-modern law school. It begins with an introduction to the law school as well as an examination of the nature of the law school which makes it a prime focus for decolonisation. This is followed by a chapter that draws together the strands of the many theories of decolonisation, and then suggests some preliminary guiding principles for decolonisation within universities. The first section draws to a close, by examining how, not just the letter of the law, but also its conceptualisations, have aided and reproduced the logics of the capitalist-colonial-enslavement project. The second section, Chapters 3–5, is an epistemic journey that unpicks these conceptualisations. Its purpose is to apply the guiding principles of decolonisation to understanding and deconstructing the colonial cleavages within legal knowledge. Therefore, Chapter 3 engages with how the law (mis)understands the human/body, while Chapter 4 and 5 considers the same in respect of space and time respectively. The final section, Chapter 6, and the book's conclusion, returns to the space of the law school to re-examine the questions that have been posed here in the introduction: How should a commitment to decolonisation be operationalised by legal academics? What does this commitment mean for the university and the world beyond it? In making some concrete suggestions, this book concludes by reminding us, that we are facing a structure and not an event. The capitalist-colonial-enslavement project was built to last. If we do nothing to rethink it, it may bring to fruition the end of humanity and the earth upon which we currently precariously survive. While ending this project may seem to be an impossible task, the bounds of human possibility are only limited by human knowledge and human experience. Neither has proven to be finite. A final note, before you dive in. This book is not meant for legal 'experts' only. We are all subject to the law. Therefore, it is up to us all to collectively discern the very nature of the law, its history, and use, so that we may together determine where we want it to take us.

1

Theories of Decolonisation; or, to Break All the Tables and Create the World Necessary for Us All to Survive

> The essential thing here is to see clearly, to think clearly – that is, dangerously – and to answer clearly the innocent first question: what, fundamentally, is colonization?
>
> Aimé Césaire (2001: 32)

> Another world is ... necessary, for this one is unjust, unsustainable, and unsafe. It's up to us to envision, fight for, and create that world, a world of freedom, real justice, balance, and shared abundance, a world woven in a new design.
>
> Starhawk (2008: 8)

Introduction

As Césaire notes, any engagement with theories of decolonisation requires an appreciation of the spatial–temporal contexts in which the colonisation/decolonisation co-constitutive relationship has evolved. In addition to this, Starhawk points us towards a desirable direction for decolonisation. Therefore, it must be understood, that without a longitudinal and planetary study of different context-based evolutions of decolonisation's theories, action that purports to engage with it will be superficial, unable to grasp the contingencies, exigencies, purposes, and limitations of their analyses. Therefore, this chapter focuses on a detailed examination of the colonisation/decolonisation interrelation, especially theorisations that conceptualise the normativity of the colonial in constructing theoretical and practical opposition to it. This examination proceeds through the different contexts in which this colonisation/decolonisation relationship manifests itself: settler states, post-colonial states, as well as within colonising states, such as the UK. Special attention is paid to the spatial–temporal continuities and overlaps within these structures and their refusals … noting that the long survival of the logics and praxes of ongoing colonialism is due, in part, to its ability to co-opt the other, adapt itself, and evolve when necessary. Therefore, context-based refusals have always also had to adapt and evolve, especially to the contexts in which they find themselves and the tools to which they have access. Thus, Baldwin noting these continuities in structure and refusal, invites us to imagine and accept that the civil rights movement in the US was just another in a long line of slave rebellions (1979). In the same vein, prison and police abolitionists narrate the end of formalised racialised slavery, not as a break, but a point of continuing evolution of new forms of racialised capitalist exploitation (Leroy 2021: 8). Similarly, postcolonial theorists and indigenous writers have always reminded us that colonial control is ongoing (Hall 2017: 24). Consequently, the propensity of evolving colonial regimes to co-opt languages of refusal also manifests in the infection of radical writing and praxes with the same structure that is being refused within them. This is evidenced by Global South scholars canonising decolonisation theories when these theories gain prominence in the Global North, effectively building 'an empire within an empire' (Cusicanqui 2012: 98). Hence, radical language is diluted and misused by political and academic praxes that reify the logics they claim to refuse. This chapter critically summarises these theoretical refusals in this light. The approach adopted does not attempt to exhaustively define decolonisation – this in neither possible nor desirable. Rather I recognise decolonisation as a set of strategies whose instant expression and articulation respond to the relevant space–time manifestation of the evolving and mutating superstructure it refuses.

It should be noted that the inherent nature of theories of decolonisation, and therefore an examination of them, is one of disobedience to dominant theory and practices of frame-working. Theories of decolonisation operate against normative method and the purposes and interests of colonial ideology. Decolonisation seeks the abolition of the ongoing and evolving structures of violent exploitation including the epistemologies that keep them in place. So, this is also a chapter of disobedience, that refuses to comply with the standard expectations of theoretical framework. It hopes to find purchase in the uncertainty of the in-between spaces, where hope is manufactured in the dark, in places where we cannot see each other, yet together dream of the light of the possible world to come. Therefore, while Euro-modern law is an intricate co-constitutive part of the push and pull of the social (re)production of colonisation/decolonisation, this chapter takes a step back from it to focus on the big picture of the world of the colonial and its refusals. It should always be remembered that decolonisation as a language, logic, and praxis, emerges as a specific political project, instituted in response to a specific structural and global injustice, but also describes 'a radically transformed future for denizens of both colony and metropole' (Gopal 2021: 881). Thus, decolonisation is inherently and irrefutably present, forward-looking, and anticolonial. While the rest of this book traces how the ongoing colonial structure bleeds into Euro-modern legal knowledge in the academy, this tracing is intentionally not its entry point into the conversation about decolonisation. By centring itself in decolonisation, the academy in the Global North ignores its own power and complicity in ongoing colonialism, and thus continues a history of co-optation of the radical language of decolonisation and anticolonial resistance. This chapter attempts to step back from that centring.

How did we get here? A brief voyage of colonial discovery

Colonialism is used here to mark the continuities of the capitalist-colonial-enslavement project, whose inauguration is dated to 1492. This coincides with the inception of the New World voyages such as Christopher Columbus' first journey to what has now been named the Americas, Jan van Riebeeck landing in what is now known as South Africa, and Captain James Cook's arrival in the now-named Australia (Fernández-Armesto 2013: chapter 1; Seed 2015: 58–82). Sylvia Wynter dates European imperial activity earlier, as beginning with the Portuguese invasion of Senegal West Africa in 1444 (2003: 257). These 'discoveries' of not-missing land, resources, and people has had a drastic effect, globally and conceptually, on all three. At the opening of 1492, civilisations had existed in (places we now call) the Americas, Africa, Asia, and Oceania for many generations. Europe was one among many. Each civilisation had its own concept of law, of philosophy, and religion – of being, of thinking, of knowing. At that time, living standards across the world were comparable to each other, with continental Europe accounting for 15 per cent of global GDP (Hickel 2017: 58–63). African polities had steadily risen in affluence, enjoying intra-regional trade and intellectual advancement (Niane 1984: 1–14; Rodney 2018: 33–48). This level of activity was also replicated in Oceania and Asia; the volume of intra-regional trade precluding necessity for wider exploration (Fernández-Armesto 2013: 210; Dalrymple 2019: 57). With the invasion and violent settlement of the Americas came the globalisation of the extra-spatial 'Europe-as-idea' (Glissant 1992: 2), and a European dominated market. Globalisation, thus, was initiated by the extermination of indigenous populations (and their knowledges) for their land and resources (most prominently gold); the introduction of epistemologies that maximised production from land, resources and people; and large-scale enslavement of survivor indigenous populations which utilised dehumanising ideas about who could be properly included in the narrowly-conceived category 'human' (Hickel 2017: 58–63). These ideas and the actions they inaugurated were extended across the world. For example, in Oceania, Europeans invaded, exterminated, and replaced the local population (Roberts and Westad 2013: 659). Syndemic massive **population loss** and destruction of structures of living were common features of Europe's encounters with the rest of the world. The Great Dying in the Americas is estimated to have resulted in 56 million indigenous deaths from new diseases, violent invasion, and the disruption of pre-existing ways of living (Koch et al 2019: 13–36). Heralded by Magellan's voyage in 1520, similar causes resulted in Oceania's indigenous population loss of about 40 per cent (Caldwell et al 2001: 35). In Asia, the most major population changes are associated with colonial administration rather than invasion. For example, a high estimate of 29.3 million deaths were said to have resulted from colonial maladministration of famines in India (Davis 2002: 7). The most significant population loss in Africa, however, started in the late 15th to early 16th centuries and involved the kidnap, forced transportation, and enslavement of Africans.

The trade in enslaved Africans was initiated to provide a source of cheap (unfree) labour in the Americas to enable the exploitation of land expropriated from the indigenous population, and to replace the exterminated population as a source of coerced labour (Rodney 2018: 78). The already lucrative and thriving markets in what is now called Asia were violently and forcibly subsumed into a totalising unitary idea of 'The Market' which ignored and extinguished alternative and pre-existing ways of commerce (Waites 1999: 59–90). This market – essentially the global colonial economy – was responsible for forging still extant economic connections among nations in the Global North, predicated on wealth gained from racialised enslavement and exploitative colonisation, using manufactured logics of racialisation as a technology for accumulation and dispossession of thus racialised populations (Bhambra 2020: 1–16). In other words, European nations not directly involved in the enterprises of enslavement and colonisation still benefitted from them, and the logics that prompted them. It is important at this juncture to understand European colonisation of the rest of the world as a unique form of colonisation which operates as continuation of the logics and praxis of enslavement and not a break from it. Consequently, Arendt makes a distinction between properly expansionist empires of Ancient Europe and the exploitative empires introduced in the late modern European period (1973: 130–2). In exploitative empires, slow death is spatially removed from the metropole and the market for unfree labour and manufactured goods is widened, but not much else distinguishes it from racialised enslavement. Thus, the spatial containment of slave plantations was replicated in the colonies. Best distinguishes these as empires of conquest, exploitation, and settlement, where exploitation occupies a halfway point between the other two – more than administrative control and less than complete control (1968: 283–326). The exploitative empire in both Arendt and Best's readings does not settle, but uses all its tools – military, legal, administrative, and epistemic – to extract like a vampire. Consequently, I designate non-settler colonisation as exploitative, relying as it does on targeted dispossession for the purposes of boundless extraction.

This deep intimacy between enslavement, colonisation, and accumulation weds them inexorably to universalising the market and the emergence of capitalism, as well as local and global inequality. The global market that emerged contingently, required universalising legal regulation which was introduced in part through the legal control of trade and the introduction of company laws to allow corporations (such as the East India Company) to administer enslavement and colonisation on behalf of European empires (Tharoor 2018: chapter 3). Families who benefitted from the global colonial economy were also most likely to be represented in the legislature of their nations, and thus be able to argue to protect familial financial interests, as was the case with William Gladstone. Gladstone, who later became Prime Minister, was influential in enabling legislation for Joint Stock Companies. His father, John, had been one of the largest owners of enslaved labour. He held nearly 3,000 enslaved people in chattel captivity and received over £100,000 in compensation for the loss of their coerced labour (current equivalent of about £83 million) (Hall et al 2014: 8, 140, 275; Ireland 2018: 379–401).[1] This largesse was funnelled into rentier shareholding.

Therefore, a significant aspect of this totalising of the capitalist-colonial-enslavement project is its impact on Africa – the continent, its peoples, and the very idea of Africa. Kidnapped Africans were simultaneously made lucrative objects as well as valueless humans (Williams 1988: 16). This enterprise of devaluation of life resulted in a population loss for Africa and a capital gain for Euro-modern polities. Eltis surmises that the numbers of *enslaved arrivals* from Africa in the Americas during this time, was just over 11 million (2001: 17–46). In between the population loss occasioned by violence in kidnapping Africans for slavery, detaining them before transportation, and death during the voyage, Rawlings and Behrendt, consider the population loss to Africa 'incalculable'. (2005: 365). This absence of figures of lives lost reflects a logic of un-mattering of Black life that continues presently. Thus, the increase of the economic power of Europe was accompanied by a devaluation, of not just the agency of African polities and peoples in the market, but also the value of Black life itself (Williams 2014: 306). In other words, the ascendancy of Eurocentrism was and is contingent on anti-Blackness. Eurocentrism

---

[1] See also: 'Legacies of British Slavery' https://www.ucl.ac.uk/lbs/ (Accessed 21 February 2022).

thus reveals itself, not as a universally natural tendency for ethnocentrism, but as a dominating force subsuming and subordinating in degrees, any epistemology or entity considered to be non-Europe … Blackness most of all. Eurocentrism describes and inscribes white supremacy as a longstanding political project – a 'racial contract' between populations racialised white or white adjacent … thus, underlining the populations whose consent or political will keeps the political project in place, which populations are agents of the racial contract, and which populations are the object of this contract (Mills 2014a: 3, 7, 11–12).

Yet, the lines between agents and objects become blurred as do the lines between the period of appropriation and accumulation by racialised enslavement and the period of appropriation by colonising territory. Colonised territory was needed for plantations for which enslaved labour was used. When racialised enslavement was ended by those who introduced it, to maintain monopoly over the wealth acquired therein (Williams 2014: 306), pre-existing colonialism gained dominance in global relations as colonisation/empire. Thus, by the end of the 19th century, most of what is now designated the Global South was governed by an imperial European power. This process was effected by non-recognition of indigenous populations, their law, and their epistemologies. Designation for colonisation was racially coded and was accompanied by dubious legal mechanisms for racialising people and acquiring the land occupied by the thus non-recognised (Anghie 2007: 52–114; McCarthy 2009: 8, 24, 64). These mechanisms included opaque treaties and conquest on questionable pretexts. 'Race' emerges through this process not as a biologically significant category with unfortunate political uses or implications, but as 'a political category that has been disguised as a biological one' (Roberts 2011: 4). Quijano posits that the artificial production and historical use of race as a political technology, originating in 15th century colonial encounters, creates and reproduces contrived material distinctions between groups of humanity (2000a: 534). Race-making originated in Europe, was initially applied as a technology of power to populations now racialised white, before being solidified into current ideas linking race to skin colour (Robinson 2000: 10–24). This process of making race significant involved deploying an overlapping triptych of 'Commerce, Civilisation and Christianity'. 'Christianity' was a mask for the minimal educational opportunities offered to the colonised, which helped ease colonial administration, but universalised Eurocentric cultural values (Adebisi 2016: 433). 'Civilisation' was promoted as encouragement to the colonised to mimic what they could never become – the image of impossibly-superior-masquerading-as-normal-but-unreachable Europe (Said 1994: 22–31). These were coupled with the promise of commercial affluence to the racially dispossessed, which involved further opening up colonised territories to the global market. This required, for example, building railways to transport goods from the hinterland to the coast for onward transport to the imperial metropole (Eichhorn 2020: 204–9).

In its ascendancy, the absence of the United States from this global market and its desire to be included and dominate it, contributed to international political moves for 'decolonisation' (Nkrumah 1966: 239). In other words, the radical anticolonial language of decolonisation was co-opted for use for the evolution and continuation of the capitalist-colonial-enslavement project. 'Decolonisation' was used to describe activity that was not anticolonial. Administration of territories was thus followed by a rapid period of what is called decolonisation, in the middle to end of the twentieth century, but this period actually witnesses and more accurately describes the efficient transformation of the capitalist-colonial-enslavement project (Nkrumah 1966: 239–54). This process, triggered by the dual forces of anticolonial movements and increasing globalisation, saw many new states morphing from colonies to nations and proclaiming self-rule. However, there was no accompanying dismantling of the global power structures, logics, economies, and epistemologies that had driven the amalgamated practices of colonisation or racialised enslavement. These include logics of commodification of space–time and the human. This performative gesture to decolonisation limited the meanings to which its praxes could be put, by restricting its actualisation to Euro-modern nation states as the sole juridical source of emancipation. A failure to dismantle empires completely, means that their logics and praxes are ongoing yet evolving. Physical and overt political manifestations of imperialism and unfree labour were removed from sight, but the epistemological, geopolitical, and financial mechanisms remain in place. Thus, I distinguish 'colonisation' – the administrative control of the territory of the 'other', from 'colonialism/coloniality' – the power structure that enabled and survives both racialised enslavement and exploitative colonisation.

Essentially, from 1500 till the present, through legal, conceptual, and academic non-recognition of personhood, as well as capture of pre-existing class and racialising–dehumanising narratives for the purposes of accumulation, colonial logics continue to be (re)produced. This is the 'colonial matrix of power' Quijano describes (2000a: 533–80; 2016: 10–23). This colonial matrix is assembled, Quijano explains, by the Eurocentric practice of racialising populations which creates social relations of domination between the coloniser and colonised, between the master and the one forced to provide unfree labour (2000a: 534). Our present inequalities are marked by and in the continuing search for unfree labour for the purposes of accumulation and the various socio-legal tools for adducing value to labour and resources. Therefore, as racialised enslavement, colonisation and neo-colonisation operate on the same epistemologies of person, and space–time, they (re)produce innately similar geopolitical inter-dynamics. Colonialism appears, thus, not as an event (colonisation), but as an interruption and reordering of human interactions and relations with the planet. Euro-modern legal knowledge appears as the handmaiden of this old–new order and the unwitting architect of its reproduction. The consequence of the introduction of this mode of organisation of the world was to also restrict the possibilities to which humanity and the earth could aspire. The capitalist-colonial-enslavement project resulted in 'societies drained of their essence, cultures trampled underfoot, institutions undermined, lands confiscated, religions smashed, magnificent artistic creations destroyed, extraordinary possibilities wiped out' (Césaire 2001: 43).

At the dawn of 2022, in which I write this, 'civilisation' has acquired a unitary Eurocentric meaning. There is one civilisational concept of law, of philosophy and religion – of being, of thinking, of knowing. The living standards across the world are now tremendously incomparable. There is a clear abyssal line almost irrevocably dividing social realities in the South from the North (de Sousa Santos 2016: 70–1). The Global North accounts for at least 42 per cent of global GDP, despite having only a 17 per cent share of global population (Solarz and Wojtaszczyk 2015: 812; IMF 2021: 37–42). In addition to this, accounting for lost growth, it is calculated that since 1960, the Global North has drained from the Global South resources worth $152 trillion (Hickel et al 2021: 1037). Yet, Global South states are beholden and dependent on the Global North through aid, debt, and for ways of being, of thinking, and being known. Non-European participation in the market is simultaneously trapped in the paradox of lucrative objects (their resources and labour) and disposable life. This paradox is evidenced by fortress-like practices of 'borderisation', which reduce previously colonised places into modern-day plantations, from which the populace cannot move, without being hunted down for return. Into this world decolonisation cannot be introduced as a metaphor but must offer theories and praxes for us to imagine and build new worlds. Thus, contemporary demands for decolonisation (no matter how varied), embed within themselves a temporal-spatial breadth, that manifests not just in representational requests but invites a confrontation with and disruption of the reproduction of colonial logics.

Decolonisation or how we get out of this here: an analogy on the colonial table

Despite their temporal-spatial breadth, theorisations rejecting ongoing colonialism often arise out of specific contexts. Therefore, the praxis, conceptualisation, and language adopted by thinkers and workers of decolonisation often reflect these specific contexts. Decolonisation can therefore be described as a collection of anticolonial strategies and trajectories whose boundaries are delineated, not only by the manifestations of the specific colonial manifestation contested, but also the structural and epistemic tools contextually available. To illustrate the convergence and departure points within this collection, I have often found it useful to offer an analogy of a table: Picture a large dining table. The table is laid with as much affluence as our imagination can manage. In this analogy, the table itself and the feast upon it, represent the material and structural benefits of colonialism. Access to the table is the privilege that whiteness/white supremacy provides – notwithstanding how one is racialised. Note that, as with all analogies, this is not perfect. Some anticolonial critiques do not confront or name colonialism directly. There are overlaps and divergences across and within critiques. Nevertheless, I find this analogy useful to explain how decolonising movements sometimes seem to contain divergent aspirations, and decolonisation may sometimes be heard as a collection of contradictory demands.

Decolonisation I: Give us an equal seat at the table/we want our own table/you made a table out of our lives

Decolonisation I represents varied critiques of colonialism from postcolonial states, mainly in Africa and Asia. Most notable here is 'postcolonialism'. As a critique of colonisation and colonialism, it is sometimes written as one word to denote the *longue durée* of resistance to colonial logics within postcolonial states. Thus 'postcolonial' here does not describe the endpoint of colonisation but defines postcolonialism as an immediate response at and to the moment of the colonial encounter, that also continues after the formal end of physical occupation (Gandhi 2019: 3). One of the main concerns of postcolonialism and similar related theories, is exploring why full liberation was not achieved upon the physical exit of the colonising powers. This is often illustrated by distinguishing such liberation from 'flag-independence' – which is identified as a transformation of colonialism and its enduring control (Nkrumah 1966: ix). The main concern of postcolonialism is a diagnosis of the inner workings of colonial permanence, but there has still been room within that diagnosis to imagine the end(s) of colonialism. Thus, Fanon though describing decolonisation, carried out in practice, as a superficial replacement of the old-colonial with the new-postcolonial, argues, nevertheless, that any movement towards new anticolonial worlds is progress that challenges colonial power (2007: 2). Consequently, contesting colonialism, no matter how seemingly unsuccessful, disrupts its complacent claim to control.

Furthermore, the geographical span of the postcolonial world results in immense diversity within postcolonialism that renders its available means and desired trajectories equally diverse. Surprisingly, postcolonial hopes have been almost uniformly frustrated. This frustration is explained by Memmi as pervasive and complete (2006: 67). This is often baffling and disappointing, because, by being forced to retain the laws, structures, and epistemologies of the coloniser (Darian-Smith 2013: 247–64; Darian-Smith 2015: 647–51), it is expected that the benefits that citizens of the coloniser state enjoy(ed) will eventually and naturally accrue to the newly independent populations. In other words, because they have mimicked the coloniser, the coloniser's benefits should be mimicked in their realities. Yet mimicry never becomes mastery. As Bhabha states, 'the disavowal of difference turns the colonial subject into a misfit – a grotesque mimicry' (2012: 107). The colonised is not himself, but he can never really become the coloniser either. Thus, gaining colonial benefits is impossible because of what Nkrumah describes as neo-colonialism – where a state's economics and politics are directed by more dominant external forces (1966: ix). Consequently, there is an overlap here with Decolonisation II, as indigenous scholars also argue that epistemologies of time, place, and person have been distorted for colonial purposes and must be repatriated for true decolonisation. So, as is the case with settler colonialism, 'decolonisation' by handover of colony and colonial government to externally controlled local autocrats does not become liberation. Veracini argues that this type of decolonisation is 'the culmination, not the discontinuation, of colonialism' (2014: 622).

Beginning in the 1960s and '70s, many postcolonial political leaders, who were also prolific writers on the postcolonial condition, considered the possibility of flag-independence becoming economic and political emancipation from colonialism. For example, Thomas Sankara of Burkina Faso described the heavy financial burden of debt on African countries, as a 'cleverly organised reconquest of Africa' (1988: 375) and urged African nations to collectively refuse to repay their debts. He was assassinated within a year of making that statement. In Tanzania, Julius Nyerere introduced a Freire-inspired farm-school system based on institutionalised practices of *ujamaa* – a principle of familyhood that emphasised the collective over the individual – as well as the University of Dar es Salaam with its postcolonial curriculum aimed at the masses (Ibhawoh and Dibua 2003: 62; Mayo 2012: 44–51). These social experiments have not been resounding successes. Yet, many anti-colonial activists in this vein, including, Mahatma Gandhi and Amílcar Cabral, recognised that liberation required more than physical departure of the colonisers but also psychological reclamation of the 'native self', as well as continued cultural and economic resistance to colonialism, especially its inherent subsumption of non-West bodies, languages, knowledges, and spaces to the needs of the Market (Wa Thiong'o 1992: 4–5; Cabral 2016: 115–39).

Unfortunately, this desire for reclamation has sometimes manifested as a distortion of decolonisation that is evidenced by rampant hierarchical financialisation, violent exclusionary nationalism, and xenophobia. In Côte d'Ivoire, for example, *ivorité* – authentic Ivoirian identity – was codified into law as a stipulation that political candidates and voters must be born of two native Ivoirian parents. This led to widespread political and electoral violence, most notably between 2010 and 2011 (Ipinyomi 2012: 157). In India, this type of nationalism, which co-opts and distorts the language of decolonisation, is exemplified in the long-historied rise of Hindutva – a form of right-wing nationalism that has occasioned violence against anyone who is considered 'other' to the constructed 'pure' national identity (Basu 2020: 163). Further East, the contrivance of 'Asian Values' has been used as an authoritarian justification for buying into the economic benefits of free market growth without implementing political freedom (Welzel 2011: 29–30). The root causes of waves of violent xenophobia in post-apartheid South Africa directed against immigrants from other parts of Africa have been linked to national beliefs in South African exceptionalism resulting from adopting the settler-colonialist's anti-Blackness (Mapokgole 2014; Tella 2016: 142–58). This turns away from Biko's Black Consciousness, in which he seeks solidarity among all people racialised Black in refusing integration into the standards, values, and practices of colonialism (1981: 133–42). In short, these distortions co-opt the language of decolonising in ways that mirror colonial practices of hierarchisation, power, and control.

Fanon, therefore, blames liberation leaders who fail to complete the work of emancipation by refusing to imagine the mechanics of transition to a world no longer dominated by colonialism, for the failure of decolonisation (Fanon 2007: 1–51). These leaders fell back into bad habits of political and social control that they had learned from the colonisers, while expressing surprise that the tool of oppression which they had taken control of, continued to oppress. In fact, Fanon argues that nationalist flag-independence is often only of concern to the bourgeoisie who aspires to a status comparable to the bourgeoisie of the coloniser country. Therefore, the colonised-bourgeoisie enlists the colonised-proletariat to his cause of 'decolonisation' – only for the colonised-proletariat to realise that the status wished for by the colonised-bourgeoisie is dependent on the oppression of his accomplice–proletariat. Thus, this type of nationalism, as well as distortions of radical language, reveal themselves, not as a repudiation of colonialism, but a demand for a share of (control of) it. So, Cabral cautioned against interpreting stepping into the shoes of those in colonial power as liberation, where oppressive hierarchies remain (2016: 77–8). In response to these internal colonial tendencies, the concern of subaltern studies has been to reposition intellectual analyses of the postcolonial condition from the perspective of the subaltern – placed as they are at the bottom of the social, political, and economic structures of society (Saldívar-Hull and Guha 2001: 42; Gandhi 2019: 2). However, Spivak in her critique of intellectuals who purport to represent the subaltern, notes that the mechanisms through which academic thought is parsed, inherently places the subaltern in shadow (1988: 271–313). Purportedly liberatory intellectual thought, in its attempt to represent, and emancipate, has not been able to divorce itself from the logics of colonialism, its mechanisms, and epistemologies, especially its entanglement with commodification and erasure. Thus, for the postcolonial, decolonisation has meant confronting the continuities of the colonial in all postcolonial spheres. Imagining beyond-colonisation from Decolonisation I, emphasises ways to describe the postcolonial condition, but fewer ways to go beyond it. Therefore, Decolonisation I often seeks a seat at colonialism's table or the freedom to lay its own.

Decolonisation II: Give us back our table/that is not even a table, genius!

Decolonisation II describes critiques of colonialism that mainly emanate from indigenous peoples in settler states – North America, Oceania, Palestine, and South Africa. Settler colonialism – characterised by invasion and replacement of indigenous populations – is quite distinct from other forms of colonialism (Veracini 2011: 5). Here, settlers arrive as colonisers. Then they decide to stay, not as immigrants, but as sole recognised authorities in the territory they now understand as theirs. The territory gets new names, new modes of government and living. The settlers' epistemologies and ontologies of life take pre-eminence in that territory. In other words, 'settlers become the law' (Tuck and Yang 2012: 6). Veracini compares the distinctions between settler colonialism and non-settler colonialism to the difference between viruses and bacteria (2014: 617–30). Both are harmful, but bacteria can live inside or outside a body, while viruses need a host to survive. Thus, the settler often denotes their moment of 'decolonisation' as the state of no longer being controlled by an external force, as well as the granting of equal rights to those from whom land was appropriated, while simultaneously, the mechanism of settlement continues the process of invasion and replacement of the indigenous population. Settler colonialism needs the host to survive. Consequently, Wolfe describes settler colonialism, as 'a structure, not an event' (2006: 388). As structural manifestation, the law's architecture is complicit in the establishment and continuation of a settler state. Therefore, for the indigenous population replaced, decolonisation requires action materially specific to their situation, which responds to the specific vulnerability to extinction in which they find themselves.

To achieve settler colonialism, indigenous jurisprudences, epistemologies, and ontologies are erased and/or reworked to produce new and dangerous relationships between individuals and nature as well as between individuals themselves. Among other things, 'land is remade into property and human relationships to land are restricted to the relationship of the owner to his property' (Tuck and Yang 2012: 5). The indigenous population is under constant danger of extinction as the logical progression of settler colonialism is to extinguish the settler–indigenous demarcation by permanently disappearing indigenous peoples (Wolfe 2007: 147; see also Veracini 2011: 3). Thus, for those indigenous peoples, decolonisation means the end of settler colonialism – the unworking and revival of indigenous jurisprudences, epistemologies, and ontologies; the permanent undoing of the settler identity and its contingencies – their ownership of the land and their legal authority. In other words, decolonisation 'requires the repatriation of Indigenous land and life' (Tuck and Yang 2012: 21) and necessitates 'the bureaucratic, cultural, linguistic and psychological divesting of colonial power' (Smith 2013: 101) It is material *and* long-term, because, settler colonialism is not a temporally restricted event, and neither is its negation. Giving back the table, requires new meanings and modalities. There is an overlap however, between Decolonisation II and III, therefore, the analogy continues in the next section.

Decolonisation III: What if that was not a table?

Decolonisation III is located within the Latin American and Caribbean decolonial school of thought (LACDS). This school, particularly, uses 'coloniality' and 'decoloniality' to describe the ongoing colonial condition and the means for transitioning to a world beyond it (Maldonado-Torres 2020: 117–32). There is a commonality within this context and the first two – all three are reactions to the permanence of the colonial project. However, the trajectory of thought here departs from the other theoretical positions, especially in how the 'beyond-colonial' condition is imagined. This departure is mainly occasioned by intellectual articulation of the failures of other attempts at decolonisation in the region and elsewhere. Furthermore, while the geographical area encompassed by the LACDS can be described as both postcolonial and settler-state, here, the length of time after physical occupation differs from Africa and Asia. Finally, the diverse nature of colonial interaction involved more hinterland incursion. In essence, inter alia, Portugal and Spain ran their colonies differently from France and Britain. These provide possible reasons why in the time since flag-independence, the main intellectual concerns in the region have evolved from postcolonialism to dependency and development (Coronil 2015: 177). This process helps to uncover the inadequacies of certain forms of pseudo-decolonisation that actually reify colonialism. This reification led Getachew to make a distinction between the conventional view of decolonisation as nation building, to recast it as 'world-making' – the creation of a 'domination-free and egalitarian international order' (2019: 2). Thus, post-coloniality in the region combined with the historical use of unfree labour, the specific nature of regional settler colonisation, as well as erasure of indigenous populations and epistemologies in this region, inaugurated a diversity and complexity of responses to colonialism that decentre Anglophone colonialism by adopting a wider and longer worldview which deliberately includes regional contexts (Mignolo and Escobar 2013: 16; Escobar 2013: 33). Therefore, planetary analyses as opposed to nationalist ones, emerge quite strongly within Decolonisation III. As the nation state, border-thinking, and their emergence are intimately implicated in the exclusionary trajectory of colonial processes, these analyses unseat the nation state's predominance in beyond-colonial imaginings (Sanjinés 2013: 160). Consequently, while postcolonialism sometimes seeks equality with Euro-modern thought, within decoloniality 'it has become indispensable to globalize the periphery' (Coronil 2015: 189). Therefore, rather than aspiring toward-Europe, Decolonisation III's questioning of Europe-as-idea that universalises itself, is imbued with intentionality in globalising the critique of coloniality (Escobar 2013: 41). Thus, the inevitability of both capitalism and modernity as well as their ensuing effects, are called into question, including the markers of state success and human development (Coronil 2015: 189). This troubles the position of the nation state as the key site of our analysis of juridical life, especially its continued utility beyond-colonialism (Sanjinés 2013: 160). Put differently, Decolonisation III is particularly concerned with the accumulation of power implicated in the emergence of the big picture of the current world, entangled such as it is with coloniality/colonialism, modernity, and capitalist exploitation, and also characterised by inequality, Manicheism and epistemicides (Maldonado-Torres 2007: 244). Of particular interest here is their critique of the design of the world and the complicity of Euro-modern legal instruments and knowledge in, through appropriation, bringing about and reproducing this present state of a world that cannot account for lives lived beyond its epistemologies (Escobar 2013: 50; Mignolo 2013a: 364).

This critique also troubles the promise law offers for world-redesign for purposes other than those which are predominately allied to power and the injustices that that alliance produces. According to Decolonisation III, Euro-modern law is implicated because the world that coloniality produces is characterised by the introduction of race as a technology for hierarching humanity; the globalisation and latitudinal demarcation within a singular market based on dispossession of land and unfree labour; the destruction of non-European epistemologies; and the coloniality of gender (Maldonado-Torres 2007: 244; Lugones 2013: 369–90). These produce, seemingly in perpetuity, differential hierarchised material results along (and compounded) socially constructed demarcations such as race, gender, class, and sexuality (Quijano 2000a: 544–5; Mignolo 2013b: 3). Essentially, because Euro-modern coloniality inaugurates itself as a system that hoards power along these lines by normalising and normativising itself (Boatcă 2013: 224), it imposes itself, over other ways of living and knowing as, 'the pinnacle of a progressive transition;' through 'the colonization of space and time to create a narrative of difference' (Mignolo 2013a: 324). Decolonisation III is quite intentional about disrupting supposed inevitabilities in patterns of power. Thus, 'coloniality', describes: 'long-standing patterns of power that emerged as a result of colonialism, but that define culture, labor, intersubjective relations, and knowledge production well beyond the strict limits of colonial administrations' (Maldonado-Torres 2007: 243). These patterns of control are kept alive through varied mechanisms of power in the modern world which rely on colonial logics – therefore, modernity is suffused with and underwritten by coloniality (Mignolo 2011: 1–2). Everywhere we go coloniality follows us. Everywhere we stand is colonial ground.

Decolonisation III describes the dismantling of the colonial matrix of power and relations and presuppositions that arose from it. This is because Euro-modernity requires complicity with the matrix, especially as regards the structures that ensure the governability, regulation, replication, and legitimation of and within the matrix. For example, development discourse is beholden to nation state structures whose configurations materialise and solidify with the colonial project (Quijano 2016: 10), and thus must accede to civilisational and modernising narratives which are themselves predicated on racialisation and Manicheanism. Consequently, it is understood that coloniality introduces as well as globalises domination and exploitation into social relations between groups of people, across genders and sexualities, by creating false universal epistemologies regarding ways of knowing, doing and being. In response Decolonisation III asks for these modalities of life to be completely unworked (Mignolo and Walsh 2018: 17). Furthermore, by overemphasising the importance and exceptionalism of the human in the world, coloniality introduced over-exploitation into human relationships with each other and nature. This is characterised by use of unfree labour for maximum productivity, destruction of nature, overconsumption and false scarcities which are all implicated in environmental disasters and climate emergencies, essentially, 'the negation of earth' (Vázquez 2017: 78; also, Jackson 2020: 2).

One of the suggested epistemic responses to the foregoing from Decolonisation III is transdisciplinarity or suspension of disciplinarity – recognising the complicity of the academe and its disciplinary divisions in fragmenting reality and enforcing inevitability, especially in the emergence and maintenance of coloniality (Gordon 2014: 81–92). Decolonisation III also suggests decentring/delinking of knowledges that have been used to dominate. This is not an argument for replacement, but a demand for an equality of knowledges, as well as the languages which carry them. Language plurality recognises the untranslatability of epistemologies that do not require their knowledge to be parsed through colonial languages. This aspiration for pluriversality borrows its ideas from indigenous epistemologies of the Zapatistas, who fight for 'un mundo donde quepan muchos mundos' (a world where many worlds fit) (Escobar 2011: 139). A more legal-political suggestion from Decolonisation III is the concept of *vivir bien* – to live well – a way to rebalance relationships that have been distorted by coloniality (Vásquez 2012: 241–52; Ranta 2016: 425–39; Dolhare and Rojas-Lizana 2018: 19–29). *Vivir bien* has been adopted – with limited success – into state policy in some Latin America nation states and arises from an interpolation (and slight misreading) of various indigenous epistemologies from Latin America. It rejects the Euro-modern presupposition that the human/individual is dominant and strives to make the good of planetary community predominant by grounding life in practices that promote harmonious respect of all life and nature (Dolhare and Rojas-Lizana 2018: 20–21).

Despite the lofty ambitions of Decolonisation III, its scholars have often been accused not only of being abstract in their aims but also of co-opting and diluting indigenous thought, especially as regards their responses to settler-colonialism. By focusing on the 'decolonial' and not the 'anticolonial', scholars run the risk of translating indigenous epistemologies and ongoing resistance to colonialism, not into action but into mere performance. These translations that emphasise pluriversality, often ignore the universalism of anticolonial movements which critiqued Euro-modernity's pretentions to universalism but did not decry universalism themselves (Gopal 2019: Introduction). The internal class hierarchies within most decolonial discourse result in scholars based in Global North ivory towers, granting themselves the spotlight and deradicalising the conversation (Cusicanqui 2012: 101–104). They thus build lucrative academic careers by misinterpreting indigenous thought and action. This gives them a platform to create new comfortable canons, within which the subaltern still cannot speak. So, decolonial scholars, demanding citation and representation, become authorities for conversations that centre themselves instead of those who are doing the actual intellectual and physical work of dismantling colonialism in the everyday, wherever they are. Decolonisation III, like all theorisations of decolonisation, runs the risk of being an exercise in navel-gazing that can never amount to liberation. Therefore, while Decolonisation III requires an ontological deconstruction of the table and requestioning of its purposes, this is also a question turned inward.

Decolonisation IV: What can be said from the table?

Decolonisation IV describes critiques of colonialism that come from within the heart of empire. This critique of colonialism is fraught with tension, because its emergence is forever imbricated with the logics of what it is trying to dismantle. So, it is very likely to stray into an altruism that replicates colonial logics. For example, paternalistic developmental support, which, to stretch the analogy, tells people how to build their own table while preventing them from building the table. Yet while Decolonisation IV runs the highest risk of co-optation by colonialism, it also reflects a long history of decolonisation movements within empire which have been diversely peopled. This is directly influenced by the multicultural nature of the imperial machine. Therefore, different traditions and consequently different directions of decolonisation are more likely to find themselves represented in Decolonisation IV. Where there have been attempts to theorise the demands of decolonisation, these theorisations have relied on the three other schools of thought for articulation of scholastic imperatives. So, apart from the more superficial attempts at decolonisation, which amount to no more than cursory attempts to diversify while maintaining hierarchies, Decolonisation IV responds directly to Decolonisations I-III. Where the demand from below the abyssal line has been 'Give us back our table', Decolonisation IV says 'Give them back the table'. This is particularly exemplified in the campaigns to return museum items acquired through colonial violence (Hicks 2020: 235–42). Decolonisation IV's response to Decolonisation I is often radical inclusion. This has manifested mostly within academia and has not been replicated as much within political and economic spheres. Decolonisation III invites Decolonisation IV as an accomplice. In other words, Decolonisation III requires an ontological deconstruction of the table and the requestioning of its purposes. And yet, it is still a question turned inwards. What world do we wish to produce from our work?

Decolonisation X, or things that do not fit on the table

There are other schools of thought that do not fit precisely into the table analogy. The conditions they theorise are intimately linked to its structure, even when they do not always implicate empire in their emergence. For example, Critical Race Theory (CRT) and the Black Radical Tradition (BRT). These two strands of **Decolonisation X** (designated here as Decolonisation^{CRT} and Decolonisation^{BRT}, respectively) find their origins in the USA, mostly as a reaction to the precarious modalities of life of Black people in the United States, resulting from racialised enslavement, 'Jim Crow' legislation and contemporary concerns relating to police brutality and over-incarceration. These historical and contemporary positions should not be divorced from their eventuating factors, such as the annihilation of indigenous peoples, the appropriation of indigenous land, and the use of unfree labour to cultivate it.

CRT arose mainly as a trenchant critique of the pretensions of the legal system in the US to race-neutrality. The foundational tenets to CRT implicate law in the (re)production, entrenchment, and normalisation of socially constructed race. The process through which race is constructed essentialises and naturalises the materiality of hierarchised categories. Thus, 'Whiteness' is identified as a system of both material and psychological advantage, yet its invisibility allows the quotidian functioning of structural racism to remain uninterrogated. Societal focus is only captured by the most blatant and often violent isolated instances of individual racism. Consequently, what is considered progress towards racial equality only happens because of 'interest convergence', when the interests of those racialised white converge with the interests of those racialised as not-white (Delgado and Stefancic 2017: 8–11). 'Intersectionality' is also of particular importance to **Decolonisation**^{CRT}, as it highlights how the essentialisation of identity renders the legal system unable to attend to the combination of vulnerabilities (race, gender, sexuality, class, ability, and so on) that are themselves often a product of social forces (Crenshaw 1990: 1241). Thus, Decolonisation^{CRT} plays close attention to how the meanings of identities are distorted by social forces and produce attendant material effects. For example, the meanings attached to Whiteness exceed variable skin colour thus racialised. These meanings include innocence, competence, trustworthiness, financial fluidity, and so on. They place themselves in direct opposition to a particular articulation of Blackness. Whiteness, therefore, has a particular value, reserved meaning, and specific place (Traber 2007: 13; Leonardo 2009: 92). Whiteness operates as material property in its capacity, not only to adduce material benefit, but also to exclude and include (Harris 1993: 1736). Blackness is articulated as the opposite of Whiteness.

On the other hand, the Black Radical Tradition (BRT) or Decolonisation^{BRT}, whose thinkers include Marcus Garvey and W.E.B. DuBois, departs from CRT on certain foundational aims. Firstly, Decolonisation^{BRT} articulates a meaning to Blackness that fundamentally departs from racialisation's reproduction of *being black* as essentially, irretrievably, and completely negative and inherently linked to racialised enslavement and the property-making that chattel slavery and its afterlives relies on. Decolonisation^{BRT} also includes Black Marxism as theorised by Cedric Robinson, which questions the atomisation and demarcation of class analyses from racial ones. Robinson argues that racial violence is not an incidental nor anterior factor of capital accumulation but is permanently implicated within it (Robinson 2000: 9–28 see also Kelley 2017). Thus, where Decolonisation^{BRT} departs most from Decolonisation^{CRT} is in its deconstruction of the role of the state and therefore the futures that can be imagined through the lens of each theory. By recognising the emergence of the state as linked to the colonial and racialisation processes through which wealth was extracted from Black unfree labour and through dispossession of indigenous land, Decolonisation^{BRT} questions the adequacy of the state as a vessel for achieving emancipatory justice. This structural implication informs Gilmore's definition of racism: 'the state-sanctioned or extralegal production and exploitation of group-differentiated vulnerability to premature death' (2007: 28). If the state is permanently implicated the (re)production of racial violence, can racial justice be achieved through it or even within it?

One could argue that because Decolonisation^{CRT} is focused on the US and its law, its theorists have not been able to make a wider historical and spatial analysis. Yet, Decolonisation^{CRT} has introduced some of the most sophisticated studies of law and race that transcend the USA. So, Meghji argues for a theoretical synergy of decolonisation and CRT to broaden and deepen the spatial-temporal ambit of our understanding of racial inequalities (2020: 1–18). This would allow the combination of micro and macro analysis of colonialism, especially in intragroup disparities across constructed identity traits. Nevertheless, though the inclusion of indigenous CRT within Decolonisation^{CRT}'s multiverse manages to embed some aspects of theoretical decolonisation into its analysis, scholars within Decolonisation^{BRT} pay closer attention to the settler nature of the US nation state and therefore the colonial dispossession of indigenous land. So, BRT scholars reflect a more spatial–temporal breadth due to the range of contexts upon which they draw (Andrews 2018: Narayan 2019: 945–67).

Summarising Decolonisations I–X

To conclude, all these schools of thought that critique the capitalist-colonial-enslavement project, identify logics that were put into play by it, and that have had continuing material effect. Nevertheless, the major distinctions between (and even within) theories of decolonisation relate mainly to ontology, means, and ends. While, the positions converge as material and epistemic repudiations of the colonial, that seek within their articulation an 'after-colonial' time and reality, the main ontological question is whether colonialism is the inescapable condition of humanity. Consequently, some of Decolonisation I (and to some extent Decolonisation^{CRT}) argues for a share in colonialism – even when the demands are not phrased in that way. Therefore, this narrative of inevitability and inclusivity within colonialism feeds into a misunderstanding of the implication of emerging global powers. To misunderstand the conceptual, ontological, and spatial–temporal entrenchment of colonialism is to perceive the emergence of China for example, as evidence of the *end* of dominance of colonial logics and praxes, rather than as a tussle for *control* of them. A rigid spatial–temporal colonial logic divorces effect from cause in geopolitical relations (Quijano 2013: 30). Thus, the emergence of new global powers operating on colonial logics, replicates smaller scale diversity measures that entail nothing more than reifying power by diversification. One of the main aims of this summary is to unveil the limitation and diversity of critique, as well as fragmentation within anticolonial movements. For example, the global anti-apartheid movement, was anti-racist, but not necessarily anticolonial or anticapitalist or antipatriarchal. New South African decolonisation movements in the 21st century have paid more attention to the continuities of capitalism, colonialism, and patriarchism. Furthermore, this summary aims to reduce the seeming impossibility of the task of decolonisation by tracing its various trajectories, its triumphs, and travails. This is because there needs to be, at the very least, an understanding of the differing pathways that demands to 'decolonise' can set off. But putting to use all anti-colonial tools within schools of decolonisation is of necessity a planetary endeavour that requires, not just global, but transdisciplinary conversations and solidarities – especially 'South-South' ones. Legal epistemological involvement in these must realise that they are in service to the survival of the world – the service of designing normativities for a world of living, thinking and being otherwise. As we face the great challenges confronting interhuman relationships and the relationships between humanity and the planet, a redesign of this world is urgent and must be made possible.

To reiterate, 'to decolonise' encapsulates a collection of connected activities and purposes that seek to fundamentally unseat colonially produced structures of coercive power and technologies of permanent dispossession and dehumanisation that threaten human and planetary survival. In other words, colonialism, as the currently dominant mode of world-making, underwrites accelerated accumulation through dispossession. Conversely, decolonial strategies seek new ways of living, thinking and being in the world, that enable earth and its inhabitants to exist in harmonious relation and not brutal dispossession.

Defining decolonisation for higher education in the Global North: some guiding principles

The summary given illustrates how both colonialism and decolonisation simultaneously operate as logics and praxes. The tools deployed in decolonisation are often dependent on the structure it is refusing. These complexities require more than what representation, equality, diversity, and inclusion offer in response. They can be good measures of the progress of decolonisation, but using them as goals destroys their utility as measures. This use also disregards the fact that to be effective, colonialism has always and continues to include within its working, quislings, and unwitting agents from beneath the abyssal line. Diversifying the face of coercive power is not the same as dismantling it. What needs to be interrogated more closely in extricating the subsummation of anticolonial politics from representational rhetoric, is the historical and contemporary entanglement between knowledge and power, across space–time, as well as the evolution of resistance to this entanglement. Therefore, I posit that contemporary movements such as 'Black Lives Matter' and 'WhyIsMyCurriculumWhite' emerge on the other side of a long history of property-making and un-mattering of Black life, and dispossession of indigenous and colonialised peoples, as a specific demand to recognise this history and undo its consequences. To understand this point is to avoid an atomised approach to decolonisation. To recognise this history is also to acknowledge that the recent proliferation of decolonising movements in the Global North is a wave in an ocean, not an isolated moment, but a continuation of previous activity across space–time. Consequently, in defining the boundaries of what decolonisation means within universities in the Global North, it is important to recognise the place of these universities in the long history of anticolonial intellectual production and praxis that has often happened in the Global South, or has been done by indigenous populations, or marginalised populations in the Global North (Ndlovu-Gatsheni 2018: 44; Moosavi 2020: 332–54; Pimblott 2020: 211–12). In this, I include indigenous action to disrupt the exploitation of nature – indigenous peoples' protests against the Dakota Access Pipeline, for example. I also include anticolonial work that (sometimes) recognises the colonial continuity in the (re)production of disposable populations in the use of unfree labour, across Africa and Asia particularly. Examples of this includes local movements protesting working conditions in mines in the Democratic Republic of Congo and South Africa, as well as theorisation of the foregoing. Local movements for political, cultural, and economic sovereignty of indigenous people within settler and non-settler states are also implicated in defining and enacting decolonisation. So, anticolonial intellectual thought and praxis have broadly in space–time, been revealed in activity such as independence movements, anti-slavery struggles, uprisings against enslavement, anti-apartheid global movements, and Pan-African organising. As has been argued previously, the institution of colonialism as a structure of power and domination, triggered an immediate and continuing response to repel and resist it. Which is essentially how decolonisation, however it is couched, can be understood – as an immediate and continuing political and active anticolonial response seeking to dismantle ongoing colonialism. It is contended, in this vein, that contemporary action in higher education owes its present appearance to, and hence is not divorced from, this history. In other words, in the same tradition, contemporary action seeks to respond to the dominance of power abstracted from and through this colonial history and present. Therefore, to be true to its theoretical origins, what is called 'decolonising' in Global North universities must, firstly ground itself in this history and praxis and not consider 'decolonisation' some recent discovery by the westernised university. This helps to avoid superficial critique of decolonisation which misunderstands and misuses the concepts with which it engages. Engagement with decolonisation on the same superficial grounds, will result in cursory curricular redesign, that does not connect deeply with the conceptual questions raised by the logics and praxes of (de)colonisation. As with the independence of colonised states, this form of 'decolonisation' is an impediment that closes the conversation and demonises those who wish to reopen it as unsatisfied troublemakers. *They become problems and locations of problems because they expose institutional inadequacies* (Ahmed 2012: 63, 158–9).

Consequently, the task of academics in the face of the foregoing, is to translate varied theories of decolonisation into action, while avoiding mistranslations into mere performance. This must be done while untangling the complicity of disciplinary dictates and conceptual methods from the emergence and maintenance of colonialism. In other words, we cannot escape the potential futility of attempting to decolonise using the very structures we are attempting to decolonise. Therefore, from within the law school, decolonisation requires us to redesign our work (teaching and research), so it redesigns the world. Yet, like Frankenstein and his creation, redesigning the world requires us to move beyond the colonial logics from which we have emerged. Just like the law school, the creature is forced to depend on the master's logic as the sole source of creativity and freedom. Still the lines between creator and creation are blurred, as the creator basks in the glory of his creation, and the creature's yearnings demand, 'Is there still possibility in my body?' We are warned against running back to the master's house for this possibility and power. Rather, to decolonise is to look to the future, to take responsibility for building newer and meaningful worlds for all.

Therefore, decolonisation tells us there is still power and possibility in dehumanised bodies, spaces, and temporalities. And so, I conclude this chapter by outlining some guiding principles that help me to translate decolonisation in academic spaces and which I use to unpack decolonisation and legal knowledge in the ensuing chapters. The first fundamental is a direct confrontation with and reiteration of the colonial nature of the world. Decolonisation has a particular register, that recognises colonialism as a structural condition and not an isolated spatial-temporal event without broad spatial-temporal consequence. Action to decolonise also recognises that the power of colonialism comes in part from its appearance as normal and natural, how 'as modern subjects we breathe coloniality all the time and everyday' (Maldonado-Torres 2007: 243). Therefore, the continual unveiling of colonialism as the engine of coercive power is essential to decolonisation. Thus, its key register is anticolonial – a refusal. A refusal of the colonial requires returning (ceding) stolen power – one limitation of diversity as a substitute for decolonisation. However, ceding power is not meant to result in inverse replacement, in which those who receive power operate on the same logics as those who have ceded power. Decolonisation invites us to think of power differently. Therefore, it is disruptive. Decolonisation requires discontinuation of the epistemologies that have produced colonialism.

Decolonisation demands dismantling, delinking, decentring, or disobeying epistemic coloniality of power and the reproduction of hierarchy upon which it proceeds. So, that the *uni*versity may be superseded by an equal *pluri*versity of knowledges.

What I mean here is that we must question how our disciplines and intellectual traditions can be put in service of redesigning a world whose ways of thinking and doing and being, do not reproduce the structures from which we wish to disengage. Therefore, inherent in some critique of decolonisation is an inability to rethink the current structure of the world – in that sense, I feel that a lot of intellectual resistance, among other things, arises from a lack of imagination. In other words, an inability to conceive of a world and a reality radically different from the one we have now, without the structures and oppressions and designs that reproduce colonialism. This is because, within higher education especially, there does not yet exist, fully developed epistemic tools to imagine and build new, just, and inclusive worlds. So, the second fundamental principle is imagination. Decolonisation's response to structural injustice is to require us to unveil the present by looking to the past, for the purpose of flourishing futures. Or as Benjamin admonishes us to, 'imagine and craft the worlds you cannot live without, just as you dismantle the ones we cannot live within' (Benjamin 2019: 14). At its most radical, decolonisation involves the dismantling of worlds that those disadvantaged by the current darkness and those who dream with them of worlds otherwise, cannot live within. Shadowed as we are by environmental disaster, decolonisation involves imagining and crafting the worlds we all cannot live without.

Finally, we must not forget that decolonisation has had a long history – at least from 1492. And so, to achieve anything within its purview, we must, with commitment, build on previous work. Decolonisation remains 'an insatiable reparatory demand, an insurrectionary utterance, that always exceeds the temporality and scene of its enunciation. It entails nothing less than an endless fracturing of the world colonialism created' (Modiri 2020: 172). This *endless fracturing* brings with it uncertainty. Very often decolonial approaches within institutions fail to disrupt, and their imaginative potential freezes. One of the reasons for this is the uncertainty of success when asked to abandon the familiar, even when the familiar is undesirable. We know the worlds we are fighting to escape. Requiring clear and certain alternatives to them, before we abandon them, precludes the responsibility for new possibilities and binds us to current logics. The creature cannot completely forsake his master. Yet, decolonisation embeds within it an imperative to act and think generatively. The lack of certainty as to what our actions may produce reflects their broad potential to create beyond the worlds we are fighting to escape. Closed thinking 'turns disciplines away from reality in their quest for controlled outcomes' (Gordon 2020: 39). Rather, we should think of decolonisation as responsibility, to not only communicate across space and logics, but also across time. So, Gordon in his reflections on the purposes of such action, for which no victory is ascertained, cites *action* itself as the imperative, irrespective of outcome. In other words, undertaking with persistence, an imaginative responsibility that disrupts the reproduction of injustice, grounded in past intellectual work, is in the present, 'loving, by virtue of action, anonymous generations to come' (Gordon 2020: 29).

2

What Have You Done, Where Have You Been, Euro-Modern Legal Academe? Uncovering the Bones of Law's Colonial Ontology

> In order to know what it [law] is, we must know what it has been, and what it tends to become. ... The substance of the law at any given time pretty nearly corresponds ... with what is then understood to be convenient; but its form and machinery, and the degree to which it is able to work out desired results, depend very much upon its past.
>
> Oliver Wendell Holmes (1923: 1–2)

> The law is also memory; the law also records a long-running conversation, a nation [and a world] arguing with its conscience. ... What is our community, and how might that community be reconciled with our freedom? How far do our obligations reach? How do we transform mere power into justice, mere sentiment into love?
>
> Barack Obama (2004: 437–8)

Introduction

An appreciation of what the law is, what it has been and the possible directions it could take humanity, requires, as Holmes and Obama note, a deep excavation of its history and ontology. In other words, to understand how the conditions of life introduced and globalised by colonialism have become normalised and woven into the structures that reproduce the current world, it is important to understand the role of Euro-modern law in shaping global structures as well as human behaviour and standards. Without a detailed examination of this, decolonisation will fail to properly engage with the power and possibility produced by Euro-modern legal knowledge. In thinking through decolonisation and legal knowledge, Sara Ahmed's writings on 'use' are very instructive here. She writes that 'use' can sometimes become a subversion of 'function'. The way a thing is used can subvert or even obliterate its supposed function. 'The more a path is used, the more a path is used' (Ahmed 2019: 41). 'Use' is how the past lives on in the present. Use is how lawful becomes normal, becomes natural, becomes just the way things are. Therefore, this chapter examines the nature of Euro-modern law and how this nature enabled/enables legal knowledge's (re)production and maintenance of colonial logics and praxes. Confronting law's historical and contemporary use in service of the colonial, invites us to view law as an uninterrupted continuum across space–time, which carries with it certain instances and ways of world-making. To enact decolonisation within and with legal knowledge is to pay closer attention to the academe from which colonialism emerged and the academe which emerges from colonialism. Consequently, this chapter is a general examination of how Euro-modern legal knowledge is, historically and ontologically, implicated in producing ongoing colonial conditions and modalities of life. The three chapters that follow unpack the specifics of this complicity further, with emphasis on the human/body and space–time.

The lawful production of epistemic injustice, or the legal academe from which colonialism emerges

Euro-modern law as a product of modernity is unavoidably infected with the methodologies and ideologies of its darker side – the capitalist-colonial-enslavement project. So, Euro-modern law's power is demonstrated not just by its pretensions to liberalism on its lighter side, but also by its coercions and violences in and beyond its darker side. By obscuring its darker side, law's worldmaking produces a world that 'described in its images and categories' appears as though it is 'the only attainable world in which a sane person would want to live' (Gordon 1984: 109). However, the maintenance and reproduction of this described world is one that requires commitments and investments from those subject to its design. These buy-ins allow inequalities and injustices to be rationalised behind a veil of universality and objectivity … a veil that hides the maldistribution of power and possibility across manufactured hierarchisations of life naturalised within legal knowledge. Thus, more potent than Euro-modern law's coercive power to control and punish human behaviour within and beyond the nation state, is its ability to compel people globally to accept that the necropolitics, inequality, violence and destruction that are the outcomes of the capitalist-colonial-enslavement project, are natural and inevitable. Mbembé defines necropolitics as '[t]he ultimate expression of sovereignty [that] largely resides in the power and capacity to dictate who is able to live and who must die' (2019: 66). Anticolonial movements and other resistances from below, responding to this power-driven differential access to flourishing life, have often contributed to producing emancipatory legislation, progressive judicial judgements, and increasingly supposedly liberal social attitudes. However, we must also recognise that the role of Euro-modern law in this claim to progress, has often been to manage and control the outcomes of resistances to its coercive power … within its coercive power.

To confront Euro-modern law's managerial features, means to consider how its code is entangled in the legitimation of hierarchisation through microregulation of the body and space–time, and thus the (re)production of colonial logics. The legitimation of law provides ongoing colonialism with its tool of justification, regulation, and normalisation. This legitimation can be identified in many ways, including how humanity is personified in Euro-modern law, in the dictates of law and order and crime, in normalising what is of value in the eyes of the law, in creating legal ontologies about land or whose work and what work has value. The superiorisation of Euro-modern law over other jurisprudences, including indigenous jurisprudences, results in epistemicides of law – killing off of othered legal knowledges and the predominance of Euro-modern law (de Sousa Santos 2018: 8). Yet even though othered legal knowledges have been and are being killed, Euro-modern law itself does not emerge on the other side of this epistemicide unscathed. Through and for its colonial missions, Euro-modern law was and is saturated with Eurocentrism and 'methodological whiteness' (explained in what follows), resulting in a self-destructive discipline and field.

It is important to examine, in this vein, the process through which Euro-modern law emerges from and through colonialism, to explain the rationalities and mechanisms behind continuing inequalities within a system of dominant imposition of parochialism masquerading as universalism. In this way, we refrain from engaging in simplistic arguments that historise and individualise prejudice and values, while simultaneously appreciating the inevitable connection between a scholar and the seemingly neutral epistemologies they claim to produce. The scholarship that has produced a necropolitical world cannot be remedied by just excising the 'bad bits' and not interrogating the benign sections. Thus, we put in question our trust for justice, freedom, peace, and non-necropolitical worlds placed in the very analyses that produced the necropolitical–colonial world from which we wish to escape. In other words, historising values that underpinned colonialism by labelling discriminatory values as merely 'standards of the past' in academic scholarship, ignores the structural teleology of such discrimination. These discriminations functioned/function to normativise and naturalise global and structural inequality, across space–time, along lines of artificed human categories, behind a mask of feigned objectivity and impossible neutrality. Consequently, the 'bad code' upon which some of this scholarship is written and produced may also be hidden in the non-excisable sections of it. Furthermore, historising and spatialising values in this way, restricts our examination of the production of present inequalities through such epistemologies to the epistemologies that produced those inequalities. The question for us in this regard should be: How tainted is legal knowledge by the process through which it emerged?

The effect of the intellectual labour of colonialism and its logics was to totalise a particular and often necropolitical worldview and make it the only valid episteme – in essence, launching a series of epistemicides through physical and epistemic superiorisations. Epistemicides often preceded or accompanied the imposition of necropolitical conditions that resulted in immediate or slow death for populations placed below the abyssal line. So, the imposition of Euro-modern legal standards for conceptualising reality was important in inaugurating, validating, underwriting, formalising, maintaining, and advancing these deadly social conditions. For example, to establish that English law operated in Australia upon its settlement by English colonisers, the Privy Council described the land, prior to occupation as 'a tract of territory practically unoccupied, without settled inhabitants or settled law' (*Cooper v Stuart* 1889: 5).[1] Yet, the indigenous population of Australia before contact has been estimated to have been at between 1 and 1.5 million people (Miller et al 2010: 175). Unrecognition of indigenous occupation illustrates how the history of structural inclusion/exclusion in humanity, had and has material effect and continues to be reproduced in and by temporally bound statements about the past. Therefore, through a distortion of realities, present and future conditions of annihilation persist as: '"the other side of the line" vanishes as reality, becomes nonexistent, and is indeed produced as nonexistent … abyssal thinking is thus the impossibility of the copresence of the two sides of the line' (de Sousa Santos 2016: 118). For the statement in *Cooper v Stuart* to be true, that Australia was unoccupied, the indigenous people had to vanish, both epistemically and physically. Thereby, producing a pristine land for the settlers to inherit. Consigning to history the present legal effects of intellectual tools of annihilation, by labelling them temporally bound and of differentiated values, is a false alibi

---

[1] A similar approach to indigenous titles and peoples was taken in *Milirrpum v Nabalco Pty Ltd* (1971) 17 FLR 141 where right of occupancy was recognised by the land being found 'desert and uncultivated'. See also *Re Southern Rhodesia* (1919) and *Wi Parata v Bishop of Wellington* (1877).

that invisibilises the continuities of injustice that live on in contemporary dehumanisation and dispossession. Those on the other side of the line are persistently overtly and covertly denied co-presence with those placed on this side of the line.

To illustrate the origins, nature, and evolution of this intellectual production, Eze, collected some of the most notable enlightenment-era thinkers' theses on 'race'. From Carl von Linne's 1735 hierarchisation of humanity by race, to GWF Hegel's 1820s essays which extend the same logics to argue for a correlation between scalation of humanity, climate difference, and capacity for rationality, Eze's exploration demonstrates the intractability of scientific racism and Euro-modern legal philosophy. Many of these scholars completely denied the possibility of non-white/Black rationality (Eze 1997: 55–7, 63, 85, 91–4, 97–103, 105, 124–42); consequently, almost unalterably linking skin colour to inexorable sociopolitical, socioeconomic, and sociolegal destinies. For example, Kant describes a person, 'quite black from head to foot, a clear proof that what he said was stupid' (Eze 1997: 57). An entry to the 1789 Encyclopaedia Britannica, listed the traits of the 'Negro' to include: 'idleness, treachery, revenge, cruelty, impudence, stealing, lying, profanity, debauchery, nastiness and intemperance' (Eze 1997: 94) Also cited by Eze is Hegel who argues that, 'The Negro is an example of animal man in all his savagery and lawlessness, and if we wish to understand him at all, we must put aside all our European attitudes' (Eze 1997: 127–8). Academic method and theory are erroneously and devastatingly fused in these articulations. 'I think, therefore I am', results in unrecognised personality being contingent on unrecognised epistemologies (Mudimbe 1991: 178; Maldonado-Torres 2007: 252). In other words, the human/being whose thinking is venerated is also venerated; the human/being whose thinking is despised, is also despised. It should be noted that Eze's collection also includes the then-contemporary disagreement of Beattie and Herder with scholarship that relied on colonial ideologies of race (Eze 1997: 34–7, 71–8). This inclusion demonstrates that the dominant values of any time are always contested, and it is misleading to historicise values that continue to be contemporarily held that were vigorously disputed within the time to which they are often historicised. It should be noted further that Eze's collection does not include non-white scholarly and non-scholarly disagreements with racist ideologies such as indigenous litigation against enslavement (van Deusen 2015: 125–46), intellectual debate between indigenous peoples and European colonisers (Franks 2002: 558), as well as uprisings and rebellions of the enslaved and the colonised (Heuman 2010: 220–33; Gopal 2019).

The type of discriminatory scholarship already discussed, had their fingerprints all over the development of exploitative colonial projects in Africa and Asia. Settler colonial projects in the Americas and Oceania had begun slightly earlier (1492–1497 in the Americas, 1770 for Australia)

(Miller et al 2010: 28, 96, 174), and were enacted by the slow and immediate extermination of indigenous populations. However, the economic success of the use of coerced African labour for enslavement, especially in the Americas, quite likely contributed to a willingness to adapt the preceding colonial logics to the next stage of colonialism. In other words, the same hierarchisation of humanity could be deployed as justification to accumulate land and coerce unfree labour without the need to transport, accommodate or feed the unfree labour. In the aftermath of colonial administration, those same colonial logics were once more deployed to exploit labour and resources, this time without the added cost of colonial administration.

From enslavement to colonisation and neo-colonialism, these evolving processes required an expansively macro-structural rethinking of the world, humanity, and political operationalisation, that could not have been achieved without legal machinery, epistemologies, and academic justifications. Therefore, these processes and adaptions illustrate the complicity between formations of power/power structures, legal knowledges, and epistemological orders. These macro-structures were and are underwritten by micro-regulation of the human and space–time. Foucault explains how, by the seventeenth century, sovereign power (including the colonial matrix of power) becomes concerned with treating the human body as a machine and thus state-owned technology – physical and intellectual – and so disciplines and exploits the body for state/sovereign purposes (Foucault 2013a: 44). The figure and body of the racially enslaved person provides an apt illustration of the human body as this state machine. Understanding the Euro-modern empire as global sovereign, through the universalisation of 'metaphorical Europe's' cultures and beliefs (what Derrida calls 'white mythology' [and Moore 1974: 11]), leads us to cast this disciplining lens globally wider and thus interdict racialisation as integral to the global world order and intellectual labour that produces it.

One way in which structural hierarchisation of humanity and space–time within evolving frames of Euro-modern legal knowledge is invisibilised from within legal knowledge, is through the apparent nescience and persistent absence within it, of the significance of racialisation to the emergence of intellectual content, value, and method. Bhambra calls this 'methodological whiteness'. This is a study of the world that does not 'acknowledge the role played by race in the very structuring of that world, [which] treats a limited perspective – that deriving from white experience – as a universal perspective' (Bhambra 2017: webpage). Similarly, Mills describes 'white ignorance' as both a false belief and absence of belief held by people racialised white, a worldview and racial frame, about racially othered people in the world (2007: 26–31; 2014b: 18; 2015: 217–27). This white ignorance underwrites the production of the racial contract, underpinning the global political structure of white supremacy, but also makes its production invisible, unquestioned, immutable, and immovable, especially within and by legal intellectual knowledge systems. Consequently, through methodological whiteness and white ignorance, a significant amount of Euro-modern legal epistemological production has not been designed to understand the world but is a continuing unsuccessful attempt to remake and regulate the world in Europe's image – a white patriarchal, property-owning image. Anything that does not fit is exploitable or disposable ... or both. This powerful hidden structure requires/required a technology of reproduction. So, Maeso and Araújo indict the law in their definition of Eurocentrism as 'interpreting a (past, present, and future) reality that uncritically establishes the idea of European and Western historical progress/achievement and its political and ethical superiority, based on scientific rationality and the construction of the rule of law' (2015: 1). Epistemological Eurocentrism, relying on Euro-modern legal knowledge, produces a world out of itself that never existed, does not exist, and cannot exist on its own. It cannot exist without a trail of bodies in its wake. And it does not count the bodies that through this worldview do not count.

Thus, our disciplinary divisions are unable to truly understand the world or provide useful solutions to its problems. This futility is a condition described by Gordon in his conceptualisation of disciplinary decadence in academia. Disciplinary decadence, according to Gordon, arises when a discipline, rooted in colonial practices, considers itself complete, self-created, entirely method-dependent, immortal, and omniscient about all other disciplines (2011: 98; 2014: 86; 2015a: 4–5; 2018: 241). Any critique of such discipline can therefore only be acceptably justified by reference to the discipline itself. Hence, this decadence specifically exposes a methodological lacuna for disciplines in the Euro-modern academy, in respect of populations objectified at the time the discipline's method and thought was formulated. 'Problem people' will not 'fit' into disciplines' purportedly universal and objective method. So, we try in vain, using diversity measures, to fit such people into the strict dictates of the discipline, yet the field keeps on spitting them out, across space–time. In other words, within this intractable adherence to colonial method and logics, 'non-normative people, become problems, instead of people who face problems' (Gordon 2014: 81–92). It seems easier to question the legitimacy of people whose 'problems' fall outside the sacred method of our discipline, than to question the method and presumptions that underpin the discipline – the soul of the discipline itself. Because to question the discipline is to question the (vision of the) world (it has created). In other words, we fall back on colonial logics of hierarchisation and delegitimisation of humanity to excuse the outcomes of the discipline – the necropolitical creation of death-worlds. This is what de Sousa Santos defines as abyssal thinking that relies on hierarchised binaries of life and death, of which he indicts Euro-modern legal knowledge as being particularly guilty (2016: 120).

Within the academy, Euro-modern legal knowledge production has mostly ignored the effects of long histories of unfree labour and appropriation of indigenous land on the legal meanings of seemingly universal concepts and methods. For example, land justice for the coloniser is not the same as land justice for the colonised. Euro-modern justice for the coloniser is often actual injustice to the colonised. The coloniser's right to private land historically relied on dispossession of indigenous land. But who those lands pass on to by succession and inheritance is determined, not by a universal understanding of justice, but by law's adherence to order and authority. The law emerging from colonialism is thus subordinated to norms more protective of itself and the aims of the capitalist-colonial-enslavement project, than of life on the planet. True justice requires rethinking the norms of legal knowledge and not merely increasing the membership and demographics of our discipline (Gordon 2020: 38). Therefore, adherence to decadent method means that we are unable to adapt our epistemologies for different futures that do not follow on from the necropolitics of the colonial. This is what Gordon means by decay – turning from living thought. By trapping our discipline in thought that crystallised during a time when race science was used to abstract property out of humanity, through the legalised processes of racialised enslavement and colonial dispossession, we trap our world into reproducing the accompanying injustices of those modes of extraction and epistemologies along those hierarchised and geopolitical lines. This is because, disciplinary decadence operates along colonial lines, creating zones of closure, settlement, and negation of human possibility (Gordon 2018: 238). This is what I mean by the necropolitical production of death-worlds. Colonial logics and metrics produce especially narrow and limiting visions of humanity, including the space–time within which humanity exists, existed, will exist. So, the universalisation of a specific 'particular', results in the slow death of all other 'particulars' and the loss of utility of the chosen 'particular'.

Consequently, by trapping human possibility within rigid disciplinary dictates, transformation is rendered almost unachievable. Rather than justice, anything that exists on the other side of Grosfoguel's 'dividing line', beyond the abyssal line, in the zone of non-being, is either eliminated or partly transformed to resemble this side of the line (Fanon 2008: 2; de Sousa Santos 2016: 120; Grosfoguel 2016: 9–15). This stark division and negation of copresence is what makes 'the claim of the universal translatability of the English word "justice" ... an extraordinarily presumptive one' (Gordon 2013: 70). Neutrality and universality are insufficient here, as epistemic injustice that arises through the obscuring of racialised knowledge cannot be assuaged by further obscuration of racialised knowledge. To mean anything at all, our quest for enduring justice through legal knowledge must be preceded and accompanied by an exploration of how the law's present ontology was produced through colonial epistemologies, including language and spatial-temporal use and practices. To prevent further disciplinary decay, we must unpack colonial logics – their methods as well as the fundamental building blocks of their assemblage. Thus, in relation to legal knowledge, we must ask ourselves where the law has been, what it has done and if there is enough left of the discipline to ensure that all humans are law's humans, that all of space–time is legible to legal knowledge. We must even be able to contemplate the destruction of the discipline for the benefit of humanity. In other words, let us ask, even if only hypothetically, if we are willing to let the discipline die, if it dies in service of the destruction of death-worlds and the creation of life-worlds? Is the law that has brought us this necropolitical death-scape, able to provide the design for flourishing future life-worlds?

Euro-modern law's three-part journey immiserating the wretched of the earth

Euro-modern law's colonial ontology beyond and within the nation state

In the colonial encounter, the first thing to go and the first thing to arrive in the making of the colony is Euro-modern law. Invasion through dispossession, dehumanisation, and killing of indigenous populations requires violation of the foundations of the norms underpinning Euro-modern law (Mills 2014a: 4). Successful invasion also requires the legitimation and introduction of the coloniser's law as well as concurrent de-legitimation of the law of the colonised. In the abstraction of and from time that produces the colonial moment, the laws of those colonised (indigenous laws) are re-written as culture and myth. Simultaneously, the laws of the colonisers are imposed and expanded as The Law, The Only Law, and Nothing but the Law. I describe this as 'Euro-modern law' to underline law's intimate enfoldment with legitimising and universalising Euro-modernity. Thus, Euro-modern law is law which began in Europe, but also arose out of colonial activities in the Americas, Africa, Asia, and Oceania. The ontology of Euro-modern law places Euro-America at the centre of the world (Eurocentrism) and is intimately tied to these historical and contemporary origins and uses (Darian-Smith 2013: 247–64; Darian Smith 2015: 647–51). Thus, in teaching and researching law, we currently adopt a narrow, anthropological understanding of what amounts to law. As Todd suggests, 'law is for the west, culture is for the rest' (2020: webpage). As with the capital market and the global political structure, colonialism introduces and maintains a universalising approach to law, whose effect is to erase other ontologies, axiologies, methodologies, and epistemologies and normativise itself, its interests, purposes, goals, desires … above all others. Accordingly, people (especially colonised and indigenous people, but also other marginalised peoples within and outside the metropole) experience Euro-modern law mainly as a system of oppression and opaque officialdom. Known only through encounters with enforcement and strict administration of land, resources, and people, consequently, 'many Indigenous peoples have come to associate "law" with power, punishment, hierarchy, and bureaucracy' (Napoleon 2007: webpage).

So, Euro-modern law is implicated in the structures that (re)produce and maintain global abyssal thinking – stark disparities in conditions of living and on the planet. For example, Anghie charts the origins and current character of international law, as a fundamental tool in universalising Euro-modern legality. He does this through an examination of the lawful processes of appropriation of indigenous land, coercion of unfree labour, the administration of nation states, and the emergence of the current global and commercial order (Anghie 2007). This international legal order has produced and continues to produce differentiated global realities and outcomes for the peoples of the world so ordered. For some it protects, for some it makes wretched. It produces a 'compartmentalised world … a world divided into two' (Fanon 2007: 3). Thus, Linarelli et al argue that international law establishes and maintains a permanence of misery, driven by capitalist need and greed, that is inaugurated by a world structure advancing on classifications of humanity into hierarchies, geographies, and acceptable orders (2018). What this means is that the nature of law, especially international law, relies on an unequal global order and thus colonialism is to law, 'not simply of historical, but rather, of ontological interest' as the colonial encounter, 'generated a set of mechanisms … which operate to empower certain societies and exclude others' (Anghie 2014: 140). In other words, we must concern ourselves, not just with what international law has done, but what international law *is*, that makes it continually do what it does. International law, accordingly, in comparison to domestic/national law, has more often been implicated in the colonial encounter and therefore the emergence and reproduction of an unequal global order. Not accounting for this complicity in the emergence of human rights reduces its utility in maintaining a discourse of resistance and liberation. Human rights under Euro-modernity have consequently been designated 'white men's rights', which decry cultural diversity as a problem and reduce the scope of humans, human rights can legitimately protect (Shelley 2001: 13–35, 213).

The entanglements between colonialism and national legal jurisprudences are not as easily identified. State law is not often thought of as an integral part of the structures of ongoing colonialism. States, and their laws, though considered to be the key agents and producers of international law, are treated as emerging mostly from the will of the people within each state's boundaries (Eslava and Pahuja 2020: 118). Therefore, one can imagine the law that operates within those boundaries is insulated by those boundaries from the colonialism and immiseration of international law. However, state borders and their creation have actually been of vital importance to international law and cannot exist without international law. Thus, one can argue that international law and therefore colonial logics, also heavily influence law's ontology, not only beyond state borders, but also within them. As Anghie's thesis suggests, which states were and are considered sovereign is a product of the universalising logic of colonialism that provides restrictive Euro-centred standards for political being internationally (Anghie 2007: 196–244). It has also been argued that our current notions of and rules for statehood are heavily inspired by principles that emerged through the processes by which European states exited from their empires – what is called political/administrative decolonisation of colonies. This form of decolonisation, according to Kreijen, was achieved by a 'legal trick' that attempted to normativise into states, the borders of colonies that were no more than 'mere legal fiction' (2004: 148). In other words, flag independence is thus exposed as colonisation/colonialism reifying itself, bleeding into and across imaginary borders, evolving to meet the demands of a changing world, while still maintaining and benefitting from its powerful hierarchies. So, d'Aspremont claims that the current principles for statehood arose, not in the antiquity of international law, but in the second part of the 20th century, and they are based on an imaginary genealogy and anthropomorphism put into service of alleviating the post-colonial anxieties of Euro-modern states faced with an influx of new non-Europe actors into the international legal sphere (2018: 139–52). These anxieties were triggered by the desire to maintain the abyssal line as well as the colonial loot and subsequent riches abstracted from its creation (El-Enany 2020: 130–1). Thus, the idea of nation states with definable borders reveals itself as a recent, possibly transient, development, as well as a colonial continuity. State laws that cohere around the concept of the natural border reproduce the hierarchies of human and space–time that characterise colonial logics of commodification and exclusion. In this case, not only excluding the colonised from what was stolen from them through racialised enslavement, colonisation, and ongoing colonialism, but also making objectified bodies further abject, by narrating certain bodies as permanently exploitable/disposable. The border and its violences are colonially transmitted conditions, spread through the colonial encounter and reified by law as the only acceptable modality of existence. Thus, it is important to note that for states formerly colonised, independence and recognition within the international sphere was often dependent on adopting Euro-modern legal structures and political forms (Darian-Smith 2013: 255; Darian-Smith 2015: 647). This recognition by Euro-modernity was vital for trade, travel, and development. It forced non-Europe to continually operate on colonial logics. Consequently, for most of the world, the misery and coloniality of international law, produces the conditions within the state as well as the conditions that keep people bound within the state.

Put differently, not only is the internal order of nation states also predicated on colonialism, but national law and the very existence of states and violent borders are produced by colonial logics. As Goldberg contends about the 'racial state', racialisation is essential to all aspects of the formation and maintenance of the modern nation state, its borders, and its composition (2008: 233–58). Thus, this racial state in the Global North is characterised by its exclusion of racialised others in order to construct homogeneity, and it internally maintains, through various legal means and invented histories, a racially hierarchised polity. For example, as El-Enany explains, 'immigration law is the tool that ensures that dispossessed peoples have no claim over what was stolen from them,' (2020: 2) and 'must therefore be understood as being on a continuum of colonialism' (2020: 5). As offspring of the colonial encounter, both the nation state and the law that maintains it, are also infused with colonial logics and subject to the abyssal thinking. Just like with hierarchisation of humanity, the absolute other state can never become the venerated Euro-modern state. Consequently, to unsettle this reality, we need to think beyond the nation state (González 2018: 138). We must concern ourselves, then, within legal education and knowledge, not just with what the law has done, but also what the law *is* that makes it do what it does, and what the law can be beyond this.

Nevertheless, Euro-modern legal knowledge's enfoldment with doctrinal law makes conceptual re-imagining of legal knowledges challenging, as well as its alliances and investments with lines of power originating in the capitalist-colonial-enslavement project. Thus, Euro-modern law, whether described as national or international, reflects, maintains, and reproduces patterns of power built on social–political violent abstractions. Euro-modern legal knowledge continues to champion imperatives that privilege the expedition of the freedom of the market, private property ownership, and the value of corporate power to capital, above and over life (human and non-human) as well as the planet. Accordingly, to understand Euro-modern law as a product of colonialism, (that is, the fusing, globalising, and universalising of the market) and racialisation as the dominant mode of control (Quijano 2000b: 216, 230), requires a conceptual excavation of Euro-modern law. How the character of law produced through the furnace of law-forged colonialism emerges on the other side to structure the world in a particular design.

Euro-modern legal journeys in enslavement

To protect the interests that emerge and underwrite the capitalist-colonial-enslavement project, Euro-modern law has constantly sought to govern space–time, and the person. This it has done by regulating what passes as law, to support the profligate accumulation that results in dispossession for those necropolitically placed on the other side of the abyssal line. The introduction of Euro-modern law regulations in these processes often followed the customs, 'social practices and assumptions' of the powerful (Handler 2016: 235). In other words, whatever the powerful did to accumulate and dispossess, was subsequently and ultimately legitimised by legal codes, judgements, academic commentary, or conceptualisation. With enslavement, this is evidenced by the globalisation of what had been a localised practice of labour use across the world. For example, in the 1620s, the East India Company (the most powerful corporation in history) began to use enslaved labour (mostly from East Africa and parts of Asia) in its factories in Asia (Allen 2018: 153–4). Thereafter, in 1663, Charles II of England granted a Royal Charter to the Company of Royal Adventurers of England Relating to Trade in Africa.[2] The membership of the Royal Adventurers consisted of people with significant political and cultural capital including, as the name suggests, people close to the Royal family (Pettigrew 2013: 25). The granting of this Charter is accepted as the crystalised start of the Transatlantic trade in kidnapped Africans. The effect of the Charter was to grant to the named persons within it, 'the adjacent islands on the west coast of Africa from Cape Blanco to the Cape of Good Hope, for a period of one thousand years' (Zook 1919: 144). The Charter, therefore, granted the Royal Adventurers a monopoly on the trade in kidnapped Africans (Zook 1919: 148). Enforcement of the terms of the charter included the legal establishment of admiralty courts on the African coast (Pettigrew 2013: 24–5). Thus, laws were used to validate actions that had begun long before their enactment.

Law was implicated in enslavement of Africans in other ways. Legal definitions, procedures, and justifications were necessary to regulate the commercial side of the trade – principles of business, insurance, value, exchange, and so on. But most notable was probably the permanently evolving legitimation of the demarcation between the minutiae of the lived conditions that separated, in perpetuity, the enslaved (and the enslave-able) from slaveholders (actual and potential). For example, in 1685, Louis XIV of France introduced the French Code Noir to govern the lives of enslaved people in French possessions in the Antilles and later in Louisiana. These codes restricted the expressions of life of the enslaved, preventing them from holding public office, testifying in court, getting married without their masters' consent, public assembly, selling sugarcane, from practising any religion apart from Catholic, Apostolic, and Roman religions, and so

---

[2] Company of Royal Adventurers to King Charles II, Feb. 26, 1663, Colonial Office (CO), 1/17, no. 4, National Archives, Kew.

on.[3] The codes were important, because as Palmer explains, they 'revealed the belief system of European society including its fears, values and moral blindspots' (Palmer 1995: 363; see also Stewart 1995: 227–45).

The most significant mode of governance and legitimation of demarcation of human categories is revealed in the nebulous and evolving legal definition of status within the slave economy. Throughout periods of enslavement, it was convenient to not closely define the status of the enslaved or enslavement. However, when defined, the enslaved were considered, inter alia, 'real estate', 'personal chattel', or 'freehold property' (Sirmans 1962: 462–3). In most cases of use of enslaved labour, law ostensibly followed actual practice. In other words, law was used to regulate and regularise a pre-existing condition of 'natural enslavement' of people racially identified as 'Negroes' or otherwise enslave-able (Moore 1941: 171–202). These purportedly natural legal predestinations, while not solidly codified, showed up in unwritten presumptions that impelled particular legal outcomes. This ambiguity is, therefore, reflected in cases which considered what made enslavement justifiable. For example, the court in *Butts v Penny* (1677: 518) decided that enslavement/property-fication of Africans was permissible due to their religion (they were considered heathen) and not due to how they were racialised. Van Cleve reports that similar decisions were reached in *Lowe v Elton* in 1677 and in *Gelly v Cleve* in 1694 (2006: 614–15). Yet, in 1706, Chief Justice Holt in *Smith v Gould* stated that people racialised Black would be treated no differently by law and no property lay in them (338; see also Lorimer 1984: 123). *Smith v Gould* conflicted with reality and illustrated the fictions and contradictions Euro-modern law sometimes produces. The different treatment accompanying racialisation as Black was obvious. In essence, the exchangeability of 'religion' and 'race' in this parlance relies on an equivocation attempting to distinguish racialisation from the now debunked 'biological race'. It is a move to innocence that endeavoured to justify the lawful dehumanisation of a significant proportion of humanity. The religion of Black Africans was designated 'heathen' due to how they were racialised (as non-white) within Euro-modernity. In comparison to the British Isles, during this same time, judicial decisions on enslaved status in the US tended to be more prescriptive, sometimes relying on heritability of status and physical traits as well as presumption of freedom/enslavement depending on how one was racialised. *Hudgins v Wright* (1806) is discussed in this vein by Powell (2005: 100–9; see also Lopez 1994: 1–2). Nevertheless, the socio-legal operation of racialisation is important here, as it denotes 'the way in which racist attributes and hierarchies come to determine the

---

[3] Le Code Noir ou recueil des reglements rendus jusqu'a present (Paris: Prault, 1767) [1980 reprd. by the Societé, d'Histoire de la Guadeloupe]. Translated by John Garrigus. https://s3.wp.wsu.edu/uploads/sites/1205/2016/02/code-noir.pdf

everyday meaning and common-sense valuation of an entity or phenomenon' (Shilliam 2018: 4). Thus, the legal meanings given to the belief-systems of the enslaved were a result of how they were considered to fit into a racial hierarchy, thus giving rise to specific moral and social destinies.

Euro-modern law's propensity to transform itself in the face of expediency for capital accumulation, is also illustrated in the introduction of the doctrine of *partus sequitur ventrem* – meaning, 'that which is born follows the womb'. This was a legal doctrine adopted, beginning in 1662, in many English slave-holding territories in the Americas, which decreed that a child born of a female enslaved person was themselves born a slave (Spillers 1987: 79; Morgan 2018: 1–17). The doctrine was adopted soon after Elizabeth Key, a woman of colour, won her freedom in court in 1658, by relying on her white father's free status as provided for in English common law (Morgan 2018: 6). In response, *partus sequitur ventrem* operated irrespective of the status of the father and in direct contradiction to pre-existing English common law, where status was inherited through the father. Consequently, slavemasters were provided with a commercial incentive and legal alibi to assault those they held in slavery so as to enhance their own capital wealth. So, this doctrine sanctioned rape and sexual violence against enslaved African women and girls, whose labour was already coerced and unfree and whose humanity was already ignored and denigrated. Thus, the production of human commodities through the violence of abstraction was assured by legal processes, in repeated acts of cruel violation, brutally reducing the human body to a unit of labour and to the goods and services they could produce.

These legalised and racialised mechanisms that generated differences in human status showed up in other ways that underlined the normalising of the power of white supremacy. Servants racialised white were not routinely separated from their families, were subject to less severe punishments, and served specified indenture periods before attaining freedom not underwritten by racialisation (that is, as opposed to 'former slave', their subsequent identity was not as often noted as 'former indented') (Handler and Reilly 2017: 42–5). These differences illustrate that the foundations of what in contemporary discourse is referred to as 'white privilege' do not describe effusive advantage but an absence of a specific disadvantage that accompanies being racialised below the line of the human. In other words, the fact that 'white privilege' is not more accurately described as 'white racial non-disadvantage', illustrates the limits of the languages within which we work.

The strategic use of imprecision in legal language to shift meanings between human-slave status was also evident in court proceedings. One example is in the summary of the initial trial of *Gregson v Gilbert* (1783; see also Faubert 2018: 127; Ward 2019: 233–48). Due to diminishing water and food supplies, the captain of the ship *Zong* ordered approximately 130 enslaved African captives being carried on the ship, to be thrown overboard. Thereafter, the ship owners attempted to claim in court, the deaths in insurance (£30 per enslaved person) as lost cargo. The underlying unquestioned presumption was stated by the Solicitor General John Lee in his statement before the court, 'a portion of our fellow-creatures may become the subject of property' (1783: 629–30). But what remains unanswered is how it was determined *which* portion of humanity may become the subject of property. Law relies on certainty, until it does not. Therefore, *Gregson v Gilbert* turned not on the status of the 'cargo' (despite this unanswered question) and their murder, but on whether the facts of the case – potentially running out of water and food while carrying African captives – arose to a necessity, without fault, which permitted the deliberate drowning of the kidnapped Africans. By narrating the captives indisputably and unquestionably as 'slaves', the court failed to engage with the question of *when* the Africans became property. At the point of capture? When they left the shores of Africa? Nevertheless, the trial court thought that there was enough evidence to suggest that throwing the captives overboard was a necessity. Consequently, the lives of the Africans drowned could be claimed on insurance. After much agitation, including from anti-abolitionists, the appeal court, finding fault on the part of the crew for the shortages of food and water, disagreed with the finding of necessity, and ordered a new trial. The appeal court in doing this accepted that there were situations in which drowning their captives would be justifiable (Krikler 2007: 36). The appeal court managed to not only leave the question of the human status of the enslaved unanswered, but by proposing a justification for the drowning, the court 'kills the victims of the Zong a second time' (Krikler 2007: 37). Similarly, two years later, in *Jones v Schmoll* (1785 summarised in Krikler 2007: 34), the court held that insurance could be claimed for the deaths of kidnapped Africans resulting from the crew repelling the Africans' rebellion during a transportation voyage, but not for those deaths resulting from Africans who had starved themselves or who felt forced to jump overboard (see also Ward 2019: 236). According to Lord Mansfield, the distinction arose from a point of legal principle. In essence, for recovery, 'it is necessary that the loss shall be a direct and immediate consequence of the peril insured' (quoted in Krikler 2007: 34). The difference between recoverable deaths and non-recoverable ones turned whether the outcome was immediately or remotely consequent upon the danger against which the insurance had been taken – trade in enslaved people (Krikler 2007: 34–5). The underlying presumption that human beings were cargo, allowed for the insurance contract itself to exist. However, the peril occasioned by human beings naturally rebelling against captivity in different ways also existed in friction with the previous underlying presumption of 'humans as property' that granted these processes their aura of legality.

The legal principle of loss and peril itself survives. And like many legal principles, denuded and deracinated of any consideration of the questionable social considerations under which they arise, concerns about clarity and certainty prevail over all ambiguous 'sensitivities' about the variable human condition. These elisions also allow claims of universality, neutrality, and objectivity to be incontrovertibly made through erasures and silences about the legal processes and factual matrices which produce these principles. Furthermore, these types of cases illustrate the increasing and continuing legal innovation required to extract maximum value from African bodies (Kish and Leroy 2015: 642). Therefore, they invite us to examine how this type of legal innovation continues into the present, reworking and bolstering evolving structures of power, marking bodies and space–time as exploitable/disposable, while limiting possibilities for the increasing scope of those who find themselves cast into the sacrifice zone.

At the root of these legal cogitations, therefore, is the tension that arises from law following and adapting itself to the wishes of the powerful, including their desires to commodify all things for the purposes of capital accumulation. The law is not able, in the same breath, to provide justice for the dispossessed as well as to protect private property which also happens to be the dispossessed. While legal genealogy within Euro-modernity begins without a solid legal definition of 'slave' (or what makes certain humans enslave-able), the legal deliberations already considered had to proceed on the presumption that the 'property' subject here is also possessed of 'personhood', albeit limited (Rupprecht 2008: 265–77). This deliberate definitional deficiency not only responds solely to the needs of the powerful, but also has enfolded into it an unsettled temporal ambiguity. When does the African become enslaved and thus property? At the moment of kidnap on home shores or the moment of sale to slaveholders under unfriendly skies? This is compounded by a spatial and socio-political distorted understanding of African polities as lawless, indubitably inferior and uncertain. In other words, the law is so attached to protecting the interests of the powerful – in this case their untrammelled right to private property – that it distorts itself and must necessarily conflate the legal ontology of the person with the legal ontology of property. Reversing this process requires more than granting liberty to the dispossessed, if that liberty remains conditional and limited by the language in which salvation from slavery is being wrought, which also happens to be the language upon which their perdition was predicated.

Therefore, this desire to protect private property while still performatively proffering Euro-modern law as a source of succour to dispossessed peoples, is reflected in the guarded and territorially-limited statements of Lord Mansfield's earlier judgement in *Somerset v Stewart* (1772: 509–10; see also Van Cleve 2006: 635). The court ruled that Somerset – he had been enslaved by Stewart, had escaped when they both travelled to England and had subsequently been recaptured – could not be legally compelled to leave the country, as slavery was not enshrined in law therein. In other words, slavery was allowed in territories where it was enshrined in law, but not in England. However, despite congratulatory academic and popular literature to the contrary, it is suggested here and elsewhere, that the judgement in this case does not present the triumph for abolition of enslavement that is often suggested. Some abolitionists considered this to be a victory for their campaign, providing that enslaved people seeking freedom could find a way to England (Webb 2014: 458). This is despite the fact that there were very few people enslaved in England – most were in the Americas and could not even begin to hope to find a way to England to claim this dubious freedom. This marked the judgement as having only symbolic effect in the abolition campaign. On the other hand, pro-slavery legal thinkers understood Somerset as setting down regulations for the constitutional practice of enslavement by establishing jurisdictional limitations (Webb 2014: 482). Consequently, this judgement also underscores the ever-moving fungibility and move to innocence in the legal position concerning the status of enslave-ability of those racialised as non-white/Negro/enslave-able, accompanied by an uninterrupted desire to protect private property. Whatever the interpretations put to the law, the enslaved person was never really free. In fact, that same tendency to performative duality extended itself into questions of the ambiguous legal status of the over 200,000 Africans 'rescued' by the British Admiralty between 1807 and 1867, after the self-congratulatory abolition of the Transatlantic trade. The rescued Africans were actually repatriated to colonial territories under a legal regime of apprenticeship that was so equivocal in character and enactment as to amount to unfree or coerced labour. This uncertainty was predicated upon, among other things, the long historical conflation in legal meanings between being racialised Black/African life and being considered mere units of labour (Ford and Parkinson 2021: 827–46).

Euro-modern law's tendency to be undecided, at least performatively, as to whether its primary goal is to protect private property or recognise the humanity of the racialised was also demonstrated within the borders of the metropole in England. This is evidenced, for example, by the establishment of the Thames River police in 1800 to protect goods brought into England as part of the Triangle trade – goods produced by enslaved labour (Moore 2021: webpage). Erasing this body from the origins of the police allows us to conceal the historical links, especially within the United Kingdom, between the police and enslaved labour. These links are clearer in the US where several academics have traced the origins of the police to slave patrols tasked with capturing enslaved persons who escaped (Reichel 1988: 51; Hadden 2003; Turner et al 2006: 184–85). This same use of the police was to be replicated later under colonial administrations, to quell protests and exact exorbitant taxation from indigenous populations (Killingray 1986: 411–37; Brogden 1987: 4–14). Therefore, narrating as benevolent the actions of state organs tasked with the use of force, can often hide more problematic outcomes in the relation between private property and dehumanisation.

It is unsurprising, considering this legal history, that the UK Slave Emancipation Act (1833) contains an example of an almost conclusive equivocation on the legal status of enslaved persons. The full title of the Act is: 'An Act for the Abolition of Slavery throughout the British Colonies; for promoting the Industry of the manumitted Slaves; and for compensating the Persons hitherto entitled to the Services of such Slaves.' The title reflects a continuation of the same tradition of spatial–temporal internal legal incoherence, which involves navigating a balance between a minimal concession to recognising the personhood of the enslaved while, fundamentally recognising them as chattel/units of labour for the purpose of protecting rights to private property and consequent accumulated wealth. While this equivocation may be incoherent in legal terms, it is not in fiscal terms, as the outcome of the Act illustrates. The Act provided that the slaveholders be compensated in the amount of 40 per cent of the estimated market value of each enslaved person (£47million in total) (Drescher 2009: 264). This valuation inadvertently solidifies the enslaved as property in the legal imaginary and thus permanently de-personifies them. Valuation of an entity considered priceless – the human – renders the entity valueless and 'beyond the bounds of humanity' (Williams 1988: 16).

Furthermore, this compensation has had and continues to produce significant and completely divergent outcomes for the descendants of the enslaved and those of slaveholders. The British government paid out £20m to compensate some 3,000 families that held people in slavery for their loss of 'property'. The balance of £27m was paid by the enslaved themselves in unwaged labour. The initial sum of £20m (£17 billion in today's money) was paid through a Treasury loan and reimbursed back to the government in taxation (Hall et al 2014: 609; Gillman 2015: 6–7; Olusoga 2018: webpage). This means that the formerly enslaved and their descendants, who paid taxes in the UK till 2015, over and above the unwaged labour required, also financially contributed to 'compensating' the people who had held them and their ancestors in slavery. The slaveholders' descendants lost nothing by setting their captives free and were thereafter, able to build upon a foundation of affluence for their descendants. The foregoing history puts a new complexion on the experiences of what is known as the 'Windrush generation'. These are descendants of formerly enslaved people from the Caribbean, who were invited to fill labour shortages in the UK after World War II. They were met with overt racism and even in the 21st century have experienced disproportionately high levels of deportation and brutal denials of citizenship (Taylor 2020: 1–21). This illustrates the continued conflation between racialised non-humanity and racialised units of cheap labour. This history also unmasks the misguidedness of public discourse that engages in binarily questioning whether disparities arise from 'race' or 'class'. As the preceding illustrates, especially in relation to compensation, racialisation operates to make poor/make rich, or to place racialised populations in the permanent condition of units of labour. These logics are blunt tools often extended from and to, those who are racialised white, but also dehumanised. Therefore, any analysis of 'race' and/or 'class' that divorces itself from an examination and re-examination of this history is bound to conflate and demarcate inaccurately. Recourse could be made instead to research like that done by the Centre for the Study of the Legacies of British Slave-ownership at University College London, which explores how slaveholding and compensation impacted on a vast array of British families with present day effects.[4] Research such as this enables us to trace how Euro-modern legal logics are manufactured and distorted to enable economic–political power to reinvent and maintain itself. It also demonstrates how entangled with the law, economic and political power have been and continue to be.

Euro-modern law ventures into new colonial lands

Therefore, the process of acquiring colonies after the end of formalised enslavement should be understood as a continuation of these logics, and not a departure. Firstly, in the immediate aftermath of the end of the trade in enslaved persons, imperial financial might was consolidated through banking structures, industrialisation, and the use of unwaged/poorly waged labour (Lowe 2015: 98). In the ensuing periods, Euro-modern legal processes underwrote pursuit and justification of the interests of might-driven and pre-existing acquisitions of territory in most of non-Europe, as well as the preservation of trajectories of economic power, through, among other things, the use of trading companies to administer territory (Allen 2018: 151–76). This involved the introduction of colonial plantations in Asia and Africa, whose operations resembled chattel enslavement in the Americas, relying as they did on land dispossession and coerced labour (Sundiata 1974: 104; Allen 2017: webpage). Thus, the neoliberal idea of the 'freedom' of the labourer to grant their labour, in the post-slavery period, actually furthered and extended logics of property-making of racialised people, while naturalising the artificial need of capitalism to over-rely on alienable labour. This allowed for a reduction in responsibility, on the part of employers of labour, for the welfare of the person who had no real choice in providing labour (Allen 2017: webpage). So, Leroy argues that the 'free' labourer, post-enslavement, was placed in increasingly inescapable conditions of exploitation, coercion, and economic vulnerability (2021: 169–84). Left undisturbed was the

---

[4] Centre for the Study of the Legacies of British Slavery https://www.ucl.ac.uk/lbs/

furtherance of a global legal, economic, and political structure that had seemingly been irreversibly plunged into logics of commodification centred around narratives of racialisation.

In other words, Euro-modern legal epistemologies operated to shore up Euro-modern economic and political interests beyond Europe's shores. The 'Scramble for Africa' specifically illustrates this reconsolidation. The trade in enslaved Africans and use of their unfree labour tapered out – from the 1830s till a few decades thereafter. Europeans from various nations then began to explore hinterland Africa, beyond the African coast. The discovery of valuable resources therein led to attempts to claim those lands for European nations in ways that mirrored how lands had been claimed in the Americas and Oceania (Harlow and Carter 2003: 1–5).

Terra nullius (a legal term that allows for the first discoverer of land to claim possession of such land) had often been used not as an anterior justification for appropriation of land, but as a subsequent legitimation argument for prior colonisation in Oceania and the Americas (Fitzmaurice 2007: 1–15). It only provides a viable explanation where the legal personhood of indigenous and colonised people is not fully recognised. Building on earlier legal experiments with *terra nullius*, in the phrase *territorium nullius*, Euro-modern legal experts adopted a different legitimation of appropriation with the colonisation of Africa and parts of Asia – recognising some property rights but not full indigenous sovereignty (Fitzmaurice 2007: 12–13; Anghie 2007: 55). *Territorium nullius* was sufficient for colonial purposes, but it did not meet with the same critique as *terra nullius*, and so enabled lawful recognition of legitimate agents in the scramble. Thus, the major conflicts that were recognised in the scramble – despite the brutal repression of the indigenous populations – were only those between European nations/actors and not resistances to colonisation (Anghie 2007: 69). This non-recognition distorted the perception of European activity in Africa as sporadic adventurous expeditions that occasionally turned violent. To unsettle this narration, Hicks re-describes the period between 1884 and 1914 as a 30-year World War Zero (Hicks 2020: 49–56) – large-scale European warfare against African polities which involved the 'removal of kings, armies and indeed whole human landscapes of towns and villages' (Hicks 2020: 53). This overlaps with a longer timeframe from 500 years ago to the present, that has been described as *Maangamizi/Maafa* – the African Holocaust.

Once again, the equivocation within legal logics should be noted in how law's ontology invisibilises its implication in racial injustice and violence. Even though it seems to be the case *in practice*, it was not widely argued *in theory* that how Africans were racialised was what allowed for this warfare and for African lands to be claimed for Europe. Rather, the differences between African political structures and Euro-modern ones were relied upon to deny sovereignty to African polities. Yet, it was accepted that there was sufficiently recognised sovereignty for treaties with African political leaders to legitimise colonisation, though this sovereignty – in the eyes of Europe – did not extend to full recognition (Gershoni 1987: 293–307; Burton 2020: 143–50). Therefore, only Euro-modern actors rose to full recognition as legitimate agents in world politics in the late nineteenth century, despite prior African engagement in the world sphere (Irwin 1975: 81–96; Orukpe 2019: 45–8). To prevent reignition of intra-European conflict due to their 'adventures' in Africa, these recognised stakeholders met in Berlin in 1884 (without African representation) to decide which European power should own what part of Africa. The General Act of the Berlin Conference 1885 thereupon gave legal recognition to the previous pseudo-legal arrangements made in Africa and with some Africans, and thus culminated in administrative and physical colonisation of the continent. European states agreed that colonisation of a territory would be recognised, inter alia, by effective occupation/control of said territory by a European power (Fitzmaurice 2007: 10). Effective occupation/control was often evidenced by settlement and the presence of administerial apparatus and utilisation of imperial law with differential racialised treatment under the law (Gershoni 1987: 293–307; Pfister 2006: 68).

This process effectively abstracted the colonised out of time, placing them in a prior time/period, where they try forever unsuccessfully, to catch up with Euro-modernity. Africans and other colonised peoples were in effect, through logics of racialisation, severely written out of both time and space. One example of this was the almost complete alienation of pre-existing property rights as illustrated in the Judicial Committee of the UK's Privy Council's judgement in *Re Southern Rhodesia* (1919). Cecil Rhodes' British South Africa Company (BSAC) had acquired land on behalf of the British Crown between 1893 and 1918. As some of the land in what was then known as Southern Rhodesia remained unallocated, representatives of the indigenous African populations asked the court to be granted back this land. Lord Sumner's response to this request inter alia was as follows:

> The present case ... raises no question of white settlement among aborigines destitute of any recognizable form of sovereignty. Equally little is there question of the rights attaching to civilized nations, who claim title by original discovery. ... Some tribes are so low in the scale of social organization that their usages and conceptions of rights and duties are not to be reconciled with the institutions or the legal ideas of civilized society. Such a gulf cannot be bridged. It would be idle to impute to such people some shadow of the rights known to our law and then to transmute it into the substance of transferable rights of property as we know them. ... By the will of the Crown and in exercise of its rights the old state of things, whatever its exact nature, as it was

before 1893, has passed away and another and, as their Lordships do not doubt, a better has been established in lieu of it. Whoever now owns the unalienated lands, the natives do not. (1919: 215–16, 233–5)

This violent engagement between Europe and Africa would not have been possible without the preceding centuries of trade in enslaved Africans which was enabled by anti-Black ideology. Recognising this does not discount the contribution of individual Black quislings and co-conspirators to enslavement and empire for immediate profit. However, the difference between African experiences of imperialism and other colonially dispossessed territories, re-emphasises the intra-hierarchy knitted into unstable technologies of racialisation, whereby Euro-modernity also conscripts underlings by holding out the elusive promise of whiteness to non-Black populations of colour. Despite these blurred lines, a similar process of effective control, sovereign alienation, and intimate regulation, as described already was replicated in Asia, where the periods of enslavement (of mostly Africans) in the New World had happened in parallel with the deployment of European trading companies across Asia. Most notable of these was the East India Company which had brutally subdued most of Asia prior to the formal colonisation of India in 1858. The East India Company, duly legally incorporated in law, engaged in such ruthless suppression and vast plunder in Asia that its activity has been described as 'the supreme act of corporate violence in world history (Dalrymple 2015: webpage), that demonstrates 'how powerful corporate actors and the state can engage in large-scale robbery' (Moore 2020: 496).

Thus, the visible legalistic and bureaucratic processes of colonialism very often belied the exceptionally violent nature that colonial administration required before and during effective control. Hence World War Zero. Settler colonisation in the Americas and Oceania had resulted in deliberate and indirect near extinction of the indigenous populations (Maybury-Lewis 2002: 45–6). Mismanagement and the application of colonial logics of land use and human value in India resulted in devastating famines – 1.5 million people reportedly died in the Great Bengal Famine of 1943 (Sen 1982: 52–85). Peaceful anti-colonial rebellions were violently extinguished, for example the Hut Tax War of 1898 in Sierra Leone and the Aba Women's War of 1929 in Nigeria (Abraham 1974: 99–106; Uchendu and Okonkwo 2021: 245–54). According to Elkins, 1.5 million Kikuyus were detained and tortured to suppress the Mau Mau uprisings (Elkins 2005: xii–xiii). To maintain lucrative hold on rebellious colonies, defence budgets of colonial administrations often surpassed, by significant proportions, any other spending budget (Killingray 1986: 420; Rodney 2018: 197–198). So, large scale violence was an integral, but oft-forgotten, part of colonial administration. Apart from this unmarked loss of life, resource removal and use of unfree labour impoverished populations in Africa and Asia. This included punitive taxation, extractive industries as well as the use of coerced labour to build infrastructure to transport goods back to the metropole. An example of this is the construction of colonial railways. These railways were built mostly for the sole purpose of extraction and often ran from the coast to plantations, farms, industries, mines, and so on (Rodney 2018: 209). As such, these much-vaunted railways were unable to get food to prevent deaths from starvation in India during the Great Bengal Famine (Tharoor 2018: 174). Furthermore, most of these infrastructural 'gifts', were mostly financed through punitive taxation and constructed by unwaged labour (Oshin 1988: 123–38). All these were lawfully operationalised through Euro-modern law.

The realisation of these inadequacies of Euro-modern legality contributed to many colonised people's agitation, firstly for more involvement in colonial rule and later for independence. However, the language of anticolonial agitation was co-opted to label as 'decolonisation' the use of law to grant administrative control of these colonial constructs to local representatives. However, the fact that recognition as states required the adoption by former colonies of Euro-modern legal and political structures, underlines the continuation and not interruption of structures of power (Darian-Smith 2013: 253; Darian-Smith 2015: 648). Using South Africa as his example, Modiri argues that the continuation of what is described as postcolonial nations, institutionalises and constitutionalises the white supremacy at the heart of conquest and invasion (Modiri 2018: 300–25). In other words, the continuing existence of the colony is a reification of the racial hierarchies and violences that institute it and flow from it. This reification is further compounded by observing the continuities of financial accumulation and demarcation in the period considered post-Empire. Financial and legal mechanisms were adapted and conscripted to maintain the economic ascendancies that had been attained through different prior periods of colonialism (Palan and Stern-Weiner 2012: webpage; Oswald 2017). In other words, strict control over the financial terms of global relations have legally kept impoverished nations both poor and trapped in colonial structures, while leaving rich nations free to hold on to their colonial loot, restrict the movement of the colonised, at the same time as endangering the planet (Sankara 1988: 373–81; Hickel 2017: chapter 3; El-Enany 2020: 130–1). Therefore, through the colonial global economy, legal, political, and financial structures reproduce 'slow-violence' effects along the abyssal line ... as if immutable destiny (Bhambra 2020: 1–16). Thus, even though the hope of statehood and protection of human rights keep on being held out to those designated 'formerly colonised', legal epistemologies fail to answer their most pressing concerns or bring justice for ongoing colonialism. For example, Euro-modern legal epistemologies for defining atrocity have not been adequately deployed to recompense the at least 50 per cent population loss (a drop of 10 million people) in the Congo under Belgian rule (Hochschild 1999: 244–5; Maybury-Lewis 2002: 46), or Germany's near-extermination of the Herero and Nama people in what is now called Namibia (Maybury-Lewis 2002: 48). This resulted in 100,000 people killed – a genocide in any other language – and yet still not comparable to the millions of enslaved (11 million) and deceased Africans (incalculable) drawn into the savagery of kidnap and enslavement for the accumulation of capital (Eltis 2001: 17–46; Rawley and Behrendt 2005: 365). Justice for the coloniser in Euro-modern law is not justice for the colonised.

Euro-modern legal knowledge beyond and on the other side of colonialism

The purpose of this chapter has been to demonstrate how despite apparent transformation and liberalisation, orders of power and subjectivity are preserved, reproduced, and naturalised in and by Euro-modern legal epistemologies and technologies. This normativisation operates to, inter alia, place strict limits on discourse in this area. The logics of colonialism can only be acceptably critiqued by the logics of colonialism. Consequently, it is concerning that strategic confusions between personhood and property, valuation of labour and the position of enslavement as a lucrative economic model have not been sufficiently deconstructed within Euro-modern legal knowledge. In other words, we need to better consider what conditions of life have flowed from legal epistemologies perfected in the fires of racialised enslavement and exploitative colonisation. What intangible technologies of dispossession are distilled from the refineries of accumulation and continue to systematically enable appropriation in the ongoing necropolitical structure? Refusing to engage with these questions critically and in depth, while preaching equity, is a way of inviting us to change the players, but never the game – or more importantly as regards Euro-modern law, not changing the rules and language upon which the game is played. Therefore, the following chapters pay close attention to the construction of the human and space–time within the logics and praxes of a Euro-modern jurisprudence that emerged from colonialism, to consider how we may think through their reconstruction within legal knowledge ... while refusing the boundaries of the field.

It should not need to be said, that this chapter is not arguing that Euro-modern legal knowledge is a field of complete toxicity. As someone who has practised, studied, researched, and taught in the field for many years, I find the concept of law to be quite beautiful. I am asking us to look beyond the strict boundaries of what we consider 'law' to make better what is not yet perfect. In this we can consider other conceptualisations of law, such as indigenous jurisprudences. There remains a persisting myth that indigenous peoples (broadly defined across the world) did not have organised legal systems prior to being colonised. This myth served, and continues to serve, as justification for the imposition of Euro-modern law on indigenous and colonised societies. This imposition, accompanied by the erasure of local jurisprudences, has been described as a gift that would enable future civilisation and modernisation of previously 'lawless' peoples. Yet, as I explain in Chapter 1, many indigenous communities had existed with recognisable political, economic, and legal organisational systems for thousands of years prior to being colonised. In the colonial encounter, these systems were either annihilated, demoted to myth, or subordinated to the colonial legal authority that never really left. The future which that authority predicted has brought admonitions for the colonised to 'move on' from the past. Yet many indigenous systems survive the colonial encounter. They have moved on, standing in sharp contrast to the ontology and purposes of Euro-modern legal knowledge which is trapped in its past. Sometimes in attempting to justify the legitimacy of these plural systems of jurisprudence, there has been a tendency to draw similarities between their structures and those of Euro-modern law. In other words, arguing for their legitimacy by pointing out how some patterns replicate structures of Euro-modern law. However, it is their points of departure that hold out more promise for the directions in which an anticolonial reading of law may travel. For example, Graham describes two concepts that underpin aboriginal jurisprudence in Oceania, firstly that the land is the source of law, and secondly, no one is alone in this world. (1999: 105–6). This is echoed by Black who explains the necessity of 'feeling' the law (2009: 199). These examples illustrate how many indigenous knowledge systems rely on beliefs that emphasise the connectedness of human beings, not just to each other, but to other living beings, nature, the earth, and the universe. They emphasise the ways in which, within their corpuses, the body and space–time are not relegated to the background of the concept of law (Graham 1999: 111). Thus, indigenous law and custom are often 'intrinsic to an intersubstantiation of humans, ancestral beings, and land' (Moreton-Robinson 2015: 84). For indigenous peoples across the world, law operates beyond the order of the sovereign and micro-regulation, and is also about thinking, feeling, and doing in ways that emphasise 'the law of reciprocity, of regeneration, of mutual flourishing' (Kimmerer 2013: 173). These jurisprudences give us room to think of the concept of law differently from what has been examined in this chapter – that is, the consolidation of disparate access to life through hierarchisation, dehumanisation that follows the orders of power. However, we must also remember that there are a great many different indigenous knowledge systems and jurisprudences across the world (Napoleon and Friedland 2014: 226), whose concepts of living and being will often differ from each other – so we are contemplating a vast plurality of thought by bringing indigenous jurisprudence into a conversation between decolonisation and Euro-modern legal knowledge. Nevertheless, we must not shy away from complexity if it opens up possibilities for doing better justice for humanity and the earth.

To reiterate, decolonisation within legal knowledge is a question of present ontology not of ancient history. Understanding this allows us to engage with how most of the contemporary violence of colonialism emerges from everyday micro-regulation of space–time and humanity – an automated systemisation of brutality that often does not require individual malice. The absence of teaching and research on race and colonialism should be concerning in any discipline, but more so for law, as this absence obscures the utility of the field in its lack of understanding of where we are and how we came to be here. Legal knowledge, in its silences, ensures the reproduction and continuation of harm, while simultaneously leaving us powerless to end them. As Euro-modern law emerged in intimate and violent collaboration with the globalisation of colonial logics, law cannot without more, merely rebrand itself as an egalitarian field, obscuring its ongoing complicity with the aftershocks of the colonial earthquake.

Ultimately, I am asking us to rethink legal knowledge and our role as legal academics in this world, in new, interesting, and dynamic ways. As law's logics are intimately linked with the reproductions of particular violent definitions of the human and space–time, a decolonial unknowing of it requires a fundamental disruption of form, content, and purpose. The preceding analysis is not just about historical legal knowledge of where law has been, but it also raises ontological, axiological, and legal design questions. But most importantly, we must ask what world we want to emerge beyond colonial logics, at the end of this necropolitical condition, on the other side of this deathscape. To answer this question, we must go beyond engaging with colonial logics produced in substantive and procedural distinctions within Euro-modern law and its legal meanings. We must also deal in the areas between those distinctions and meanings, while considering jurisprudences, concepts, methods, and experiences that we do not often concern ourselves with in law schools. This means considering what lies beyond, in spaces undefined and undefinable by Euro-modernity. In times made unintelligible to coloniality. Through bodies unseen by this death zone. In the silence after the disturbed waters. In the spaces of a dying planet. In desolate and sunken places. In words that the subaltern cannot speak.

3

Defining the Law's Subject I: (Un)Making the Wretched of the Earth

> They enslaved the Negro, they said, because he was not a man, and when he behaved like a man, they called him a monster.
> C.L.R. James (1989: 362)

> It is not the differences between us that tear us apart ... it is our refusal to examine the distortions which arise from their misnaming, and from the illegitimate usage of those differences which can be made when we do not claim them nor define them for ourselves.
> Audre Lorde, in Byrd et al (2009: 202)

Introduction

A fundamental prerequisite to the emergence a world in need of decolonisation, is the, (as James and Lorde note) misusing of difference and the creation of monsters and subhuman humans in epistemologically damaging ways. Thus, the entanglement of Euro-modern law with the design and spirit of colonialism – focused as it is on accumulation through dispossession – is characterised and operationalised by hierarchisation, dehumanisation, as well as control and disciplining along the abyssal line. In other words, through logics of enclosure and valuation, a teleological co-optation of life and nature was instituted and is reproduced by Euro-modern epistemologies. Hierarchisation, in particular, results from marking and creating human groupings through manufactured categorisations and making them accordingly increasingly vulnerable to 'group-differentiated death'. Consequently, this chapter, and the two that follow, focus on three modes through which Euro-modern jurisprudence (re)produces a knowledge system of epistemic dispossession contingent on accumulation. Primarily this happens by adopting definitions of 'human', 'space' (as well as 'place' and 'property') and 'time' in law, which function in close alliance with the purposes of capital appropriation, fragmentation, constriction, and commodification. Unsettling these definitions situates body–space–time within a larger conceptual and structural system that constitutes reality, especially Euro-modern law's worldmaking through ideology and coercion. Though these three frames are overlapping and co-constitutive, it is instructive to identify and define some of the ways in which each frame individually thus constructs reality ... even as they collapse together as they fold themselves into our reality. This enfoldment makes itself known in many places, but very few are as poignant as the 'Door of no Return' – the last place and time in Africa where captured African bodies were still at home. This is the place where the racialised body first encountered the beginnings of being translated into property and being abstracted from time. Similar overlaps in body–space–time inevitably appear in these chapters.

This examination fundamentally invites an unsettling of the conceptualities that produce the conditions of our present, which may be represented to create new conditions for possible futures. This negates the presumption that current conditions of life are natural and immutable. Thinking more thematically in this way, prevents the silofication that characterises contemporary decolonisation discourse in UKHE, allowing us to simultaneously trouble the discipline while continually crafting theories of decolonisation. Therefore, rather than ask, for example: 'how do we decolonise the law curriculum?', we are able to question the possibilities that eventuate the emergence and social production of the content of the curriculum and its underpinning normativities, as well as conceptualise what future possibilities that such questioning may lead us to in our teaching, research, and practice. To this end, to underline the devaluation of life inherent in colonial thought, I start this analysis with the body. The body/person/human is central to the workings of Euro-modern legal thought; it is 'the bedrock on which the social order is founded' (Oyěwùmí 1997: 2). Consequently, it could be argued that the main concern of Euro-modern legal knowledge is regulating the human/body. I use the designation of 'human/body' here to signify the uncertain definition and conflation of human–body–person in law as its central concern. (Whether this concern should be the case – as examined by writers of the Anthropocene for example – is a different though related consideration. See for example, Grear [2015: 225–49]). Nevertheless, the human/body – howsoever framed in law – occupies centre stage in its imaginary. Nature, or non-human life, are often only considered as important with regards to their utility to the human/body.

Therefore, this chapter focuses on how concepts of the human/body emerge from or are infused by colonial legal knowledge and logics. Thus, racialisation – the main technology of imperial power – provides the primary point of entry into this analysis, with an understanding of the ways in which other axes of human categorisation/hierarchisation are implicated in the colonial constitution of the human. The contours of the category 'human' have been profoundly shaped by colonial knowledge systems (Jackson 2017: 31). Therefore, Euro-modern legal knowledge – dedicated as it is to governance of the human and society – is necessarily underpinned by and furthers the production of this 'Europe's human' within its corpus. So, here I explicate how this production enables the creation of racialised capital and other social constructions of colonial conditions of life. In doing so, I also exposit how anti-Blackness particularly, underwrites the evolution of colonial logics and the selective destructiveness of Euro-modernity as it is inscribed by and on the human/body. This illustrates law's inherent self-incapacitation to protect life, as Euro-modernity is coded instead to protect the conditions that produce bare life and for the interests of capital accumulation. The capitalist-colonial-enslavement project is particularly detrimental to life as it operates 'through relations of severe inequality among human groups' and thus entails 'loss, disposability, and the unequal differentiation of human value' (Melamed 2015: 77). This systemised process relies on pre-set conceptualisations underlying the capitalist-colonial-enslavement project which require the legitimation of state policy also above the abyssal line, as well as legal enactment and enforcement everywhere.

Constructing law's human: the continuously continuing colonial conditions of (non)life

I am interested here in how the accumulation/dispossession couplet operates as it manifests through and on the human/body. Also important is what gives this process order and power, and how these processes implicate themselves in our understanding of seemingly objective legal concepts like freedom, liberty, justice, and order. What we understand as the human/body within law – its nature, its dictates – is co-constitutive of the social milieu within which it is placed. Therefore, what legal knowledges result from this placement and how the law is consequently understood and enforced is predicated on variate technologies of inclusion and exclusion, as well as ever-evolving lines of an artificially constructed and colonially imbricated 'law's human/body'. In consequence, I am arguing here, that it is not just that manufactured characteristics (race, gender, class, nationality, ethnicity, sexuality, ability, and so on) result in differential treatment under the law. Colonialism's effect on legal outcomes is more fundamental than that. What is contended here is that the legal constitution of the category 'human' under Euro-modern law, evolving through periods of racialised enslavement and exploitative colonisation and their afterlives, produces hierarchical colonial logics of Euro-modern exclusions from it. The purportedly neutral category of the 'human' is not as universally open to all as Euro-modern law claims. Therefore, there can be no disruption to the violent continuities of the ' "coloniality of power" without a redescription of the human outside the terms of our present descriptive statement of the human, Man, and its over-representation' (Wynter 2003: 268). Euro-modern hierarchisation within the category 'human' is woven into the language and logics of its law and thus contributes to the production of differential outcomes before the law. To put it differently, we cannot hope to achieve racial equality – for example, without rethinking the (re)production of the category 'race' and its implications, and thus imagining its annihilation as well as the annihilation of categorisation itself. Through Euro-modernity's conceptualisation of the body, colonial logics continue the work of racialised enslavement and colonisation, or 'the co-optation of a body for purposes not its own' (Bonair-Agard n.d.: webpage). Yet, the Euro-modern approach to promoting equality focuses on 'protected characteristics'. This approach, however, overlooks and does not engage with how, in the very process of the construction of law's (hu)man/body, these characteristics *became* (un)protected, as well as the mechanics by which these characteristics continue to be (un)protected. In other words, there is insufficient consideration from within Euro-modern legal knowledge for how the purported ambition to protect bodies with these characteristics is contingent on the continual *fact* of their structural lack of protection across space–time. So, rather than only trying to find ways to protect those who carry these characteristics, we should also unveil how those contingently produced (un)protected characteristics combine to signify who is most protected by the law – in other words law's ideal (hu)man body. This requires tracing the emergence of law's human/body and how that emergence happens in tandem with the (re)emergence and (re)production of the capitalist-colonial-enslavement project.

The material effects of de-personifying certain human beings within Euro-modern legal epistemology through a history of colonial logics, was explored in Chapter 2. In addition to this, we must also question if those othered humans/bodies can enter once again into the corpus of law's human/body, through merely declarative means. Does Euro-modern legal knowledge that emerges on the other side of colonialism even retain the possibility of making them human once again? What would it mean for all human life, in fact all planetary life, to be asserted as normative? Thus, we must also consider the possibility that the epistemologies that unhuman the human/body have bled beyond the nebulous and equivocal boundaries that separate the unhuman human from the sacred figure of Man. In other words, as legal epistemologies travel, do the defining logics of disconnection from humanity not diffuse themselves from internally othered populations and into the theodic figure of Man itself? Do certain qualifiers of humanity, inherently and eventually disqualify all of humanity from humanity? To put it a different way, does unhuman-ing also travel upwards and above the abyssal line? So, in our understanding of the human/body in law, we must carefully note the infectability of the logics and legal epistemologies of dehumanisation, also to groups that have historically wielded these logics and epistemologies, and thus to planetary life itself.

The primary point of entry for understanding and signifying colonial technologies for producing disparate conditions of life, is the concept of 'race'. However, in this, 'race' must be understood as artificially constructed, socially politically and socio-legally produced and not merely a biological or objectively legitimate and neutral means of classification of humanity. The concept of race as we understand and use it today emerges from a particular history and usage that is integral to the ordering of the world – using 'science' as a proxy for political ends and means. An ordering in which legal knowledges are also complicit, producing a 'transversal dividing line that cuts across multiple power relations such as class, sexual and gender at a global scale'. (Grosfoguel 2016: 11). Thus, it must also be understood that race overlaps with other classifications of humanity that also hierarchise. These hierarchisations thereafter result in amalgamating modalities of life and conditions in which the human/body is placed.

But what does race actually mean, especially in the context of the production of colonial knowledges of being? As stated already, it is inaccurate to define race *only* as a significant neutral biological phenomenon and a legitimate categorisation of humanity, without more. In other words, it is inaccurate to imply that racial identities with biological origins have moral/ character implications or on their own can tell us anything scientifically significant about racialised populations. To be fair, this approach has been largely dismissed within academic discourse. It is now accepted that there is no pre-existing scientific merit in the hierarchical and eugenicist categorisation of humans according to race that marked enlightenment scholarship. Conversely, good arguments can still be made for categorisation according to how subjectification happens in relation to racially produced oppressive structures. That distinction between these two modes of categorisation must be made clearly and overtly, lest we fall into race-neutral analysis in the face of glaring racial disparity, that falls back on the assumption that the production of human 'races' happened unproblematically. The social effects of classifying humanity into races still persist, as do many of the biological tools for classification by race, contemporarily and mainly, skin colour.

Thus, biology is not completely insignificant in thinking about race, as the skin, as a biologic marker, is implicated in the copious accoutrements of race-making. But race's relation with biology manifests most strongly as a tool or an outcome of classification, not the core of classification itself. For example, the American Medical Association, in recognising racism as a public health threat, acknowledge the biologic outcomes of racialisation (that is, giving socio-political meaning to skin colour) (American Medical Association 2020: webpage).

While defining race as biologic has fallen into academic disfavour, racial categorisations have also increasingly been understood as cultural categories instead. In this characterisation, 'race' and 'ethnicity' become synonymous. The use of ethnicity as a replacement for race quite possibly reduces the discomfort non-racialised people experience in discussing race, as it divorces the discussion from a history of dehumanisation. However, the effect of this use of 'race' also constricts the fluidity of culture, making it coterminous with the immutable destinies of skin colour implicated in eugenicist definitions of race. This oppositional conflation also dislocates itself from the historical practices of mapping colonial cartographies, which resulted in interpellated ideas of place, race, and culture (Razack 2018: 74–82). Therefore, it should be noted that the increasing contemporary desire to replace 'race' with 'ethnicity', attempts to disappear the unjust social production of racial categories, by among other things, diluting the reasons for studying race – injustice.

Within studies of racial injustice and colonisation, race is more acceptably defined as socially constructed. This is not an entirely new development. Both Alain Locke and W.E.B. DuBois engaged with the social production of race in their work – both writing from the 19th to the 20th centuries (Mason 1979: 342; DuBois 1897). This use is also mirrored in Gilroy's conceptualisation of race as a mutable social, political, cultural, and historical construct, rather than something rooted in innate biological difference (Gilroy 2013: 1–9). Social constructionism means that society, including law and knowledge producers, give moral and social meaning to perceived racial classifications, and those meanings crystallise but also evolve over time (Obasogie 2015: 345). Race is produced through the capitalist-colonial-enslavement project as a regime of domination: it is not itself an ontology (Wolfe 2016: 18). However, one limitation of social constructionism as a tool for understanding structural inequalities, is its ease of accessibility within liberal discourse as a means for the denial of those inequalities. Here, race is considered as something we can refuse to see – a wilful confusion between '*socially constructed*' and '*not real*'. Money is socially constructed (meanings and value are adduced to scraps of paper and lumps of metal). So are nations. Yet, we deny neither's power nor existence. The result – and often the point – of the wilful confusion is to refute the existence of the injustice produced by categorisation. To wit, it is instructive to note that Section 9 of the Equality Act (2010) defines race in relation to 'colour', 'nationality' and 'ethnic/national origins' but makes no room for social construction. This fundamentally misunderstands the modalities of race and severely limits the scope of the legislation to bring an end to racial injustice.

However, it must be accepted that strict definitional categories often required by false objective and universal standards will expectedly throw up difficulties caused by the problematic premises upon which the questions we ask are based. These problematic premises frequently result from faulty presumptions as well as the misusing of science and the body that is being condemned, to justify continuing structures and epistemologies of accumulation and dispossession. Therefore, it may be more expedient to examine what this category has been used for, and the evolving social conditions it produces. Race as a social construct or 'a floating signifier', is implicated in the marking of bodies and the ordering of the colonial world, explored in the previous chapter. In what is now known as the USA, for example, in 1787, as a compromise to secure the unity of the country, people of African descent were classified in the constitution as three-fifths of a person. This deployment of the signifier thereby simultaneously increased the political and economic influence of white slave-holding Southern states and marked Black people as less than human (Ohline 1971: 563–84; Humes et al 2002: 452–66). This use of race and the body as a system of dehumanisation with particular structuring and ordering functions is often conceptualised as 'racialisation'. In other words, racialisation is part of what race *does*. In essence, racialisation describes the process by which the creation of race, as a supposedly legitimate categorisation of humanity, becomes a salient and normalised tool implicated in the organisation of all social relations in all human time and all human space, for all human bodies (Garner 2007: 67; Garner 2017: 3). Racialisation is a process that marked which bodies (and spaces) could be legitimately colonised and thus the fluid racial hierarchies that persist, persist not just as afterlives of colonialism, but a continuation thereof. Creating racial categories gave continuing 'legitimacy to the relations of domination imposed by [colonial] conquest' (Quijano 2000a: 534). Through this legal process the human/body becomes 'the primary site and surface of race and representation' (Jackson 2006: 2). The racialised body becomes a text that holds social meanings capable of being read and understood by interlocutors. These meanings are then passed through space–time. All bodies are racialised. White bodies are racialised as normal or normative (Dyer 1988: 45). Other bodies, in varying degrees, are racialised as not normal and not normative.

Cartesian dualism's separation of body and soul is implicated in some of the foundational ideology of creating bodies that fit into the ideal of law's human (Maldonado-Torres 2007: 245–8). He draws on Aristotle's descriptions of the living being as 'soul and body, of which the former is by nature the ruling and the latter the subject factor' Aristotle suggests that of 'those that are bad or in a bad condition it might be thought that the body often rules the soul because of its vicious and unnatural condition' (350 BCE: 1254a19–1254b20). Therefore, the human (subject) was considered to be split into having a soul and thus reason, and a differentiated body (object), which was in a state of nature. It was believed that a division could consequently be achieved between them. Based on this belief, differential sociolegal meanings were given to persons, depending on which was accepted as 'in charge' – body or soul. This fostered, for example, gendered demarcations in understanding personhood. Men were 'walking minds' and women were said to be ruled by their bodies and therefore unthinking units of flesh (Oyěwùmí 1997: 6). These same logics were utilised to racialise and devalue the life of bodies so marked. Essentially, colonial domination and destruction of life was animated by unfeeling rationality – the separation of the daily conditions of the body from Euro-modernity's understanding of reason. In other words, the violence of abstraction separated personhood from racialised bodies and so rationally and justifiably permitted harm on those bodies more frequently and naturally. This violent abstraction for the purposes of accumulation (which included processes that made property out of life) created a new model for the category 'human' dependent on the colonial relation (Maldonado-Torres 2007: 245; Bhandar 2014: 211). The adoption of skin colour as the primary marker of race allowed for non-white populations to be marked as the visually identifiable absolute other, whose lack of rationality provided licence for their domination and dispossession.

But we must remember that though racialisation was the key technology of colonial marking of the body, it also interacts and interpellates with other markers. Therefore, 'coloniality of gender' and 'un-gendering' give us useful frameworks for understanding the ways in which other floating signifiers overlap with racialisation and also how colonial meanings have subsumed and erased pre-existing indigenous meanings of body differentiations. So, Lugones urges us to consider how the 'colonial matrix of power', as an entire structure, operates beyond narrow definitions of race (and gender, and so on) to enact the 'control of sexual access, collective authority, labor, subjectivity/inter-subjectivity and the production of knowledge from within these inter-subjective relations' (2013: 372). Coloniality of gender describes the structural selection (marking) and use of racialised–gendered bodies for the purposes of the capitalist-colonial-enslavement structure. This use created demarcations within 'othered' populations that relied on the complicity of privileged-by-gender colonised men to enforce those boundaries. These boundaries are complicated across contexts and produce pervasive material and epistemic effects. Spivak describes the body of the subaltern as subject to an enfoldment of colonial knowledge, racialised, gendered and capitalist structures (1988: 271–313). Through these structures the subaltern is deprived of testamentary life. She 'cannot speak' because her human/body has been made unintelligible by and to the power structures which make her unintelligible. Her inability to speak reduces the scope of her power and her possibility to the very limits of her structurally marked human/body.

At play here are intertwining structures that annihilate non-Europe ways of knowing and being human. For example, Oyěwùmí argues that in the Yorùbá context, gendered categorisation prior to colonisation did not carry the same social connotation as Euro-modern legal epistemologies do (1997: 35). Yorùbá society was not ordered around the body, but around social structures of seniority. Therefore, the colonial process, and its introduction of gendered categories, was achieved primarily with the complicity of colonised men. Consequently, as with racialisation and social constructionism, the meanings that attach to gendered–racialised bodies crystallise through the epistemologies of colonialism and their use, as well as intragroup connivance. In observing this, Spillers uses the concept of 'un-gendering' (1987: 77) to refer to the particular effects on the body and on society found at the intersection of being racialised and gendered away from normativity. Thus, Spillers distinguishes the process of *gendering* of White women that transpires in the domestic space, predicated on the gendered roles of motherhood and care for family, from the process of *ungendering* of African-American women that begins on the slave ship, and is predicated on captivity and coerced servitude, as well as loss of gender, family, and bodily autonomy. Ungendering, therefore, produces a body that is open to be violated by all, in all ways (Spillers 1987: 77). These erased bodies are still useful to capital, either as direct cheap labour, or through motherhood a source of reproduction of more cheap labour. For example, through practices of violation, exploitation, and disposability, enabled and justified by doctrines like *partus sequitur ventrem*.

Such enfoldment transcends a mathematical conjunction of gender and race but denotes a multi-dimensional teleological hierarchal construction of the category 'human', that places the function and vulnerability of the racialised and gendered human/body exponentially beyond the bounds of normative protection. Justice must account for these meanings and their historical trajectories, as well as the hermeneutical injustice that results from Euro-modern law's inability and self-imposed incapacitation to read bodies thus misused. Race and gender in particular, but enfoldments of signifiers in general, do not operate as legitimate flat axes of identification, they however, contain Euro-modern legal meanings that place those so labelled at unequally tiered points within the hierarchised category 'human', and thus invariably signify who is entitled to testamentary life and who can lay claim to profligate life. I use 'testamentary life' here to imply complex storied life, life as it is meant to be lived and valued, in harmony with all other life, human and non-human, and with nature. 'Profligate life', on the other hand, describes enjoyment of life beyond what one should reasonably be able to claim – an enjoyment of life predicated on the dispossession and dehumanisation of others and destruction of the planet upon which all life is meant to survive. Dehumanisation, thus describes, not only what is done to marked others, but to the category human itself.

Thus, the marking of bodies produces othered lives, which are, through the logics and practices of colonialism, unintelligible to legal epistemologies of Euro-modernity, its protection, and its justice. Euro-modern legal knowledge, in its longstanding alliance with capitalist power, has constructed itself to primarily protect profligate life and so cannot read other life or effectively protect the planet. Therefore, these body markers of gender and race (and class and disability and sexuality, and so on) function as technologies that produce particular modalities of life through the coercive power of the law that shapes behaviour and thinking globally. Their insidiousness lies in their appearance as natural, such that their outcomes – for example, making poor and making rich – also appear natural, an inevitable destiny of different marked sections of humanity. Therefore, Euro-modern legal knowledge which claims the human/body as its central subject has, ironically, through its colonial logics, made most of its subject unintelligible to itself. Attempts have been made to unravel this unintelligibility within the law, through among others feminist and queer emancipatory legal epistemologies. For example, Critical Race Feminism (CRF) emerged out of Critical Race Theory 'to expose how law has served to perpetuate unjust class, race, and gender hierarchies' (Wing 2000: 4). Thus, CRF elucidates how race, class, and other factors, correlate 'within a system of white male patriarchy and racist oppression to make the life experiences of women of color distinct from those of both men of color and white women' (Onwuachi-Willig 2005: 736). Thus both 'intersectionality' and the Combahee River Collective conceptualisation of 'identity politics' (Combahee River Collective 1983: 264–74; Crenshaw 1990: 1241–300) were developed to articulate the vulnerable position of 'women of color' subject to Euro-modern law and society. A related point is made by Spivak, but she also indicts postcolonial theory and subaltern studies as emancipatory epistemologies whose structures have similarly made the subaltern unintelligible (Spivak 1988: 275). So, we are invited to depart from the essentialisations that have epistemologically being stamped on the body, especially through the colonial process, and recognise the structural nature of oppression, as well as intragroup – wilful and unwitting –complicity with it. Furthermore, this troubles the state as the sole juridical agent for protection. This is due to the imbrication of the state's emergence with colonialism and the constructs that flow from that. Therefore, '[t]he coloniality of gender is … an invitation to consider "gender" geo-historically as a colonial construct, and not a universal condition that existed before colonization' (Icaza 2018: 66).

The rejection of Euro-modern notions of patriarchy is significant in defining our understanding of how colonialism shapes the modern world, especially the roles of gendering in extracting labour and reproduction.

Therefore, we can surmise that under colonial conditions, the body can be made an exploitable space, whose power is (un)limited by how it is marked. Lefebvre argues that bodies are ontologically productive of social space (1991: 170). This idea is examined further in the next chapter. However, of interest here is how the marking of bodies determines their spatialisation. A spatialised body is always a site of indiscriminate potential conquest (as Spillers notes). Bravo uses the examples of Truganini and Baartman to illustrate the ways in which the bodies of racialised women, in life and in death, are treated as object–property within the law (2013: 289–326). Both women were brutally objectified in life as part of colonial desires to fetishise, acquire, dominate, and accumulate both human and land as territory. In death, both were displayed – Truganini against her expressed wishes in the Tasmanian Museum. Baartman's body parts, including her genitals, were displayed in the French National Museum of Natural History till the 1970s. Though Truganini's ashes were eventually scattered in accordance with her wishes on Tasmanian soil in 1976, in 2002 her hair and skin samples were discovered at the British Royal College of Surgeons. After a long political negotiation and change in French law, Baartman's remains were repatriated to South Africa in 2002. These logics and praxis of 'thingifying' the spatial–temporal racialised and gendered human/body move back and forth between the invasion of land and the dehumanisation of the body. They continue to be replicated in experimentation and use of marked bodies across space–time (Brandt 1978: 21–9; Skloot 2017; Schroeder et al 2018: 3–7).

What the foregoing tells us is that rather than thinking only through the lens(es) of the various characteristics which are (un)protected, we should also trace how the coloniality of power writes itself onto bodies as an imperial shorthand that carries (in)decipherable messages across space–time. Then we may be able to note how these messages bleed into our legal epistemologies. An example is how racialised enslavement introduced particularly limiting ways of understanding the human/body and personhood. We can think of the infectability of colonialism's logics in this way: to lawfully steal *a body*, we must define *bodies*, even when unmarked, as legally stealable. Thus, even though we may outlaw the *act* of stealing bodies, without redefining the human/body, the *legal definition* of all bodies retains aspects of stealability. This may manifest in exploitable labour and vulnerability to slow and immediate violence usable for capital accumulation, but it is always predicated on a demarcation between the human person and the labour produced by the person. Consequently, Bhandar explains how Lockean justifications for private property and techniques of abstraction conflate property, racial, subject, and object (Bhandar 2014: 203–18). She argues that this conflation is most apparent in the body of the enslaved who is 'both treated juridically as one who can be held legally culpable for crimes but is also an object to be owned by others' (Bhandar 2014: 211). Bhandar's arguments echo Harris' who explains how 'whiteness', originally socially constructed as racial identity, morphed into a form of property which, in the past and present, is acknowledged and protected by law in the US (Harris 1993: 1707–91). Moreton-Robinson describes a similar process in the Australian context, where whiteness translates indigenous land into private enclosures (Moreton-Robinson 2015: 65–78). While this property-fication logic is key to the marking of bodies, it is not a primary and obvious organising logic in *all* events of racism. Wilderson notes, anti-Black violence, specifically, is gratuitous and thus does not require capital's immediate usability of labour or resources (2020: 216–17). This type of violence reveals itself globally in events of police brutality and Afrophobic encounters. Nevertheless, the ever-present spectre of violence provides a background coercive force to the alienation of othered labour. So, through periods of racialised enslavement and exploitative colonisation, as well as their continuing afterlives, the modalities that result from (un) protected characteristics surreptitiously uncover the inherent and sociogenic plasticity of the human/body and its vulnerability to the interests and desires of capitalist–colonial power. Hence, even within that vulnerability lies possibility. Thus, consequent upon that vulnerability, I do not consider (un)protected characteristics necessarily separatable aspects of the human/body. They share across them, not just their usability as technologies to discipline the human/body for the use of capital and under the auspices of state power, but simultaneously serve as fault lines of vulnerability to systemic and non-systemic violence.

Reproducing/maintaining law's human: the unintelligibility of testamentary life to legal knowledge

It can be argued, therefore, that Euro-modern law's premises about who can be considered law's ideal human subject, have remained largely unchanged since the dawn of colonialism – which Dussel et al put at 1492 (2000: 470). 'Man' has been that subject and other humans have merely been subsumed into that definition. Wynter describes this as the process of Man1 (bio-economic subject) morphing into Man2 (political subject), with no reconstruction of the foundational principles of normativity upon which the very concept of 'Man' is conceived (2003: 318). As Grear claims, deep within the foundations of law there is a particular universal vision of a human being for whom the law is made – the rational man (2007: 531; 2015: 231–2). Within legal education, this 'Man' frequently appears as the oft-critiqued 'reasonable man on the Clapham omnibus' in the law of obligations and beyond (Martin 1994: 334–74; Conaghan 1996: 47–68; Carlos 2011: 1–32; see *Vaughan v Menlove* 1837: 492; *Hall v Brooklands* 1933: 224). The closest actual subject to this vision of law's ideal human/body is a white property-owning, heteronormative, European man (Douzinas 2000: 97). Thus, law's ideal Man1 and Man2 evolves through Wynter's thesis and retains the actual protected characteristics – whiteness, class/economic advantage, gendered advantage, heteronormativity, and is also advantaged by ability and geopolitics and so on.

As an aside, it is important to remember that within systems of advantage so conceptually and interpellatedly ordered, it is possible to inherit and benefit from histories that are not our own, and so social-political-legal constructions, rather than individual morality are more relevant to meaning-making within those systems (Rothberg 2020: 1–21 especially). Nevertheless, the closer humans/bodies are to these actually protected characteristics, the more the law recognises their entitlement to profligate life. The further away, the closer to bare and disposable life. It matters little how bodies come to be near or far. This illustrates law's propensity to protect the interests of capitalist-colonial might (Thornton 1998: 370–2; Darian-Smith 2015: 647–51), and links it with particular technologies of power which inscribe themselves of the human/body. Consequently, the human/body most protected by colonial logics and praxes is the human/body that has been socially-politically-legally constructed to bring most capital value. This then reveals Euro-modern legal knowledge's imbrication with capital. Hence, 'colonisation' constantly reveals itself not only as a physical, spatial, and temporal project and endeavour, but also operates, almost in perpetuity, as the epistemic project of 'colonialism', an ontological project, and a normative project, with material axiologies and teleologies, that find meaning and effect in humans/bodies (and space–time) as well as through technologies of capital.

'Racialisation' thus proves a useful concept for understanding the weaving of meanings into, and reduction of meaning of, complex bodies for the purposes of adducing value for capital and the complicity of the law. It should be noted though, that this value for capital is not infinitely translatable. Thus, what is valued for life above the abyssal line is not valued below the line and vice versa. For example, the freedom to offend wielded by the powerful is mostly experienced as harm below the line. The freedom to be free from that harm below the line is then experienced as restriction on freedoms above the line. As the law inevitably allies itself with power – above the line – purported temporal protections and movement toward freer societies, manifest not as linear progressions but modifications and invisibilisations of technologies of power. In other words, human society does not really move towards freedom, but towards increasing concealment of the workings of power and attendant marking of bodies. Consequently, freedom above the line can be conceived, not as constant 'freedom from' but escalating 'freedom to'. For example, freedom to exploit labour below the line, wherever that line is found, has been a constant companion to power above the line, with changing manifestations from racialised enslavement to contemporary exploitation of low-wage and unfree labour in populations made to be socio-economically disadvantaged in the Global North and the Global South.

Thus, capital accumulation (governed by law) does not produce inequality along (un)protected characteristics marked on the body as an unfortunate by-product of colonialism's ways of being and doing, but by normative progression and inevitable contingency. This is often explained through the phraseology of 'racial capitalism' (theorised most notably by Cedric Robinson (1983), but originated by South African anti-apartheid scholars [Phiri 2020: 63–81; Al-Bulushi 2020]) to denote the ways in which racial capitalism describes 'actually existing capitalism'. In other words, conceptualisations of racial capitalism do not necessarily suggest that capitalism cannot be non-racial but rather recognise that the actual capitalism that exists in human society has always been intimately tied with racialising (very broadly defined), hierarchisation, and mythologising itself. As Leroy and Jenkins explain, 'slavery epitomized a racialized system of valuation and extraction that continues to this day' (2021:11). Thus, the marking of the human/body as assisted by legal epistemologies operates as a source of production. This is its primary function. This process is cyclical across time and space as 'the capitalist world system finds a distinctive way to reify regional and cultural differences into races in order to structure social divisions between different forms of labour' (Kundnani 2021: 63). Racial hatreds and other individualised intolerances, which equality laws focus on, emerge only as dependent on differential valuing of bodies for production. This is succinctly clarified by the Fieldses, who tell us that the 'chief business of slavery [was] the production of cotton, sugar, rice, and tobacco' and not the production of 'white supremacy' (Fields and Fields 2014: 117). In other words, inequality is an inevitable though not deliberate product of racialisation – a distinction well understood in law between recklessness/negligence and intention. Marking of bodies serves no other purpose than accumulation, and thus hierarchisation of humans/bodies is 'neither a by-product nor "negative externality" of otherwise inclusive systems, nor a remnant of old days that is dissipating with time and increased awareness. [Racism, as well as any other human/body differentiation] is resource, or a technology, on which institutions and organisations rely to achieve production' (Marchais 2020: webpage). Racism and white supremacy are required to produce 'race', as sexism and the patriarchy are required for the production of gender and so on. Put differently, the individual intolerances and malices (as well as legal sanctions against these) that are produced by the marking of bodies – in other words, 'the event of racism' (Modiri 2016: webpage), are necessary for the perpetuation of the less obvious but more systemic, structural, and necessary-to-capital, reproduction of the marking of bodies – making the socialised appear as normal and normative. Thus, Kwame Ture realises the necessity of institutionalised racism to the current order of the world when he says that to end the former is also to end the latter (Carmichael 2007: 79). Therefore, without undoing the connection between capitalism and the marking of bodies, egalitarian motives of equality and justice proceed in vain as fragmented inadequate substitutes. The illusions of linear progress hide the evolving and expanding machinery of accumulation and dispossession, for example, 'the determination of slavery to perpetuate itself … due to the folly of endeavoring to retain the new wine of liberty in the old bottles of slavery' (Douglass 2018: 488). Thus, logics assisted by legal epistemologies of regulating human life through marking of the human/body constantly reproduce the abyssal line of life and death. Uninterrogated legal knowledges reproduce a field of pain and death in the human/body and on this wretched earth.

To describe this life/death dichotomy, Foucault was concerned with the functional and legitimated power of the state-sovereign in regulating the life of the legitimate population (Davies et al 2017: 1267). For example, Foucault explains that to the state, the population presents a political, scientific, and biological problem (2013b: 66). Thus, questions of governance and ultimately law, manifest themselves in multidisciplinary modes of control, through torture and the prison (Foucault 1995: 11–13). The law is and has been necessary to determine all other spheres of governance, housing, education, health, work, maintenance of order, and so on. The repeated use of law to produce this order invisibilises its power and involvement in the process. Thus, Euro-modern law has been 'an essential feature in the illusion of necessity' (Crenshaw 1987: 1351–2). Where colonial control has been and is necessary for the appropriation of land for accumulation of imperial capital, this manifests itself in legal control of, and legitimising demarcation within, Euro-modern legal language and modes of abstraction. Foucault recognises this system of control as an extension of the conditions of the battlefield to the domestic sphere. This effectively reduces the axiology of human existence to appearing to the structure in the starkness of only either death or life (Foucault 2013b: 75). This dichotomous condition is also produced in colonial logics of commodification of person (labour) and space–time. There is no real liminal space that is not disposability. On the battlefield, the soldier who is alive contributes to the fight, and the soldier who is dead or injured has no impact on the war. By extending this death/life frame to civil 'peacetime', the concern of the sovereign in the domestic sphere is reduced to only the same concerns that pervade the warscape – some will live, and some will die. There is no in-between space. What is not usable is disposable. Euro-modern legal knowledge operating at the behest of empire illustrates this use of the human/body and space–time beneath the abyssal line. Colonial operations are not designated as wartime, so the disposability of life and the earth woven into its praxes can continue, through legal modes of control. Nevertheless, as Foucault is describing coercive power generally, the analysis does not engage specifically with how colonial logics create spaces of non-being where disposability is the dominant mode of existence.

Consequently, Mbembé's concept of necropolitics expands on Foucault's biopolitical ascription. Necropolitics operates as state–sovereign death–power that is expressed mainly in the 'power and capacity to dictate who is able to live and who must die' (Mbembé 2019: 66). Thus, Mbembé's thesis recognises the limits of a biopolitical analysis that fails to account for extreme situations arising from deploying colonial logics where, 'life was not so much being governed, as much as death itself was being sanctioned' (Davies et al 2017: 1267–8). Wherever destruction and dehumanisation is/was required for the advance of the empire, it is coded as natural and enacted lawfully – rationally. Whole swathes of abyssal populations are labelled 'must die'. We see evidence of this labelling in multi-causal large scale population loss occasioned by colonial contact with Europe – examined in Chapter 1. Thus, Nast and McIntyre describe the biopolis and the necropolis as co-constitutive and almost counterpoints of each other – zones of life and death respectively. The biopolis is constructed for the state – the afterlives of colonialism's logics and praxes – to survive at all costs (some will die); the necropolis is comprised of variously located zones of exclusion containing populations whose lives point only to death (some must die) (McIntyre and Nast 2011: 1467). In other words, in the biopolis, for survival, the death of some is possible, while in the necropolis, the death of some is inevitable. The process of identifying populations who are marked, 'must die', can be found in colonialism's appropriation-led creation of 'zones of non-being' or spaces beyond the abyssal line, predicated on materially driven gendered and ungendered racialisation (Fanon 2008: 2; Weheliye 2014: 41, 96; Grosfoguel 2016: 11–12). The spatialising aspects of these concepts will be addressed further in the next chapter. What is important to note here is that necropolitical–colonial logics rely specifically on the legitimation (through Euro-modern legal instruments and epistemologies) of death-inevitability marked populations in zones of non-being.

Therefore, both Foucault and Mbembé recognise global structural or state-sanctioned racism as not just one example of sovereign death–power, but *the* example; so, this acknowledges the role of imperial epistemologies, colonial logics, and control of the human/body in the emergence of the biopolis and the necropolis (Foucault 2013b: 74–7; Mbembé 2019: 1–5, 38). The enactment plays out in case law, legislation, treaties, and legal instruments, reinforcing and regulating the processes and space–time practices within racialised enslavement and exploitative colonisation as well as the dynamics that continue forth from them. The limits of Foucault's analysis, however, lie in the fact that his thesis, like Marx's critique of capitalism, seems to ignore how action below the abyssal line (Saldívar 2013: 199; de Sousa Santos 2016: 70–1), (contemporarily designated the Global South) not only has an effect on zones above the abyssal line, but also that conditions above the abyssal line are specifically contingent on zone demarcation. Foucault only finds racism significant when it occurs above the abyssal line (Weheliye 2014: 16). This critical lacuna causes an analytical schism, splitting the colonial from the current and fails to note how the articulation of logics that constitute colonialism – being and space–time – survive in evolved forms. Colonial logics operate as contiguous extractive and dehumanising ideologies working in tandem, creating dichotomous zones of accumulation and dispossession, along fault-lines created by the false race/racism relation. As Weheliye contends, the biopolitical function of race is racism (2014: 55–6). In other words, the division of humans into racial (and other) categories, functions to identify populations structurally coded for death – slow or immediate, whose bodies can be and are, disparately exploited for the benefit of capitalism. The nescience in noting this morphology and the attendant requirements of law's complicity in the process, ensure the survival of human hierarchies, as well as the consequent destruction of populations necropolitically marked for death. Thus, colonial logics produce the very conditions of life that elicit the emergence of (un)protected characteristics in law. So, there is often a tenuous and false relationship between the actually not objective characteristic and the condition the human/body is purportedly being protected from. For example, 'race' and 'racism'. Their relationship is often misconstrued and explained as flowing opposite to the direction it actually flows in. That is to say, the presumption is that the legitimate and natural categorisation of people by race then results in individual and collective racial hatred. Conversely, it has been suggested here that racialisation/structural racism produces race which produces individual racism (Kendi 2016: 9).

So, the messages left through the marking of humans/bodies by technologies of power produce in perpetuity the very conditions of life which technologies of power are then petitioned to protect the human/body from. Put differently, the division of humans into racial (and other) categories, functions to identify humans/bodies which can be and are, exploited for the benefit of capitalism, and to identify populations structurally coded for death – slow or immediate – through oppressions specifically implicit upon those categories. Thus, the very existence/creation of racial-gender-class-ability-sexuality categories produces the life-death dichotomy that marks the necropolitics of a world suffused in colonialism. Gilmore thus defines racism as, 'the state-sanctioned or extralegal production and exploitation of group-differentiated vulnerability to premature death' (2007: 28). The failure to acknowledge body-politics and racialisation's morphology as well as the attendant requirements of law's complicity in the process, invisibilises and ensures the survival of colonial logics and praxes, including the continuing consequent destruction of populations necropolitically marked for death. For example, this was evidenced by governmental policies in reaction to the COVID-19 pandemic which were designed to protect the economy and bodies supposedly most productive to capital, to the extent that they were productive to capital (Núñez-Parra et al 2021: 192).

In this vein, one could argue that the late 20th century emergence of borders can be considered a manifestation of hyper-legitimation of selected humans/bodies and de-legitimation of othered ones. This emergence is aided by the appearance of land as private property, which is itself deeply embedded in the identification of law's legitimate subject, in the amassing of capital (value), but also in the de-legitimation of human subjects (commodification), and de-legitimatising ways of being, as well as the emergence of unfree labour (Harris 1993: 1715–6, 1721–4; Keenan 2010: 428; Mignolo 2013a: 364; Bhandar 2018: 3–5). How these ideas manifest specifically in the emergence of land as property will be explored further in the next chapter. Suffice it to note here, that the absence of engagement within legal knowledge with these hierarchisations, present a problem to humanity and to the discipline. Unwilling to adapt, Euro-modern legal knowledge decays ... but cannot die. This is because, by keeping the flattened human/body as its subject, but not testamentary life, though it may never die, legal knowledge may never bring life. Euro-modern legal knowledge remains unable to read and protect the many-storied realities of human existence that exceed the spatial and temporal boundaries of the sovereign's regulatory epistemologies. Testamentary life is ontologically unintelligible to Euro-modern legal epistemologies which maintain an ever-moving but ever-present zone of non-being predicated on law's ideal human/body. Thus, in Gordon's reading of Fanon's conceptualisation of the zone of non-being, he argues that Euro-modern conceptualisations of the human stand 'in the way of human being or a human way of being' (2015b: 19). As a result, this particular vision of being creates zones of non-being that preclude human being and flourishing planetary life.

The particularity of past and present anti-Blackness to understanding this present darkness

The ongoing colonial world must also be understood as a fundamentally anti-Black world. By defining 'the human' as European, this meant that, according to Maldonado-Torres, colonial logics were deployed to create power dynamics and relations on the principle that '[t]he 'lighter' one's skin is, the closer to full humanity one is, and vice versa' (2007: 244). White supremacy and Anti-Blackness are thus contingent conditions, that frame anti-Blackness as a global organising principle and provide racial privilege to non-Black 'people of colour' (Grimes 2017: introduction; Jackson 2020). Scholars writing on Anti-Blackness recognise the inadequacy of 'racism' to describe the world or the social realities of those, who according to Fanon, have been *made* 'black' by being cast into the arid zone of non-being (2008: 2, 82–108; Jung and Vargas 2021: 3; Weheliye 2014: 37; Hartman 2002: 757–77). The enactment of racialised enslavement for over 400 years as the natural social condition a body racialised 'black', produced firstly, a category of person that constituted an absolute negation of humanity, and secondly, a world whose logics advance on and require that negation. This ongoing enactment has been described as the *Maangamizi* or *Maafa* – denoting a catastrophe, holocaust, or genocide against Africans racialised Black (Standford-Xosei 2019: 177). So, anti-Blackness defines, 'the extreme antisocial condition of possibility of the modern social world' (Jung and Vargas 2021: 4). In other words, the realities of Euro-modernity are contingent upon and undergirded by anti-Blackness. Therefore, the ontological delegitimisation of Black life through the mechanism of racialised enslavement, in a world that relied on Black labour, required, and requires more than the granting of liberty. Consequently, this delegitimisation remains an ongoing though evolving global organisational principle: in other words, 'relations of Black captivity are always at play' (King et al 2020: 11).

The uncritical repeated use of the word 'slave' to describe a person subjected to slavery, rather than the more accurate 'enslaved', distances the actual legal actor, and illustrates the natural/normative production of negation as a natural consequence of being racialised Black. For example, the case of *Gregson v Gilbert* (1783: 232) reports the throwing overboard of more than 130 'slaves' from the slave-ship *Zong*. Yet at the time of the events of the case, the Africans had not been enslaved, they had been kidnapped/captured. So, what made them 'slaves' in the eyes of the law? Why was this not a murder trial? How can they be unmade slaves? This negation is further reproduced in Afro-phobic treatment of Africa as a zone of absolute exclusion of humanity. A stereotyped place of 'absolute night, forgetting the existence or possibility of sunrise' (Adebisi 2016: 442). Effectively, designating Africa as the place from which slaves can be acquired, for unfree labour and accumulation of capital, grants all her descendants a seemingly everlasting inheritance in anti-Blackness, reinforced by borderisation. Borderisation is, according to Mbembé, 'the process by which world powers permanently transform certain spaces into impassable places for certain classes of populations' (2019: 99). Black people can only pass when they demonstrate their economic value. Therefore, the social realities produced from the trade in kidnapped and enslaved Africans results in them being perpetually and 'globally identifiable as the people who were appropriately designated a "slave race" in modernity'

(Mills 2013: 35). The effect of being racialised Black in a world ordered by colonial logics is to permanently exist in the category 'slave' and its changing meanings (Wilderson 2020: 15). These meanings separate the commodification of Black life from its negation, so as to render Black life, as such, negated (Biko 1981: 133). In essence, a Black person does not become no-longer-a-slave with emancipation, but a different and wider definition of 'slave' that encompasses absolute otherness, a definition that can be and is extended even to those who do not descend from peoples who were themselves enslaved. This, according to Wilderson, produces a very specific relationship of the Black person to violence, not found in other racialised groups. A Black person's 'relationship to violence is open-ended, gratuitous, without reason or constraint, triggered by prelogical catalysts that are unmoored from her transgressions and unaccountable to historical shifts … an "extension of the master's prerogative"' (Wilderson 2020: 216–17).

It should be noted that Wilderson particularly, and Afropessimism generally, has been criticised for a conceptualisation of the world that ignores hopeful possibility of new worlds, and which posits only apocalyptic ends as the termination of racial injustice (Gordon et al 2018: 105–37; Cunningham 2020: webpage). Furthermore, Wilderson's analysis is encumbered by a colonial conflation of Africa and Blackness: as he notes, 'there is no Black time that precedes the time of the Slave. Africa's spatial coherence is temporally coterminous with the Arab, and then European, slave trade' (2020: 217). His analysis thus ignores both the many years preceding the trade in enslaved peoples when Africans had complete agency in the world (Diop and Cook 2012: xiv–xvii), as well as contemporary agentive actions. In other words, while Afropessimism makes vital contributions to theorising our present conditions that cannot be ignored, its conclusions foreclose various forms of power that existed and continue to exist beneath the abyssal line, as well as the unknown possibilities those forms of power may inaugurate. Thus, we must take care in our conceptualisations of an anti-Black world when we rely on the epistemic tools produced by the anti-Black world, so that the conceptualisations do not operate to reify anti-Blackness and not dismantle it.

Other ways of being: towards testamentary life within legal knowledge

Considering how the contours of the human/body have and are being produced and governed by law, we must question if, from within colonial logics and using Euro-modern legal knowledge, it is possible to reconstitute the vision of the human/body to produce testamentary life. There is a paradox here. If this is possible, then the same constructions from which we want to break free provide the possibilities and contingencies of breaking free.

Do they remain after we have broken free? Our bodily challenges produced by the structure, determine our challenge to the structure. Breaking free may thus be impossible. But if we are going to rethink the meaning of the human/body, we may as well rethink the meaning of impossibility. Therefore, if we wish to begin a journey, however impossible, to testamentary life from within the Euro-modern legal constitution of the human, one place to start would be by unsettling its concept of legal persons. Naffine describes the constitution of the 'legal person' in law as merely an overarching definition for a recognised holder of rights and obligations (2009: 1). She argues, furthermore, that various schools of thought that conceptualise the human subject, at their most basic, make no concrete claims about the sort of beings that law is for. This raises a teleological question, as legal personality is not confined to humanity. Who then is the law for? Additionally, different conceptualisations of the human are used in different areas of law such as medical, administrative, and criminal law (Naffine 2009: 4). This teleological indeterminacy and inherent malleability have allowed the marker of 'legal personality', nebulous as it is, to become increasingly reliant on Cartesian rationality – the separation of the mind from the body and the discounting of the value of embodied knowledges. Thus, 'legal personality' as a legal descriptor, attaches itself more neatly to corporations than to human/bodies, as corporations illustrate ultimate rationality – a completely disembodied and unfeeling mind (Grear 2007: 522). Therefore, a paradox emerges where under racialised enslavement, for example, legal personality was afforded slave-trading corporations but not racialised human beings. Identification as a person arose, not from the self-evident possession of a human body, but from the attributed possession of Euro-centred thinking. As the corporation has no body, it is pure reason, mono-storied and therefore, most intelligible to the law. The vulnerable body is made more vulnerable and not subsumed into the conceptualisation of legal personality. We can surmise therefore, that human beings are more correctly read in law as legal persons with bodies, rather than humans/bodies with legal personality. Thus 'the state-sanctioned or extralegal production and exploitation of group-differentiated vulnerability to premature death' (Gilmore 2007: 28) is written into social construction of bodies along the fault-lines of 'unprotected characteristics' and so is legally (re)produced.

Consequently, legal personality itself has had varied and influential meanings and uses during the pendency of Euro-modernity and these have shaped Euro-modernity itself (Naffine 2009: 12). In other words, 'in the making of legal persons [law] continues to set the very contours of the moral and political community' (Naffine 2009: 13). The narrow definition of the legal person which excludes many more than it includes, is at the centre of rethinking the teleology of law. And so, Haraway argues for a turning away from Cartesian dualism in our understanding of knowledge and the human being (1988: 575–599). This would require the constitution of a legal person that is resituated in space–time and re-embodied (Grear 2007: 524; Naffine 2009: 144; Naffine 2011: 16–17). Mitchell argues further for the rejection of the concept of the legal person as a means to protect bodies made vulnerable to premature death, as well as slow and immediate violence (2015: 797). To protect the body, we need to move away from the lexicon 'protected characteristics' of the legal person and actually protect the human/body by making testamentary life intelligible to law.

However, it should be noted that operating from within Euro-modern legal epistemologies alone, we encounter methodological limitations in our understanding of the human/body as we must reconstitute its boundaries from within the perspective of the legal person. Therefore, we may also look to other knowledges beyond Euro-modern legal knowledges such as Indigenous knowledge systems (IKS). Understanding the effect of Cartesian dualism on IKS [adducing irrationality to them], we must also at this point, conceive broadly of what could be considered indigenous knowledges and which bodies could be considered to (collectively) hold them. The United Nations has been intentionally reluctant to restrictively define 'indigenous peoples' whose history has been marked by harmful colonial definitions (UNGA 2007: 6). So, the Martínez-Cobo study identifies indigenous peoples by reference to: pre-colonial autochthonous descent/ancestry; continuous socio-cultural distinction; distinctive autochthonous language; and self-identification as indigenous (Martínez-Cobo 1986: 6–39; see also Baird 2020: webpage).

Thus, based on these criteria, subject to application, various ethno-linguistic populations living in postcolonial states in Africa and Asia can also lay claim to indigenous identity and their epistemologies can be described as IKS. Nevertheless, the recognition of these knowledge systems as such, continues to be affected by the Western gaze. The colonial creation of categories like 'indigenous', 'tribe' and 'native', ties those categorisations temporally and spatially only to the colonial event, and so remain stuck in that space–time (Iliffe 1979: 324; Lowe et al 1997: 1–8; MacEachern 2000: 362; Parsons 2012: 66; Mamdani 2012: 3). In other words, these designations, 'indigenous' in particular, remain confined and distorted by the knowledge that tried to destroy the full actualities of what they vainly attempt to describe, such that those full actualities are currently obscured. Those designations, consequently, falsely point only to cultural communities, when they should also point to communities that are political, social, jurisprudential, epistemic, and so on (Simpson 2007: 67; Tatour 2019: 1569–93). Categorisation is revealed thus, as an almost inescapable conundrum. If indigeneity is solely defined as a counterpoint to what it attempts to escape, escape is impossible without redefinition of being. Yet it is the constant redefinition of being within IKS that reveals IKSs are not trapped in time and thus have produced, and continue to produce, alternatives to Euro-modern restricted readings of the body.

African IKS have had and continue to have varied worldviews on the human/body/person. Generally, rather placing a definitional emphasis on embodiment only, emphasis is placed on embodiment within community and the different roles various humans/bodies play within that. For example, *Ubuntu* (mostly southern African) links being human to relationality (Letseka 2012: 46–7). Ubuntu is usually illustrated by the phrase *'umuntu ngumuntu ngabantu'*, which means 'a human being is a human being because of other human beings' (Letseka 2012: 48). *Ujamaa*, which was popularised by Tanzania's Nyerere, relates being human to the 'familyhood' of African society predicated on the ideals of equality, freedom, and unity (Ibhawoh and Dibua 2003: 62; Mayo 2012: 44–6). *Umunna bu ike* (Igbo/West African) 'brotherhood is power' suggests being human arises from social solidarity, and so emphasises unity and abhors social division (Okoro 2010: 147). The idea of *Ọmọlúàbí* (Yorùbá/West African) is that being human is defined by good character, knowledge, humility, respect, hard work, and wisdom ... a person who engages in a cyclic mutual-developmental relationship with her community (Fayemi 2009: 167–9). Theorisations from African academics in the Diaspora also support these conceptualisations (Menkiti 1984: 171–82; Onyebuchi 2018: 1–18). The inference from the foregoing is that the African worldview of the human is based on the cyclic concepts of 'being' and 'belonging'. Human embodiment is its basis, but 'belonging' to community is paramount. Therefore to 'be' is to 'belong'. Not 'belonging' in a manner understood by indigenous thought, questions the purpose of 'being'. The human being is a relational being because the very essence of *being* human is dynamic and relational. In other words, the human being, by being, is active and that action is not restricted to itself but crystallises and evolves by constant relation with other beings and the earth upon which we all survive.

Thus, many IKS emphasise the importance and essence of humanity as the interconnectedness of the human being, not just to other human beings, but to non-human life and other non-living inhabitants of the planet and the universe (Kinchloe 2011: 338–41). This has been famously and arguably imperfectly articulated in South American indigenous epistemology as *'vivir bien'* – to live well (Gudynas 2011: 441–7; Ranta 2016: 425–39; Cuestas-Caza 2018: 49–63). *Vivir bien* arises from an inexact and western-dependent transliteration into Spanish of the distillation of a range of indigenous philosophies of life (Gudynas 2011: 442–3). These include *Alli Kawsay/ Sumak Kawsay* of the Kichwa, *Suma Qamaña* of the Aymara communities, *Balu Wala* of the Kuna communities, and *Ñande Reko* of the Guarani communities (Cuestas-Caza 2018: 57). These philosophies of life understand the state of human being as interdependent on all other facets of existence which include 'other beings, animals, plants, minerals, stars, spirits and divinities and is governed by the principles of relationality, complementarity, correspondence, reciprocity and cyclicity' (Cuestas-Caza 2018: 56).

As with concepts such as 'decolonisation' epistemic accelerationism has resulted in dilution of the radicality of the South American indigenous conceptualisations of the human/body, as they have become commodified and divorced from their epistemic sources. Nevertheless, *Vivir Bien* emerges as a cultural frame of reference within indigenous–culturalist epistemic communities. It denotes harmonious existence between *ayllu* (family-community) and the *pacha* (indivisible and interconnected space–time.) Yet, *vivir bien* also emerges thereafter within post-developmentalist epistemic communities as a critique of developmental theories' inextricable links with colonial logics and the conditions of life imposed thereupon (Cuestas-Caza 2018: 50). In the same vein, these concepts have been constitutionalised with varying levels of success in Ecuador and Bolivia (Gudynas 2011: 441–7; Solón 2018: webpage). The Inter-American Court of Human Rights (IACrtHR) has also adopted their paradigms in conceptualising 'a project of life' as a canopy human right. This incorporates component rights based on the core idea of human of dignity and South American indigenous conceptualisations of human being (Ipinyomi 2015: 11–14). While this attempts to extend indigenous ways of being into structures of Euro-modernity, it could also be argued that by trying to embed understandings of ways of being into structures that are diametrically opposed to those ways of being, failure is inevitable. This type of expansion, to a certain extent, relies on the assumption that indigenous knowledges are pre-modern and require the civilising structures of Euro-modernity to validate them. This suggests that 'real modernity' cannot be solely constitutive of indigenous ways of thinking.

Re-envisioning the human/body/person by turning away from Cartesian dualism, steers us towards a new-old understanding of humanity and living in the world. As Haraway invites us into embodied and situated knowledges, the body becomes more politically relevant to our understanding of the relationship between law and society and the role of law. This is also illustrated by the concept of 'body-politics' which is defined by Mignolo as 'the missing half of bio-politics' (Mignolo 2009: 174). Body-politics recognises the violence that is entailed in describing the other as violent and thus less than human. This framing removes the othered body as the object of study by a supposedly dispassionate observer and makes that human/body the knower of its own condition (Mignolo 2009: 176). Antiracist knowing, and feminist pedagogy require us to pay closer attention to the body from which knowledge is made and how knowledge is made from the body. For example, large and minute resistances to continuing colonial conditions often involved reappropriation of body functions annexed by racialisation. Hartman described, for example, enslaved peoples 'stealing away' for small periods of times to meet with other enslaved people beyond the enclosures of the plantations that held them captive (Hartman 1997: 66–9). These practices were defiant reassertions of humanity and self-ownership – taking back what was stolen ... even if just for tiny moments of time. They were free in those times. Understanding freedom from this body-political lens complicates the flattened understandings of the concept from within Euro-modern legal knowledge. In other words, how a body is marked (racialised, gendered, classed, and so on) not only places the human in a specific position, power-wise, within global and local structures, but also describes and prescribes the scope of power available to that human/body. Power in this sense meaning, 'the ability to make things happen, to make the possible actual' (Gordon 2020: 41). The more the body is marked, the less the amount of power that the human/body has access to, the less the human is able to make things happen beyond their own body. The less the body is marked, the more the human is able to make things happen.

In the same vein, Fanon and Wynter are particularly attentive in their work to the human/body and its structural reconceptualisation – how structures mark bodies. Both write as scholars within Black studies – a interdisciplinary field of study that is rooted in envisioning the world scholarly from the perspective of African and African descended people. In *Black Skin, White Masks,* Fanon tells the story of having recently arrived in Paris from the French colony of Martinique and being identified as a 'Negro' by a child on a train (2008: 84). The child tells its mother that the sight of Fanon – the Negro – is frightening. Through this story and in the book in general, Fanon illustrates how the violent othering world that those who are made Black of the earth experience always has a corporeal effect. Therefore, the body that is racialised, or in alternative ways structured as other, experiences the world differently internally and externally, contingent upon that structuring. Kinouani also examines this phenomenon when she explores how the entry of Black people into white space and becoming subject to the white gaze and white fantasies produces in their bodies a 'malaise', 'a heaviness' and a lodging of racism into the racialised body (2021: chapter 1). The othered human/body exists in a different biological, social, spatial, and temporal world from those with proximity to whiteness. In *The Wretched of Earth*, Fanon explains how the colonial context – beyond the events of conquest and political decolonisation – continually creates context-dependent men (2007: 5–20). In other words, the space–time and activity through which a human being lives will dictate the contours of their being in this world. These dictates include necropolitical structures of power, enacted colonially. Throwing off these structures and their legacies necessitates an intentional self-reclamation beyond Euro-modern claims to liberalism and progress that have mostly imposed hierarchical orders of humanity and unequal entrances into the category 'Man' for most of humanity. Therefore, true decolonisation, Fanon argues, requires the making and becoming of new kinds of anti-colonial humans. And so, he says to 'leave this Europe which never stops talking of man yet massacres him at every one of its street corners, at every corner of the world' (Fanon 2007: 235). In essence, Fanon is asking us to recognise and put to an end the global necropolitical results of not just the physical encounters that occur from universalising Euro-modernity, but also epistemological and epistemicidal ones. These encounters are, in other words, cyclical and co-constitutive. The making of a restricted category of 'Man' using neoliberal language of modernity and progress as false alibis, gives licence for the destruction of those who find themselves beyond this category. The further from 'Man', the nearer to death ... and vice versa. Wynter, therefore, describes the universalising of a 'western' idea of Man as an 'overrepresentation' and suggests that turning away from this overrepresentation requires, 'securing the well-being, and therefore the full cognitive and behavioral autonomy of the human species itself' (2003: 260; see also Wynter 2013: 30–66). Wynter's conceptualisation of the human being thus invites a broad-spectrum reanimation and resuscitation of the category of 'human' from the ruins that colonial logics have left of humanity (McKittrick 2015: 8). This conceptualisation reveals the true meaning of dehumanisation, not as a removal of marked bodies from the category 'human', but an overall misconstruction and misreading of the category 'human'.

To re-understand and reframe the human/being is to recognise the human as always being – active, changing, with power and possibility. Not just a biologic being – an isolated mind confined to an isolatedly defined body. To understand the human as relational is also to recognise the futility of atomised approaches to decolonisation that rely on (un)protected characteristics. A relational being formerly excluded, when placed within a zone of direct exclusion as an egalitarian move – Black people in white space, for example – suggests and requires structural and spatial reimagination (Gordon 2020: 47). Atomised approaches to decolonisation will result in diversifying the face of the structure we purport to change, without any real change – a difference that does not make a difference. Atomised approaches continue to put to death the body and its possible ways of human being.

Consequently, re-imagining the human after and through the death of colonial logics could be conceived as a rescue and retrieval mission (Da Silva 2015: 92) of humanity from the colonial imaginations of profligate life and anthropocentric being that threaten to destroy the planet and most of humanity with it. Thus, legal knowledges can begin by appreciating the true gradation of vulnerabilities of planetary life and the urgency of the perdition in which we find ourselves. Re-envisioning the human/body from within decolonisation envisages making actual life of human and nonhuman bodies intelligible to legal knowledges. In other words, anti-colonial, decolonial visions of the human, place the human/body and all the earth above the structure of a necropolitical society, whose survival relies on the bare life of marked bodies and the enclosure of all nature and non-humans. Anti-colonial, decolonial visions entail simultaneously thinking larger and smaller of the human. The human is not most important, but more of humanity is more important. Humanity's meaning and essence extends beyond the restrictions placed on it by Euro-modernity. As Wynter posits: '[h]uman beings are magical. Bios and Logos. Words made flesh, muscle and bone animated by hope and desire, belief materialized in deeds, deeds which crystallize our actualities' (Wynter 1995: 35). Humans are biological and cultural and metaphysical and cosmic all at once (Walcott 2015: 190). If humans are made from life and words, then each human being contains a world. Each world is always reaching out to other human worlds with their storied life to create a different version of a collective human world. Each human life disposed, is the ending of a possible world that can never be again. Each human life matters to the world that can be possible. The world can be remade from life and worlds – reimagined. Unless we seek the reproduction of the harm that humanity and the earth has suffered, rethinking the spatialisation and temporalisation of humanity, the earth, and her realities in necessary. Bodies count, but re-imagining the world is more than a body count. Therefore, the question of human bodies is also a temporal question of the past, present, and future. The question of human bodies is also a spatial question of the enfoldment of the near and far. Thus, if Euro-modern legal thinkers have not equipped the law to handle the existential and fundamental questions of who we have been, where we have been, who we are, and where we are, how then can we answer the question of who we may become?

4

Defining the Law's Subject II: Law and Creating the Sacrifice Zones of Colonialism

> To think about distant places, to colonize them, to populate or depopulate them: all of this occurs on, about, or because of land. The actual geographical possession of land is what empire in the final analysis is all about.
>
> Edward Said (1994: 78)

> A map of the world that does not include Utopia isn't worth even glancing at ... it leaves out the one country at which Humanity is always landing. And when Humanity lands there, it looks out, and seeing a better country, sets sail. Progress is the realization of Utopias.
>
> Oscar Wilde (1969: 27)

Introduction

In the previous chapter I argue that to undo colonial misusing and Euromodern untranslatability of human/bodies, these bodies should be re-understood, at the very least, as ontologically relational. This relationality applies not just to all other human beings, but also to all non-human life and non-life in and of the earth. However, colonial mapping and its cartographies, require, as Said notes, the redefinition and (dis)possession of land and thus depart from Wilde's notions of Utopia. Thus, in this chapter I take Chapter 3's argument further by focusing on how the society (space, place, and all they contain) around law's human has been and is being constituted by the influences of colonial logics and praxes. This examination takes reference from the use of race as an abstractive technology in the making of property from humanity. Therefore, I lean further into an analysis of how racial capitalism, in particular, and Euro-modern law in general are both entangled in the legal ontologies of, not just human body negation, but also contingent appropriation/redefinition of land and space. This process ties the constitution of law's human to the creation of a universalised Euro-modern legal ontology of land as a means of capital accumulation as well as human veneration reliant on this. My concern here is to explain how that process emerges, with specific emphasis on the legal epistemological interactions between human/beings, land, property, and space. I observe quite deliberately here, that one of the most significant outcomes of the legitimate property-fication of labour, land, and nature through Euro-modern legal epistemologies, is the complicity of legal technologies in continuing the colonial conditions of life that extend beyond the escalating disappearance of testamentary life into the looming endangerment of the planet.

Commodifying the land on which we try to survive

The capitalist-colonial-enslavement project tied the need to acquire copious amounts of unfree labour to a need for recognisable and legal means for the acquisition of land as property. Interestingly, in many cases, in the accumulation of colonial territories, signed treaties were used to evidence transfer of title to land, from the colonised to the coloniser. This even though the initial indigenous 'title' was often an indigenous trust over land. Yet what was 'received' therefrom was outright ownership. In other words, what was granted was not what was ultimately taken, as the meanings of what is meant by land between the coloniser and the colonised did not coincide. For many indigenous and later colonised peoples, land was not alienable property to be exploited as a capital source or for the natural resources under the land. In the words of Kimmerer, land

> was everything: identity, the connection to our ancestors, the home of our nonhuman kinfolk, our pharmacy, our library, the source of all that sustained us. Our lands were where our responsibility to the world was enacted, sacred ground. It belonged to itself; it was a gift, not a commodity, so it could never be bought or sold. (2013: 17)

Conversely, to the colonisers, secured ownership of land was essential to enacting the conditions that were necessary for finacialisation and assuming the conditions of profligate life – boundless accumulation and exploitation of the earth's resources, including human labour. This required colonial powers to be able to legitimately utilise both inexpensive land *and* unfree/unwaged labour. This explains why, while chattel slavery did not exist in colonial possessions in some regions, colonising powers who had appropriated land in those regions still operated (and/or permitted the operation of) plantation-like establishments relying on the use of unfree labour. So, 'capitalist-colonial-enslavement project' aptly describes the continuation in all three manifestations of a singular logic of accumulation and dispossession. The labour used in the colonies was almost always racialised, often coerced and unwaged, and also relied on the removal of indigenous people from their homes to be housed near or on the plantations. Portuguese colonial plantations produced goods – coffee in Timor, sugar and cocoa in Brazil, cocoa in São Tomé and Príncipe, and coffee, cotton, and sugar in Angola (Clarence-Smith 1990: 152–72; Walker 2007: 75–106; Shepherd and McWilliam 2013: 326–61;Varela and Louçã 2020: 199, 223). The Spanish had cocoa plantations in Fernando Po (Sundiata 1996: 11–14). Belgium's brutal colonial activities in what was called the Belgian Congo, involved racialised use of enslaved, enforced, and tortured–compelled labour to work on these plantations, resulting in a loss of roughly 50 per cent of the indigenous population (Hochschild 1999: 280; Juif and Frankema 2018: 313–43). There were British tea plantations across Southeast Asia and East Africa (Palmer 1986: 105–26; Wickramasinghe and Cameron 2005: 4–6). Coerced labour was also used in the British and French Empires across Africa and Asia for infrastructural development and defence: these included transport systems to extract resources from the colonies to the metropole (Akurang-Parry 2000: 3; Tharoor 2017: webpage; Daughton 2021: introduction). These examples illustrate, not just the lie of colonisation as infrastructural benevolence, but also its reality as expansion of pre-existing coercion of unfree labour that had been practised in the Americas under racialised enslavement (Wallman 2014: 51–2; Siddiqui 2020; 50–60). Colonisation did not depart from enslavement in its logics, but widened the geographical scope of racialised populations subject to dispossession of land, alienation from home, and being unfree labour. Therefore, being able to alienate land from indigenous populations was vital to the continuing economic success of a praxis of exploitative colonisation, whose logics were adapted and extended from racialised enslavement. Thus, the contemporary global economy continues to be fundamentally shaped by North–South extraction and accumulation practices that began during racialised enslavement and intensified in the formal colonial period (Feintrenie 2014: 1579; Bhambra 2020: 307–22). The unequal opportunity to make massive profits by exploiting low-cost raw materials and unfree labour creates and maintains this racial and geographical divide (Aoki 1998: 52). The legal alienation of land as property and the legal epistemologies that maintain this are crucial to preserving and reproducing this global order.

To unpack the process by which global appropriation of land for the Euro-modern machine becomes normativised, I begin our story at about the start of the 17th century. At this time Europe had not yet taken complete physical control of the land masses of the Americas, Asia, Africa, and Oceania. However, colonial desires to find new land to take control of and exploit had already been fuelling disturbances in mainland Europe, as land capable of alienation became scarce. Thus, for both the intellectual and the political classes in Europe, the question of acquiring land beyond European shores, becomes vital at this time. These desires and the conceptual logics to weaponise them crystallise in the 1600s, through the writings of scholars like Locke and Petty, (and later Hume and Adam Smith), as well as through the political enactment of land appropriation as a means to acquire private property. Prior to this time, under the European feudal system, land rights while mainly vested in nobles, were also granted in diminished form to those identified as serfs and peasants. In other words, access to land was granted unequally within this already unequal system. However, land was not treated as something from which others could be alienated completely — in other words, private property. The reasons for this are obvious. Unlike other types of choses classified as property, land is needed to ensure the existence of life itself as it provides a place to live and to produce food to live (Large 1973: 1040). So, the very experience of being human relies on access to land.

This pre-existing praxis around land meant that making land private property required a fundamental rupture in the societal functions of land, law, as well as land's legal ontology. In this vein, Cedric Robinson describes the emergence of racial capitalism as reliant on a conversion of European societal structure from retail mercantilism to more voluminous trade (2000: 18–20). This conversion could not have been achieved without enabling private ownership to land. The means for obtaining this access relied on logics for differentiating human/bodies and adducing values and fixed destinies to that differentiation, that already existed in European society (Kelley 2017: webpage). In other words, the hierarchical categorisation of human beings and bodies by class–race was already an integral part of European ways of being. This is discussed in the previous chapter. Nevertheless, it should be noted that at the time, these differentiations were not coterminous to what we now call race, as skin colour was not a key basis of differentiation, but differences were marked spatially and culturally, in religion, social class, and economics. Thus, the initial victims of racialised dispossession were Europeans — the Irish, the Roma, the working classes, and other thus differentiated populations (Kelley 2017: webpage). For example, when bankrupt feudal landlords in Scotland and Ireland increased their rents and maximised land use, they instituted enclosures of land and the removal of othered people who were already on the land. These removals — 'clearances' — were supported by scholarly reconceptualisation of not just who could be removed from land (origins of racialisation), but of the nature of land itself. William Petty (1623–1687), influenced by Aristotle, Cartesian duality, Hobbes, and Bacon as well as his own personal experiences of deprivation in Ireland, articulated a theory of value that equated land with labour (Naldi 1989: 3–36; Fox 2009: 388–404; Bhandar 2018: 36–51). Consequently, he suggested that 'all things ought to be valued by two natural Denominations, which is Land and Labour ... we ought to say, a Ship or garment is worth such a measure of Land' (Petty 1899: paragraph 18). As labour is derived from the body, this analysis, though economically profitable, reduces (in perpetuity it seems) the value of the human body to its labour and removes from the value of land its vital function as sustenance of invaluable testamentary life.

John Locke's (1632–1704) labour theory of property takes Petty's arguments a step further by also relying on a schism between body and reason, as well as a more precise mathematical valuation of labour. He posits:

> Though the earth, and all inferior creatures, be common to all men, yet every man has a property in his own person: this no body has any right to but himself. The labour of his body, and the work of his hands, we may say, are properly his. Whatsoever then he removes out of the state that nature hath provided, and left it in, he hath mixed his labour with, and joined to it something that is his own, and thereby makes it his property. ... As much land as a man tills, plants, improves, cultivates, and can use the product of, so much is his property. (Locke 1999: 117–18)

A close reading of Locke's labour theory of property reveals that it relies on several questionable foundations. First, the problematic conceptualisation of labour as property which is separate from the body fails to account for the fact that labour cannot be taken away from the body (Keenan 2010: 424; Bhandar 2014: 211). Thus, this schism relies on an idea of self-ownership that only makes sense if the human is defined only as ownable, either by the human in question or by another. By reducing the human solely to the labour produced by the body, this schism extends the understanding of prior practices of enslavement in ways that disappear the humanity of the enslaved. Furthermore, as the labour which is proposed to be mixed with the land here is intangible, Locke conflates different types of essences – labour, human, land, other tangible things – within the category of property. Additionally, the theory is used to explain the anterior acquisition of real property that had already been acquired, which had not been acquired in the way the theory posits and was not acquired thus subsequently (Quiggin 2015: webpage). Land in the Americas, of which he was writing, was acquired by violent dispossession and conquest. Once acquired, it is passed on by legal legitimation. Hence, the theory does not explain any form of acquisition of land in practice. So, the justification even though it proceeds as a legal truth, reveals itself as arising from a fictionally founded, antagonistic 'politics of articulation' and political expedience that sets the boundaries – epistemological and legal – of propriety (Devenney 2011: 152–3, 161). In other words, while the theory does not explain the actual acquisition of land, as it purports to do, by creating fictional antecedents for the origin story of land as private property, it operates to entrench a legal and proper narration of land as private property. For example, Justice Sumner in *Re: Southern Rhodesia* (1919: 233) rejects Matabele and Mashona ownership of land because their land practices differed from this proper origin story. Consequently, this narration and articulation are of vital importance to understanding colonial accumulation/dispossession of land, as Locke also places a very narrow, Eurocentric and mathematical definition on profitable labour and improvement of land that relies on racialised, gendered, classed (and other non-protected life) presumptions of who is law's human, as well as whose labour and what type of labour has value (Nichols 2005: 44–5, 48; Keenan 2010: 424; Quiggin 2015: webpage). Therefore, this narrow identification becomes a self-fulfilling prophecy thereafter of who has value and whose labour has value. Valuation in the eyes of the law and economics contingently relies on being able to amass large quantities of land and acquire large-scale labour to 'improve' said land. In essence, Locke's labour theory of property is underwritten by the presumption that colonially accumulated land thus alienated, must be made profitable by the use of unfree labour (Graham 2010: 47). The theory of property also continues to have significance for how value placed on physical labour is considered less important to capital generation as compared to fiscal labour. Finally, and very importantly, the theory relies on the presumption that land is infinite (Quiggin 2015: webpage). This presumption about the boundlessness of land and the wealth it provides, under logics of property-fication, underpins the intractable capitalist over-exploitation of both land and unwaged labour.

Consequently, we see how Petty and Locke (both writing in and around the 17th century), articulate ideas that consider the 'value of both land and human life as equivalences based on the cultivation of land' (Bhandar 2018: 36). Bentham additionally conceptualised this value as tied to the ability to sell the subject matter of value – land or labour (Ress 2020: 102). Thus, in terms of land as private property, its value is essentially linked only to claims to land that could be recognised by Euro-modern law. Native and indigenous titles and ways of being on land were completely disregarded. This is because, it was Euro-modern legal claims to land that granted the holder the right to maximise its commodity value, by alienation, 'improvement', and sale or security. Thus, racialised enslavement and exploitative colonisation became germane to the Euro-modern economic regime as the most expedient ways to accumulate capital. This process was and is bolstered by the language, organs, and structures of the Euro-modern law. So, by the end of the 17th century, the 'truth' of 'land as private property' had displaced all other land truths to become an indisputable fact in Euro-modern legal epistemology.

This legal epistemology of land as alienable property, whose use must be maximised, therefore, facilitated the colonisation of most of the world by Europe between the 19th to the 20th centuries. Relying on narratives of improvement and civilisation, European colonial powers (often through trading companies) were able to legitimately lay claim to resource-rich territories, the best agricultural land across the world, as well as unfree labour, all for the maximisation of profits (Hickel 2017: chapter 3).

Hence, it is not just the physical and administrative acts of colonisation of land and enslavement of human bodies that must be of concern to achieving decolonisation. We should also pay very close attention to how the redefinition of the teleologies of humanity and real property, as well as a conflation of the foregoing, (re)produce the colonial materialities and trap us into a temporal loop of destructive life. Just as emancipation did not end the hierarchical redefinition of human/bodies as property, the ending of administrative colonisation has not brought about a return of indigenous meanings of land. Colonised alienated land was handed over to successor states through legal technologies that continued and did not disrupt logics of enclosure. Therefore, though reification of land as private and/or alienable property through what is called 'decolonisation' manifested differently in settler and non-settler colonies, the direction taken in each case advances on the same logics of accumulation and dispossession. In most non-settler colonies, despite the dismantling of the direct administration of colonisation, the legal concept of *uti possidetis juris* ('as you possess under law') meant that inherited colonial boundaries often remained unaltered. Colonial possessions were 'handed back' intact, to ensure a continuous lineage of possession. *Uti possidetis* (initiated in Roman law) is a legal principle that evolved from being a tool to preserve the status quo where needed, to a temporary and transitionary legal mechanism to ensure stability during movement from colony to state (Shaw 1997: 492–500). This mechanism took on more permanent operationalisation in the period of transition to flag independence. This is because preservation of colonial boundaries became a significant part of post-independence politics. This was markedly so on the African continent. Through Article 2 of the Organization for African Unity's Resolution 16(I) of 21 July 1964, 'all Member States pledge[d] themselves to respect the borders existing on their achievement of national independence'. A constant narrative in both the making of colonies and their disintegration was that colonial presence and mechanisms (including borders) purported to prevent violence that existed prior to the making of colonies and that would undoubtedly erupt once the colony became states. Consequently, it could be argued that those who were in control of the post-colony had a vested interest and desire in preserving the sanctity of their new state (Kantai 2007: 119). This desire could have crystallised around a need to prove the colonisers wrong or a more calculated interest in keeping consolidated colonial benefits for themselves by stepping into the shoes of the coloniser. Either way, the result was the increasing rigidity of colonial borders. Yet *uti possidetis* works in tandem with and in reliance on *terra nullius*; the use of *uti possidetis* ensures that there is no *terra nullius*, that there is no legal vacuum in the time between colony and state (Hasani 2003: 85–6). *Uti possidetis* does not reject the problematic premise of *terra nullius* [or *territorium nullius*], that designates indigenous colonised peoples as 'nobody'. *Uti possidetis,* therefore, 'bestowed an aura of historical legality to the expropriation of the lands of indigenous peoples' (Reisman 1995: 352).

This collective reluctance to disrupt colonial borders on the part of both the colonisers and those in charge of successor states also illustrates the continuation of ways of thinking of land. This is illustrated on the part of coloniser states and their allies, by withholding recognition of new states and imposing stringent conditions of entry into the family of new states on newly independent nations (d'Aspremont 2018: 139–52). To reiterate and elaborate upon the observation made in Chapter 1, this version of 'decolonisation' was achieved by fabricating states that were neither states at the time, nor previously Westphalian states, out of independent political entities that were made into colonies *because* they were not considered Westphalian states. Through the multicausal preservation of colonial borders, the logics and praxes of enclosure that were utilised and extended during racialised enslavement, were further expanded into colonisation, and have spread even further after the end of formal control of colonies. This proliferation is spatial, temporal, and conceptual. The logics of enclosure, alienation, and improvement are now extended well beyond enclosure of land and labour, into legitimating enclosures of health, education, social care, and other societal goods. This perpetuation of logics is described as 'neo-colonialism' – the continuous control of the affairs of a post-colony by market, political, and military forces from outside of it (Rahmatian 2009: 41). This is evidenced, among other things, in international organisations urging developmental strategies that rely on maximising capital value of land and other resources narrated as unused or 'waste' (Tzouvala 2019: 245–6; World Bank 2013 xvi). Such pressure is premised on a narrow understanding of the teleology of both the human and land that ignores the deepening poverty introduced through colonial logics and praxes (Allen 2020: 109).

So, continuous control – ongoing colonialism – derives strength from the conflation in legal epistemology of the meanings and value of land, labour, life, and property. These operate as contingent enclosures of land and labour in the Global South that maximise profits for the Global North, producing profligate life for some. The borders restrict movement across them, especially to the Global North, and reproduce within them, seemingly in perpetuity, racially divergent conditions of bare and necropolitical life. These divergent spatialisations of despair are also being exponentially augmented by 'digital borders' which indiscriminately expand necropolitics into cyberspaces by relying on technologies, such as machine learning, algorithms, biometric data collection, facial recognition, and so on, to surveill, criminalise, misrecognise, and bolster the physical border (Achiume 2021: 334). The harms of these technologies are exacerbated by the digital divide between the Global North and South, as well as abject failure to reckon with the racial and other body-politics of digital technology (Williams 2020: 74–83; Birhane 2021: 1–9). The proponents of these technologies, by claiming artificial technological objectivity, presuppose that these non-human technologies must be just and fair. However, their purported objectivity often merely replicates pre-existing inability to read the complex text of the human body whose conditions are produced by the social structure and space around it. Inevitably, with specific particularities, this digital injustice is also replicated in settler colonial conditions. However, in other aspects, due to the permanence of colonial presence, the effect of enclosing of land in settler colonies differs from non-settler ones.

In settler colonies, the coloniser comes to stay permanently on indigenous land. To make a home, the settler demands access to vast swathes of land as private property. This requires, in the first instance of colonisation, the removal, through slow and immediate death, of indigenous populations (Hickel 2017: chapter 3). This is a continuing process. The fictional justification of *terra nullius* becomes a prophecy that must be fulfilled. 'Nobody's land' will be true when there are no more living bodies of indigenous peoples to be found above the land. To wit, 'invasion is a structure, not an event' (Wolfe 2006: 388). Additionally, settler colonisation also relies on epistemological and legal knowledge to make the process normalised and ongoing until indigenous extinction is achieved. 'Nobody's land' continues to speak across past, present, and future – till there will nobody left, or till the logics are interrupted. In the interim, legal knowledge is used to recast the indigenous population who have pre-existing claims to land as physically, epistemically, and legally homeless; the invader who is granted superior title is physically, epistemically, and legally at home with assured access to profligate life (Moreton-Robinson 2015: 16). This is illustrated in the stark differences in the conditions of life of both populations. For example, under apartheid in South Africa, white populations had individual access to boundless land, while the indigenous population (53 per cent of the population) was squeezed into manufactured and arid Homelands (13 per cent of the land) (Levin and Weiner 1996: 93–119; Jensen and Zenker 2015: 941). Thus, by providing Euro-modern legal guidelines for the transfer of land *inter alia*, conditions of life laid down under apartheid, continue through the recognition of the settlers' superior title. This is part of what makes South Africa one of the most unequal societies in the world today (Wilson 2011: 1–15). Remember: invasion is a structure, not an event. As with non-settler post-colonies, indigenous peoples whose ways of lives have been decimated are 'encouraged' to make profitable use of their land. In Brazil for example, destructive forest fires that destroyed the Amazon in 2020 have been linked to increasing economic pressure to open up indigenous lands to capital (Lima et al 2020: 104258). Annihilation remains the end goal of settler colonisation (Bhandar 2018: 25).

Yet, neoliberal land reform has been an inadequate fix. Manji reminds us that land reform was often introduced by colonial administrators as a defensive strategy to maintain the status quo (2006: 1–12, 39–46; 2019: webpage). The status quo retains concentration of profitable land in the hands of a few people and entrenches Euro-modern epistemologies of land (and other resources) as enclosures or enclosable. Unjustly acquired property rights are thus placed in perpetual opposition to rights that can protect conditions that can foster testamentary life, such as rights to housing, water, food. Any professed 'decolonisation' that does not reconceptualise the meaning of land, continues the injustice of dispossession.

The reproduction of commodification: space, place, and where law's human belongs

Consequently, the late 20th century emergence of borders can be considered a manifestation of hyper-legitimation of selected bodies and de-legitimation of othered bodies within zones of inclusion/exclusion. Anzaldua argues that contemporary borders function to 'define the places that are safe and unsafe, to distinguish us from them' (1987: 3). So, the translation of dynamic space into flat financial commodity continues to reproduce itself with necropolitical results for bodies denied testamentary life. This reproduction is revealed in the creation of contingent geographical zones of necropolitical life and the increasing destruction of the planet. The abyssal line dividing what is designated the Global North from the Global South is a permanent tangible manifestation of colonial, physical, and epistemic violence resulting from recasting the human and space as alienable property (de Sousa Santos 2016: 109). From the point of creation of the line, the conditions of life in these two zones have travelled in divergent directions. Beneath the abyssal line is a 'zone of nonbeing, an extraordinarily sterile and arid region' (Fanon 2008: 2), which lies below the 'line of the human' (Grofoguel 2016: 10). Therefore, the identification of this physical space is contingent on the marking of bodies. Marked bodies mark designated space, and designated space objectifies illegible bodies. This process also produces technologies of belonging and non-belonging. Thus, Ahmed suggests that in a white world produced by Euro-modern world-making epistemologies, bodies racialised white are orientated such that they move easily and are held up by spaces around them (2006: 132–42). Bodies racialised as Black, indigenous, or otherwise non-white or non-normative, are restricted in how they are permitted to enjoy space. In other words, through the 'racing of space', globally and locally, by designating particular spaces (countries, cities, continents and locales) as naturally being dominated by persons of particular races, the social characterisations constructed in relation to those racialisations are constructed as related to those spaces (Mills 2014a: 41–53). Those countries designated 'white countries' are civilised, and 'black countries' are corrupt. This maps onto the logics of colonial cartographies which conflate space and race. These cartographical logics are extended into the praxes of internment, concentration camps, school exclusions, exile, deportation, and prison. There is, in other words, a cyclical, co-constitutional and perpetuating relationship between the marking of bodies and the marking of spaces.

Not only are these spaces directed to separate destinies, but these destinies are also designed to deepen and disseminate. Hickel describes European colonies as 'sacrifice zones', (argued here to be an ongoing designation). Sacrifice zones are areas where, '[n]o loss of human life, no amount of suffering, no degree of degradation was too much, so long as the economic interests of colonial companies and states were served' (Hickel 2017: 99). The use of the word 'sacrifice' here, leans heavily on mythologies of 'pagan offerings', disrupting our perceptions of the divide between the 'ancient' past and 'civilised' present. Modernity has not brought with it a civilisation that values human life. The bodies of the 'other' are still being sacrificed for the good of 'our' land. The earth and waters are still swallowing bodies and drinking blood. Dispossession of land and life operates in perpetuity. Euro-modern law is the grease that oils the wheels of this process, by continuing to recognise land rights and ways of knowing land that have been unjustly derived. But zones of non-being such as these are also dispersible. Pockets of zones of being are created within zones of non-being and vice versa (Grosfoguel 2016: 12). The tragedy of Grenfell Tower illustrates such a zone of non-being within a zone of being. In 2017, the 24-floor Tower was destroyed by a residential fire that was accelerated by unsafe cladding and structural safety concerns which had gone unheeded … resulting in 72 recorded deaths. The tower was inhabited mostly by people from racialised and disadvantaged socio-economic backgrounds. The area surrounding the tower was contrastingly quite affluent. Sometimes, these zones of non-being are not invisible to Euro-modernity. Yet logics of enclosure for profit continue to extend themselves necropolitically as bodies on fire fell from the sky. Bodies made illegible and valueless to Euro-modernity. Furthermore, these conditions of life are also the conditions of the planet on fire. The destruction of the planet and unequal vulnerability to climate catastrophe also result from the subjugation of land and nature for the use of humans/

bodies legible to Euro-modern legality (Yang 2017: 29). This planet may yet fall through a sky on fire.

In essence, Euro-modern legal knowledge renders itself unable to make these links to explain how, for example, the content of immigration law, environmental protection laws, land law, housing rights among others, are all co-contingent on marking of bodies and spaces. Thus, to re-make the world, legal academics could engage more closely with how flattening land to mean capital only, empties it of multivariate meaning including its relations to 'place' and 'space'. 'Place' has been defined *inter alia*, as a location where things happen, reflective of aspirations of peoples, coproduced by humanity and nature, resulting from interaction between humans and other inhabitants of the planet, consequently, an integral element of being and experience (Escobar 2008: 42; Degnen 2018: 93, 95–6). Place can also be defined as 'lived space, meeting place, site of social reproduction ... personality' (Tuck and McKenzie 2014: 32). Place is not static; its value is relational to what is happening in it and who is on it. So, place gives space its meaning. Space is the abstract foundation upon which place builds, but its meanings and boundaries are also produced by law, among other things. Thus 'space is a practiced place' (Certeau 1984: 117), a 'product of interrelations ... predicated upon the existence of plurality' (Massey 2005: 9). It is an 'indissoluble set of systems of objects and systems of actions' (Santos 2021: 5). Space provides subjective, political, and ideological room (Lefebvre 2009: 171) for relational human beings to build places in which to aspire to testamentary life. Therefore, testamentary life requires dynamic and communal access and use of space. Conversely, restrictive control of space is fundamental to the exercise of coercive power (Razack 2002: 10). So, we must pay closer attention to how coercive power creates its spaces, through legal mechanisms and language. We must also take closer account of how through the same means, coercive power orders the conditions of life that happen or do not happen thereupon. As the major historical and continuing exercise of coercive power in the world, colonial epistemologies of land instituted new spatial relations on the ground that crystallise into irrevocable reality (Mbembé 2019: 79). Thus, the logics and praxes of colonisation as an ongoing event, contribute to how space manifests in divergent conditions of life that are governed by law, including the making of property by flattening the meanings of land and life.

Unsettling the relationship between land and life is key to deconstructing this flattening. The etymology of the word 'property' presupposes a fusion between people and place (Graham 2010: 92). In this original articulation, the relationality of human existence extends to what it is surrounded by. This could be described as follows: "I am, therefore, place is; land is, therefore we are." This extends the articulation of Ubuntu ways of living: "I am, because we are," to include relations with the earth around the human. The use of Euro-modern property law and its development in tandem with exploitative colonisation and racialised enslavement, through indigenous removal from land and reworking the meaning of land, severed the link between people and place – especially for racialised, colonised, and indigenous peoples thus removed (Graham 2010: 91). The universalising of Euro-modern legal epistemologies of land results in a spatial collapse of the near and far (Massey 2005: 92). Specific legal spaces and experiences are created by the afterlives of colonial administrative regimes. For example, the common law practiced in Kenya and Ghana was introduced by British colonisation, and so these spaces produce similar experiences of law and space, even though they are geographically far apart. Yet, Ghana shares a border but vastly different social realties with its French post-colony neighbour Côte d'Ivoire (Kedar 2014: 1010). This undoing also contributes to the illegalisation of Black presence in various ways, from confinement to plantations, to strict immigration laws, to creation of white spaces (Anderson 2015: 10–21; Mbembé 2019: 79; Moore 2020: 1946–60). This colonial spatial ordering of the world produces very specific realities and conditions of life and therefore contingent understandings and experiences of what it means to be human. In other words, '[t]he colonial world is a compartmentalized world,' 'inhabited by different species' (Fanon 2007: 3, 5). The restriction of certain bodies to certain spaces is an inflection of rights to space and mobility across space as well as a constant telegraphic replay between space and bodies. 'The colonial subject is a man penned in' (Fanon 2007: 15). The restricted body is held perpetually in space, without power beyond this confinement, to use space for its own and communal possibilities. In contrast, Euro-modern law's perfect person – the corporate body – is the ideal subject to hold rights to law's perfect flat fiction of property within a legal epistemology that creates property relations which themselves 'establish and maintain inequality' (Devenney 2011: 161–2). This resonates with the crux of Harris' argument in 'Whiteness as Property' which revolves around the conflation of meanings between property and person (1993: 1707–91). Whiteness is property, because it operates to exclude from it, persons not socially constructed to own it. As a resource, on a global scale it informs access to land and space, and the possibility of creating places. This in turn informs, among other things, legal epistemologies of citizenship, subjectivity, ownership of resources, access to territory and property, as well as criminalisation with spatial inferences (Devenney 2011: 162).

Thinking the world anew, therefore goes beyond equitable redistribution of land – if land is still narrated as enclosable and its value relating only to financial improvement. To rethink the world and the meanings of land and space, we can learn from resistances to spatial ordering that are mounted through rearticulation of the uses of bodies and spaces – for example, acts of self-ownership that are also enunciated from place. These include anti-mining activities in the Andes and the Dakota Access Pipeline protests as well as present continuous resistance to the capitalist-colonial-enslavement project (Hartman 1997: 66; Jenkins 2015: 442–60). These forms of resistance to restrictive making of meanings confront and defy the ideological separation of people from space and place. These resistances recognise that place is needed to give meanings to testamentary life, even when the structure of the world is designed to distort or deny those meanings (McKittrick 2006: xiii). In other words, these re-orderings of the world make clear that land rights and spatial relations are not or should not be legally ontological facts. So, if humanity has made the world we have, we can remake it beyond isolated pockets of defiance. This would involve rethinking, not just legal epistemologies around space and land, but around the nature of the law itself – where it comes from, what it can do, and how it defines property.

English law's definition of property that relies on 'transferability and durability' does not recognise the (possible) dynamism of space and place and the intractable connection between them and (the destruction of) testamentary life (Grear 2003: 37). Thus, abyssal thinking that produces contingent spaces, spatialises law because, despite producing space, law proceeds by presuming space to be static (Lamble et al 2017: 88). Yet, law and space are inseparable and co-constitutive (Philippopoulos-Mihalopoulos 2014: 4). Euro-modern law (property law especially) works in space, creates space, works on bodies, marks bodies, and creates the conditions bodies are subject to in space (Bhandar 2018: 4). This has been an essential feature of the capitalism-colonial-enslavement project. As Yang states: '[p]roperty law is a settler colonial technology' (2017: 27). However, through its regulatory aspect, this legal regime also creates and flattens reality – using its world-making ability to produce a world that does not actually exist and cannot survive (Shaw 2021: 70). Unequal vulnerability to global warming, environmental devastation, and climate change, all demonstrate that our use of land is unsustainable. Making land property through colonial legal epistemology serves and served to 'replace localised and physically responsive land laws with universalised and abstract land laws' (Graham 2010: 85). These imposed laws cannot easily find a solution to a problem that was produced from within them and their epistemologies – epistemologies that protect the right to exploit over protection of life.

Thinking legal spaces anew: is there place for legal knowledge in a borderless world?

Legal knowledge emerges from the other side of this analysis as a tool for creating a world of fiction – a world where imagined rules and regulations about illusory and invented borders carry more weight than actual life and death. The hope of a borderless world arises organically when we unsettle this fiction. Hard and soft borders are a feature of a Euro-modernity that is constitutive and ancillary to colonialism and its logics of commodification of the human and space. These borders remake the meanings of bodies that are susceptible to being cast to the waters. They remake the *Zong* and the Middle Passage into the waters of the Mediterranean. So, we must ask ourselves what exactly borders are for. A border that cannot be crossed is no longer a border, but a wall (Mbembé 2018). The cross-ability of a border is not ontological to the border, but to the human who desires to cross it. What invisiblises the border's reproduction as a plantation fence is the porosity it provides for particular persons and products that pass through with ease. And yet, 'the border is not a line', but a regime for the management of mobilities and interrelations (Munshi 2020: 1751). The dependence of the nation state on these border-walls, then calls into question the teleologies of the nation state as it emerges as a product of post-colonial anxieties to keep colonial subjects out of the metropole and away from colonial loot (Táíwò 2019: 61; El-Enany 2020). In other words, it is impossible to re-imagine the future or rethink the world from a position that tenaciously preserves the permanence of the present nation states. States are new creations on shaky foundations made more apparent by the existence of post-colonies that operate in perpetuity as zones for producing cheap labour without the need to shelter or feed that workforce – as modern-day plantations (Jones 1921: 50). Ongoing colonialism is cheaper and more efficient present-continuous racialised enslavement, creating wider and wider sacrifice zones and more and more human sacrifices for a land that will not survive the advancing destruction.

However, the experience of racialised people within this deepening disaster remains specific and acute. This is because, for racialised people, the border is not epistemically, 'spatially or temporally limited' (El-Enany 2020: 25). The border follows them, even when they cross it, even after they cross it, wherever they cross it to, whenever they cross it to. The world is continually (re)made white space. The settler has come to stay – everywhere, for all time. The racialised body is no longer at home. The racialised body is never at home. The racialised body is homeless. "Go back where you came from," is a command to be cast into the abyssal zone of time. It is a demand for human sacrifice. There is no non-white space that is not Hell. There is no home to go to that is not the jaws of a killing machine. Racialised bodies are trapped in the death zone, in the sunken place, continually cast beneath the abyssal line. Decolonisation is sought for the emergence of new species of humans and new contingent meanings of space and place that will not produce abyssality.

Decolonisation, especially its praxis regarding land and space, primarily requires the return of stolen land. This cannot be done effectively, however, without the resuscitation of other anti-colonial meanings of land, space, property, time, and the human. In many indigenous and colonised societies, the meaning of land is conceived as intimately connected with the persons who live on it as co-constitutive (Tafira 2015: webpage). Land bears a gravity that supersedes flat real property. Land rights in this sense and land's relation to the law are not focused on ownership, but on obligations of land being held in trust, communally, for those who are here, those who have gone ahead and those yet to come. Indigenous land epistemologies are therefore, 'concerned with people's obligations towards one another in respect of property than with the rights of people in property' (Du Plessis 2011: 49). Just as with interpersonal relations, obligations, and not rights are paramount. Rather than property-fication, these meanings of land extend into a complex interplay of economic, social, and political power within communities. Colonial epistemologies broke these links. Decolonial thinking in land and environmental justice is in essence, contingent on re-embodying the legal person and reordering law's human within space–time. The imperial geographical possession of land was achieved by re-narrating land. To undo colonisation is to undo this narration. Because, decolonisation cannot be done on the colonisers' terms, within the colonisers' meanings, in the coloniser's time and ultimately only for the colonisers' benefit.

To this end, with reference to legal knowledge, 'Land back' is also an epistemic question that takes closer account of other legal epistemologies of land. Rather, than considering law as something separate and superior to the land, Oceanic indigenous philosophies consider the land itself to be the source of the law (Graham 1999: 106). It is the land that gives meaning to human life which finds definition in community. In Andean indigenous thought, 'pacha' describes global space–time and Pachamama is the earth (land and water) as well as a goddess from whom all life emerges (Jenkins 2015: 442–60; Humphreys 2017: 459–84; Cuestas-Caza 2018: 50). These philosophies are replicated in some African communities where responsibility for land was vested in a divine head of state (Johnson 2010: 95–7). This emphasises the inseparable relationship between person and place in indigenous thought across the colonially interrupted world (Tsosie 2000: 1302). This way of relating to land was an obstacle to colonial acquisition of land. However, these epistemologies protected the earth from environmental devastation for centuries. So, to rethink and decolonise within the legal academy is to think of the possibilities that land has held and the power it has been subject to. It means to imagine, from within the academy, the possibilities land, the law, and the world can be remade into. For us to rethink land as unsettled and unsettling, we should trouble our acceptance of it as a noun that describes what is. We must conceive of space and place and land and race as verbs that describes undoings and doings (Liboiron 2021a: 43). To decolonise land and space is to make them unsettled, boundless, and free, a dynamic container and companion for testamentary life.

5

Defining the Law's Subject III: Law, Time, and Colonialism's Slow Violence

Colonialism is not simply content to impose its rule upon the present and the future of a dominated country. ... By a kind of perverted logic, it turns to the past of the oppressed people, and distorts it, disfigures and destroys it.

Frantz Fanon (2007: 149)

The colonialists usually say that it was they who brought us into history: today we show that this is not so. They made us leave history, our history, to follow them, right at the back, to follow the progress of their history.

Amilcar Cabral (1969: 63)

The defining feature of being drafted into the black race was the inescapable robbery of time, because the moments we spent readying the mask, or readying ourselves to accept half as much, could not be recovered. The robbery of time is not measured in lifespans but in moments.

Ta-Nehisi Coates (2015: 91)

Introduction

Fanon, Cabral, and Coates illustrate how the reproduction of the colonial ever-present is undergirded by colonialism's manoeuvring in time. Thus, time and temporality are essential to understanding the interplay between legal knowledge and colonialism and how colonial logics are carried into the future. Temporality (materially constructed by memory practices, but also with non-human agents) denotes a subjective movement through moments, while time (socially constructed and cognitive) represents the objective attempt to quantify, measure, and mark that movement (see generally Bluedorn 2002: 14; Hoy 2012: 92; Birth 2012: 102; Grabham 2016: 16, 34–5; Abazi and Doja 2018: 240). In other words, temporality can be described as 'the experience and perception of time' (Lundström and Sartoretto 2021: 2). Times and temporalities, therefore, connect the earth and all its inhabitants – human, non-human, and inanimate – across space–time (Grabham 2016: 30). The introduction of the clock as a record of time is intimately linked with the acceleration of modes of accumulation and dispossession, which intensified during the colonial–enslavement project and increasingly thereafter under the auspices of globalised accretion of capital. Euro-modern legal knowledge, especially within the common law, is heavily reliant on time and temporality to make its meanings. Therefore, as a tool for social order, ([past, present, and forward-looking), Euro-modern legal knowledge is then also complicit in enabling colonially and racially accumulated capital and other advantages to be retained through abstractions from time. The same is true of colonial and racial dispossession and ancillary disadvantages. This permanence of accumulation and dispossession results partly from a reliance on linearity and mono-temporality, which presupposes the inevitability of progress in ways which naturalise the effects of colonialism. Such linearity and singularity obscure and invisibilise the ongoing abstractive and extractive violence enacted through erasure of othered bodies and continuations of colonial cartographies in sacrifice zones. For example, reliance on this linearity makes it instinctive to conceive of 'decolonisation' as a matter of the past rather than a concern for the future – as merely justice for 'historical' acts rather than also a means and a language for thinking the future world anew. Thus, Euro-modern time temporally traps the colonial–enslavement project within it, masquerading it as a fixed event rather than an ongoing structure, which is still moving through its moments, affecting human perception of future, present, and past. This ordering of time is subsequently implicated in the epistemological fragmentation of the discipline into distinct areas of law. Once observed, this bending of time then becomes apparent in how we mis-narrate the current spatial–legal difference between, for example, the UK and US as a temporally distinct one; in how we narratively distance what used to be colonies as prospectively and retrospectively eternally separate and independent polities from the metropole. Hence, this chapter focuses on Euro-modern ordering of time especially, and, as well as with legal knowledge, its role in creating and reproducing the ongoing colonial order in perpetuity. Specific emphasis is placed on the technologies within legal epistemology which enable the ongoing order to be temporally permanent.

Colonial times making time colonial: the continual re-making of the colonial ever-present

Mainly, time and temporality are imbricated into colonialism through the universalisation of a particular way of keeping time – the collapse of the whole world into one time (Bell 2020: 89). With the temporal move, which was the introduction of Greenwich Mean Time and the Prime Meridian, Europe (via London) consolidated its place as the absolute centre of the 'modern' world (Nanni 2017: 219). Prior to the globalisation of Euro-modernity, each culture weighed time using its own devices, according to its own wants, needs, and desires. With the rising of the sun, the ripening of grain, the pendency of the stars in the sky, the length of the harvest, the changing of the seasons … time was measured with reference to local and not global needs. The promiscuous power accumulated and instrumentalised through colonialism resulted in an ordering of time so complete and total that its implementation, in terms of time, often operated without the physical presence of power (Edelstein et al 2020: 16). Thus, globalisation can be understood, not just as a spatial narrowing, but also the temporal collapse of non-Europe time-ways into Euro-modern linearity and temporal singularity in order to serve the purposes of commodification. This temporal collapse required the 'privileging of the historically specific legal and political infrastructure of European capitalism' (Tzouvala 2020: 4). In other words, the capacity to control time is an automated display of unmitigated economic power. Bourdieu describes this as the exercise of absolute power, manifested through the manipulation of time to deny alternative possibility to others and grant endless possibility to self (2000: 228). This control of this domain of power has also been described as 'chronopolitics', a politics which turns time into a warzone that makes present kingdoms into ancient ruins and narrates current civilisations as barbaric backwaters (Hicks 2020: 113, 190). This temporal power was deployed in the globalisation of the praxis and logics of accumulation and the subsummation of all bodies and spaces into its orbit, because a singular measurement of time was required to undergird and consolidate this expansion. Such singularity serves, among other things, to make what is contrived and constructed seem natural and inevitable. By making resistance to them seem, out of place and out of time, these new modes of living also resulted in the invisibilation of other temporalities that opposed the collapse of the world into a singular rhythm of rapid accumulation. So, the governing of time was fundamental to 'controlling, disciplining, and annihilating' non-normative bodies and spaces, trapping them into relations with time that were incomprehensible, violent, and inescapable (Shringarpure 2019: 63). Therefore, despite being in permanent competition with the cyclic patterns of testamentary life – cycles of life and death, day and night, rest and rejuvenation – linearity and singularity predominate in the public sphere and so naturalise themselves (Greenhouse 1989: 1637). This they do by subordinating all other temporalities into coercive power's disciplining of time (de Sousa Santos 2016: 165–72). Yet, this self-naturalisation nevertheless relies on cyclical entrapment and repetition. Afropessimism observes this paradox in its melancholic realisation of the inescapability of oppression within purportedly progressive cycles of violence in the colonial ever-present. Periodisations, such as 'precolonial' and 'post-racial', help to recite a change only to the outward features of injustice but they never really denote its end. Afropessimism invites us to unsettle the presupposition of the naturalness of linearity by reading as simultaneous, both 500 years ago and the present, because reading history as only of past concern comforts the privileged alone (Wilderson 2015: 435). This same understanding of the concurrence of time is also evident in postcolonial African literature which bemoans the intractability of the conditions of life into which African peoples are trapped by the persisting colonial logics of body and space–time which are deployed at home and abroad (Macharia 2021: webpage). Furthermore, Euro-modern adoption of linear time as dominant and consequent erasure of cyclical and other understandings of time, manifested differently depending on the type of colonial encounter. In settler colonies, for example, manipulation of time secured permanent control of land; while in non-settler colonies and through racialised enslavement, chronopolitics facilitated the extraction of unfree labour and resources (Nanni 2017: 13).

These foregoing varied modes of control were dependent on the colonial logics and praxes of spatiality and marking bodies discussed in the previous chapters. Yet, linearisation of time is of general but also relatively recent application. Prior to the introduction of the clock into the workplace, workers were remunerated for the value of their labour, rather than the amount of time they worked (Stewart 2012: 310; Nanni 2017: 41). Tying time to value and thereon to money required that time be made abstract – unconnected to human existence and space. This abstraction of time operates as an extension of Lockean division of labour-as-separate-value from self. The narration of labour as the prime value of the human/body is married with time as a marker of that value. Thus, the 'colonisation of time' describes time's use primarily for the benefit of the market and not for the needs of testamentary life (Shippen 2014: 2). Therefore, even though the clock was invented in the 13th century, its importance as a means of measuring time, does not become significant until the Industrial Revolution which was accompanied by colonial land and labour accumulation (Stewart 2012: 307). Consequently, colonial chronopolitics enabled the creation of, at the moment of the colonial encounter, hierarchical divergent timestreams demarcated by bodies and spaces. Euro-modernity borrowed the language and ontology of linearity from the church, this imbued the conceptualisation of time with endless linear progress (Greenhouse 1989: 1638). Consequently, these distortions and conflations of space–time mean that African bodies and colonial resources only become of value to modernity when they are extracted from 'the past of their backward locations' and incorporated into the global capital market (Fabian 2014: 94). As non-European ways of marking time were thought to be too embodied to pass the test of Cartesian dualism, the marking of time in rapid Euro-modern fashion became a sign of civilisation (129; Said 2003: 108; Nanni 2017). Euro-modern time was inculcated, globalised, naturalised, and thus made permanent, especially through the introduction of strict colonial-era schedules for transportation systems like the railways, as well as colonial schools and mission work (Hom 2010: 1164–5). These ways of 'civilised' living held no room for temporalities that did not serve capitalist-colonial purposes.

So, non-Euro-modern ways of marking time, marked bodies that were to be violently written out of time. The ascription of the time of peoples that are indigenous, racialised and/or colonised as 'timeless', marked them for extinction, disposability, and bare life. For these bodies, timeless meant being out of time or without time. Or according to Gilmore, vulnerable to 'premature death' (2007: 28). So, the very premise upon which the colonial enterprise was based was the presumption that the other lived in an incommensurable time-period to the coloniser. This is what Fabian calls the denial of coevalness (2014: 173). He identifies this as an attitude of asynchronicity in which anthropological ethnographers, even though collection of knowledge from subjects of study relies on simultaneous time and temporality, present that extracted knowledge in writing and teaching as if they and the object of study existed in divergent times. 'The Other's empirical presence turns into his theoretical absence' (Fabian 2014: xxxix). This creates a spatial–temporal fiction, that continually narrates journeys to what is now designated the Global South as if they were journeys back in time. This attitude results from constant placement of Euro-modern knowledges and disciplines and realities as the referent from which other knowledges and realities are dispatched (Bevernage 2016: 358). In other words, epistemologies of time outside of Euro-modernity are always subordinated and made unintelligible to hegemonical epistemological structures unwilling to read them, so also are the possibilities they posit (Rifkin 2017: 192). In contrast, the same fiction of time that dislocates colonised places and people from the present to the past, also relocates colonial logics to the future (Keenan 2019: 285). This is exemplified in the use of Euro-modern law to grant legal title to land to settler populations and their assignees in ways that disregard prior native/indigenous title to land and ways of being on the land. Prior users of the land are cast into a primordial past that never really existed and are subjected to conditions of bare life. In comparison, Euro-modern users of land can lay claim to the advantages of enclosure and are thus able to access means of profligate life and expectations of endless futurity.

Therefore, of main concern here for legal knowledge, are the ways in which the creation of a specific translation of modernity dislocates bodies from space, while simultaneously producing artificed time demarcations to justify and make permanent these dislocations. As a constructed vehicle for the narration of naturalness of the capitalist-colonial-enslavement project, Euro-modernity's birth can be traced to a particular place and time – Western Europe in the 17th century (Mignolo 2000: 29; Escobar 2013: 35–6). But it is now everywhere. It is: 'awakened by contact; transported through commerce; administered by empires, bearing colonial inscriptions; propelled by nationalism; and now increasingly steered by global media, migration, and capital' (Gaonkar 2001: 1). Thus, modernity was and is a provisional selective universalisation of a particular linear and singular sorting of time (Latour 1993: 76). Euro-modernity, of necessity, to reify and entrench itself, must rely on 'a belief in linear progress ... of reason and freedom' (Wood 1997: 541). Therefore, the Enlightenment and the Industrial Revolution as well as the restrictive narrative of them, shorn of the colonial and enslavement violence that they required, are key players in the emergence of this tale of modernity. Erased from this articulation of modernity is the reliance of these moments on the creation of othered bodies and necropolitical zones of sacrifice, as well as the extraction of unfree labour and dispossession of indigenous land. The result of all this is to, within our intellectual imaginary, place colonised/racialised/indigenous spaces/people into an earlier timeline, outside the developmental process of humanity (Alcoff 2007: 84), where they are eternally and futilely striving to reach Europe (both metaphorically but also physically – see the waters of the Mediterranean). This physical and temporal displacement serves to label certain humans/bodies as futuristic and certain humans/bodies as temporally anomalous and accordingly inevitably subject to extinction.

Yet, this temporal dislocation obscures the contingent nature of the temporalities of colonised and coloniser spaces. This dishonesty about their co-dependency is evidenced in the spatialisation of responsibility for colonial era crimes. By situating events in a faraway time and place – the fault and thus responsibility for them, was not that of the colonial officer, but was due to him travelling back in time to a lawless place and period. He was subject therefore, not to the rules and reason of 'civilised men', but to the lawlessness of a timeless people and place. This story of modernity fails to acknowledge the co-constitution of Euro-modernity and the other temporalities it disrupts and discards. Euro-modernity always constructs itself out of the ashes of the othered times it consigned to the fires of colonialism. In other words, left uninterrogated is how colonised bodies' experience of Euro-modernity is contingent on the way in which the coloniser enacts modernity. Or as Olaniyan says, in explaining why African poverty is 'modern' (predicated on Euro-modern extraction and accumulation), 'it is absolutely ridiculous to think that Congo is not modern, but Belgium is' (Olaniyan 2014: 3:28–3:33). As previously mentioned, Belgium's brutal colonial activities in what was called the Belgian Congo, which involved racialised use of enslaved, enforced, and tortured–compelled labour to work rubber and oil palm plantations, resulted in a population loss of roughly 50 per cent of Congolese and a stagnation of development (Hochschild 1999: 280). By dislocating the temporalities of the coloniser from the colonised, the memory of the colonial-enslavement project, as a key player in capital accumulation, is simultaneously erased and preserved. Documents necessary for the lineage of capital accumulation to be maintained are celebrated and kept alive as records and archives (Walters 2017: 181). Yet there are many absences. Several colonial administrations deliberately destroyed evidence of their activities away from the metropole. For example, 'Operation Legacy' describes the world-wide destruction of colonial reports and documents at the formal handing over of British colonial administration (Cobain 2016: chapter 4; Sato 2017: 697–719). Still, these absences in the archives sometimes speak louder for their silence (Franco and Mustafa 2019: 42–8). For inheritors of colonial violence, the archives may bleed through apertures that leak fragmented and incomplete recollections of colonial violence and annihilation. So, memories of the brutalities upon which accumulation is contingent are kept alive only as heritable bodily, communal, and spatial trauma. Sometimes, you can feel the damage and disturbance in the land, in the water and in the air. 'History is restless. Afterlives are busy. Every record is incomplete. Many records are absent. Most records. The archive is mostly omission' (Mitter 2018: webpage).

Thus, Euro-modern legal knowledge fails to reckon with the damage it has wrought on bodies and space–time. Consequently, it is that temporal contingency between the coloniser and the colonised that informs the ascription of 'Euro-modernity' that I use. This ascription signals that there are other modernities, contingent on the emergence of 'Europe as *the* modernity', that do not find within their realities, the same profligate life that is found above the line (Gordon 2020: 8, 65). Euro-modernity is thus revealed not as a noble advance-guard of universal progress, but a deceptively benign necropolitical selector of 'who must die'. In response, decolonisation invites us to unsettle the fragmentations and erasures of contingent knowledge and experientiality before the law. Within Euro-modern legal knowledge, there is a tendency for periodisation and temporal fragmentation. 'Post', one of the most common markers of the past, is reliant on linearity. Therefore 'postcolonial' casts colonisation, for Euro-modern law, in particular and the social sciences in general, as a problem for the past, not the present or future. Yet even within the articulation of 'postcolonial' the intractability of colonial logics and their ongoing enfoldment with power has been noted. 'Post' here is not 'just a matter of the passage of time', it refers instead to how power transfigures itself, while still increasing its domination, such that, 'what we are dealing with is not two successive regimes but the simultaneous presence of a regime and its after-effects' (Hall 2017: 24). This articulation of present-continuous evolving power recognises that laws and systems that grew from the past, cannot by the mere passage of clock-time, detach themselves from the logics and praxes of their roots. Legal knowledge, in seeking easy categories, has thus failed to account for how human beings actually dynamically live in multiple, simultaneous, complex, enfolded spaces, places, times, and temporalities (Mbembé 2001: 8). In other words, the study of history as a discipline and its appearance within disciplines (for example, legal history), also unveils itself as a technology of power, which takes control of global memory, and rewrites and orders those memories also into service of the colonial ever-present.

Furthermore, this temporal structure is similarly implicated in the mid-twentieth century transmogrification of the nation state and its reified consolidation as racial state. Anderson, in his thesis on states as imagined communities, explains how the emergence of 'empty homogenous time' facilitates the ability of states to imagine themselves as single homogenous units moving simultaneously and linearly through time (Anderson 2006: 24–26). This fiction erases temporalities that are within the state and external to it, upon which the state relies. One of these erasures is the fundamental significance of racialisation in the conceptualisation of insiders and outsiders to the racial state. The imbrication of racialisation with modernity ties civilisation to populations marked 'white', erasing any advancement outside of that marking (Bell 2020: 389). Thus, Goldberg implicates mythmaking and fabricated memories as important facets in the consolidation of power in racial states (2008: 234). Both rely on erasures of internally divergent temporalities as well as operations of contingency. Thus, empty homogenous time is necessary to make sense of erasure because it relies on a fiction of simultaneous and homogenous (Euro)modernity, fostered by mythmaking through media and literature. This manufactured simultaneity serves to preserve the state's aims, which are not structured to protect testamentary life or dynamic space, but the market. Therefore, ultimately, '[e]mpty homogeneous time is the time of capital' (Chatterjee 2003: 33). In other words, the state perpetuates itself, through legal epistemologies tuned to make the ongoing and manufactured, into permanent reality. Thus, time is actually an 'accumulation, rather than a passing or a progression' (Walters 2017: 181). The present always gathers the past and the future onto itself – the barriers of time are only really human creations through structures of power (Hicks 2016: 8).

The time always returns: forever in the waters of difficulty

Law, as a discipline, like history and anthropology, is intimately tied to the time and temporalities of colonialism in particular, (as well as time and temporality in general) (Mawani 2014: 65–95). A very basic understanding of, for example, judicial precedent, principles of contemporaneity, concepts of reasonableness, contract law, law reform, individuality, and personal rights, reveals the suffusion of temporal manoeuvring within law's ambit. For instance, the essence of a judicial precedent is a selective account of past and present facts through the eyes of past law, with a view to the future impact of that reading. Judicial precedent, therefore, relies on an accumulated reading of particular pasts, presents, and futures (Greenhouse 1989: 1640). Thus, legal judgement and judicial precedent produce different times and temporalities by binding the present to the past and also binding the present to the future through expectation (Harrington 2012: 496; Chowdhury 2020: 20–30, 145–6). A judicial precedent on contract law, for example, demonstrates the accumulation of time described here, as it brings to fruition past intentions of parties to a contract. *Donoghue v Stevenson* (1932: 562) also exemplifies how this accumulation of time, body, and space presents itself in legal education and its cyclic connection to legal practice. This 1932 decision laid down the framework for negligence claims across the Commonwealth. The cursory details of the case are as follows: Mrs May Donoghue had been bought a ginger beer by a friend and at the bottom of her drink, after having ingested a significant amount, she found a decomposed snail. The House of Lords on appeal found that the manufacturers of the ginger beer, for the purposes of the case, though they had never met her or been in legal contract with her, owed Mrs Donoghue a duty of care. By not ensuring their ginger beer was free of decomposing snail, they had been negligent. For many law students across the Commonwealth, this is one of the first legal cases they learn. Mrs Donoghue's body is constantly brought into law classrooms. Every time we teach the origins of the duty of care, we are forever confronted across time and space with her bodily disgust at drinking the ginger beer negligently flavoured with decomposing snail. We teach nothing much else about Mrs Donoghue. Mrs Donoghue is simultaneously present and very absent. Like many litigants, the flat version of Mrs Donoghue is trapped in legal time. There are numerous other similar testamentary witnesses to the content of our curricular research and practice. Some speak flattened testimonies, like Mrs May Donoghue. Some bodily testaments are distorted by our use of them. Some have been silenced, their testimony is absent from the artifact of law. Each time we engage with legal knowledge, we are surrounded by ghosts and spectres of (im)possibility. What does it mean to acknowledge that our present is contingent on the past and is the possibility for the future?

So, we pick and choose the pasts and versions of the past to which we wish to refer within our expressions of legal knowledge. Yet the power to articulate the past must be recognised as power to 'to take control of a memory, as it flashes in a moment of danger' (Benjamin 2009: 389). Consequently, law produces its own temporality. This means that law does not exist completely outside of time, time also exists and is instantiated within law (Grabham 2016: 14). The image created of law in time is thus contradictory: always existing, but having a singular linear referent, human but abstract, objective yet myth (Greenhouse 1989: 1640). Euro-modern law is one of the tools for what Latour describes as the sorting and production of time. A process for ordering time and creating the technologies of a chronopolitics. Grabham describes this as legal processes engaging in 'brewing times' through the interaction of human, non-human, and inanimate agents (2016: 22–3). This results in a complicity between law, time, and structures of power and social order, where 'temporality and legality are conceptually fused in the West through their mutual implications of a total order in relation to which social life acquires meaning' (Greenhouse 1989: 1631). Law assigns for itself the role of managing change, slowing it down and making it predictable (Stewart 2012: 315). For example, managing through legislation, the changes demanded by resistances to racialised enslavement, exploitative colonisation, and contingent racial injustice, by preserving lines of power through compensation, preservation of colonial borders, as well as restricted meanings of justice. By embedding predictability and naturalness within its praxes, 'law and legal temporalities assist in the fabrication of "social" and "natural" time' (Grabham 2016: 13). Time therefore arises from the presumptions inherent in state practices and the exercise of state power (Greenhouse 2018: 73). In other words, the self-actualising nature of Euro-modern law and the power it wields across the earth is such that the times and temporalities it produces are experienced as natural (Keenan 2019: 286).

The very language within which the law operates through legal definitions and jurisdictional limits is also a temporal device. The same act or legal instrument may have different legal effects depending on the time and space within which it is enacted. This manoeuvring within time was often operationalised within legal decisions to consolidate colonial accumulation, such that not only land was accumulated, but also time. For example, the judgement in the case of *Wi Parata v The Bishop of Wellington* (1877) that declared the treaty of Waitangi 'worthless', and 'a simple nullity' relied on a racially contingent reading of the past that produced divergent timestreams for its litigant. This case was concerned with determining whether the Ngatitoa tribe in what is now known as New Zealand, ever ceded land to the Crown, so that a school could be built on the aforementioned land. Chief Justice Prendergast found that the Ngatitoa had no title in land to grant. According to Prendergast's ruling, whatever rights they had to the land were superseded by the Crown's claim in the land. This despite the treaty of Waitangi – signed between the British and the Maori in 1840 – recognising Maori ownership of the land. Prendergast CJ rejected the possibility of such a binding treaty being signed by 'barbarians without any form of law or civil government' (1877: 77). A similar approach to subjectivity and re-reading of the past and law was also taken in the UK's Privy Council's judgement in *Re Southern Rhodesia* (1919) (discussed in Chapter 2). In both cases, the displacement of the racialised population had the effect, not just to dislocate them from their land, but from time, by nullifying legal agreements, their past sovereignty, as well as their future possibilities. In contrast to Euro-modern law's inherent presumption of endless continuity, in rejecting the lawfulness of indigenous jurisprudence and extending Euro-modern law beyond its initial spatial jurisdiction, these enactments relied concurrently on actual temporal disruption and mythic continuity (Peters et al 2017: 462). The doctrine of *uti possidetis* previously discussed, also serves a temporal purpose as well as a spatial one. By enfolding colonies into an artificial linear destiny that inevitably produces Westphalian states, the legal doctrine traps the boundless possibilities of peoples and spaces into one of endless colonial futures. Thus, Finnis argues that, based on laws of succession and a connected succession of laws, the overtaking of the colony by the state is not a legal disjuncture, but a settled continuity (2011: 418). The timelessness of indigenous peoples and other colonised populations is not reversed by state creation. They, their bodies, and possibilities continue to be out of time.

So, Euro-modern law sets the temporal and spatial limits of loyalty to the state, to the earth, to humanity … to everything. This temporal borderisation also turns up in taxonomies of humanity, (and their successors), linked with the colonial project, for example, 'European', 'Asiatic', 'African'. These taxonomies grant those so delineated temporally dependent access to the metropole (Mawani 2014: 69, 86). Time and temporality are not neutral aspects of social life and non-life (Greenhouse 1989: 1633); law must juggle many temporalities within itself – the temporalities of society ordered as linear, the temporality of law and laws that may take different directions, and the divergent temporalities of legal actors (Greenhouse 1989: 1642–5). Euro-modern law is always juggling unsettled pasts and multiple possible futures, but Euro-modern legal knowledge insists on making these times explicitly knowable with itself as sole referent. What is unknown or unknowable, through the eyes of Euro-modernity, did not happen. Consequently, the social production of time, backed by the power of the state and the authority of law, traps us into selected pasts and limits the futures to which we can aspire. Because legal temporalities are ideally predictable and knowable, legal construction of time restricts humanity and the earth into continuous repetition of increasingly made dangerous versions of the present, rather than the possibility of different futures that do not travel through the time of the colonial-ever-present.

This ongoing-ness or accumulation of the effect of law and time calls into question the ascription of past atrocities as 'historical injustices', as they still order present-day obligations and responsibilities. So, this ongoing-ness strongly suggests that racialised enslavement, colonial dispossession, and apartheid, as well as future responsibility for environmental devastation, all exist in the legal present (Edelstein et al 2020: 20–1). In various ways, Euro-modern law seeks to fragment and hold back temporal flows of accumulated time behind legal barriers, such as statutes of limitation as well as spatial and temporal jurisdictional restrictions. Consequently, it is in this manipulation of time, that Euro-modern law does its most powerful and most invisible work. This includes the slow violence that can be found in the imposition of conditions of life on the body and space–time, that are hostile to testamentary life and dynamic place. The enactment of slow violence is woven into the logics and praxis – the very ever-present machine – of colonialism. Not only is this type of violence slow, but it is also continuous and continuing – without needing to be dispatched, thus departing from the narrative of immediacy as a perquisite of violence. Slow violence lives in the machine. It is part of the machine. It feeds the machine. It is fed by the machine. It is, therefore, not surprising that this violence finds sustenance and permanence through the premises and effects of colonial-era laws and judgements which were simultaneously temporally and racially contingent.

Euro-modernity's work as a temporal tool of colonial domination, accumulation, and dispossession extends into the present as an enfolded instrument of memory and order that maintains the hierarchies, accretions, erasures, and realities created during formal colonisation. In not acknowledging this, its colonial ever-present, legal knowledge operates like a living memorial that ensures that 'whole cultures really were stripped of their technologies, had their living landscapes transformed into ruins – and had these moments of violence extended across time, memorialized' (Hicks 2020: 180). Thus, we stand here, in the midst of global inequality, racialised and gendered disparity, rising waters, under the shadow of a boiling sun, facing the threat of increasing pandemics. ... Humanity stands here, side by side with history's ghosts in the ongoing ruins of Euro-modernity, in the afterlives of exploitative colonisation and racialised enslavement. The way in which the law orders the world by selected temporal enfoldment and fragmentation means that through its epistemologies and devices, accumulated wealth can be lawfully transported through generations, but not responsibility for the slow violence through which it continues to be accumulated. These processes unveil themselves in the ongoing-ness of spatial dispossession of and from land. How do indigenous people experience their ongoing removal as permanent violence? How does dispossession from the category, 'human' unveil itself as constant nightmare? It is inscribed on othered bodies as festering wounds of battles that had been declared won in the past, and yet these bodies will still have to fight those battles in the future. From anti-colonial wars to slave rebellions, to civil rights protests, to a global movement for Black lives ... it is the same battle across space–time. Consequently, separation into past, present, and future is not really possible, as we live in an ever-present colonial now. Ta-Nehisi Coates deliberately and repeatedly erases the demarcations between the act and outcome of racialised enslavement in the USA. Coates argues that one main outcome of being racialised Black is the 'inescapable robbery of time' (2015: 91). This robbery of time is found in the moments lost, not just to racialised enslavement and colonisation, but all the smaller stolen moments that flow from that. The moments spent preparing for and dealing with the ongoing/slow violence that structure a world built on logics and praxis of accumulation and dispossession. It is in the moments used up arguing for the right to exist. The moments lost writing this book. This robbery of time also refers to moments of love poured into lives lost too early to disproportionate acts of racialised violence ... and the trauma that follows the loss. All this is enacted through a 'legacy of plunder, a network of laws and traditions ... a heritage' (Coates 2015: 110). Yet, Euro-modern law places strict limits on when 'robbery' (permanent deprivation through dishonest appropriation of that which belongs to another using contemporaneous application of force) would be an affront to itself. Enslavement and colonial dispossession were mostly lawful affairs (Moore 2020: 495–497). So, Coates' argument suggest that colonialism's logics imply, not just the robbery of time, but the robbery *in* and *with* time. The coincidence in the deprivation of personhood for accumulation during the pendency of racialised enslavement, and the deprivation of personhood as disposable marked bodies, only becomes apparent with the repair of the schism of fragmented time. Thus, in the USA, it is accepted without irony that Black lives had more value as enslaved property than they have now. This 'truth' sits beside another contradiction – that enslavement was the time of unfreedom and now is the time of freedom.

What we can surmise here is that in confronting hegemonical acts of periodisation, we are able to turn away from hasty distinctions in time frames. This has strong implications for the language that we use in the discipline and the realities that flow from them. For example, we then realise that with the removal of the obscurantism of periodisation, 'absolutist distinctions between slavery and freedom are untenable' (Hartman 1997: 13). Furthermore, monolithic and fragmentary periodisation obscures the roots of not just environmental degradation, but places climate justice and social justice in false adversarial corners, while colonial logics continue to simultaneously and concurrently brutally abstract from both those corners. Humanity, the earth, and all their possibilities in all their complex multiple temporalities are always 'becoming free'. Othered bodies and spaces are bent out of sync with Euro-modernity, out of the rhythms chosen by the machine of accumulation and dispossession. A lack of alternative futures is the offspring of Euro-modern temporal (mis)management. A narrowing of future possibilities into one future labelled 'perdition', where humanity is in jeopardy, and the earth is in geologic crisis.

Therefore, justice for the earth and the peoples of the earth, cannot be achieved without critically unveiling the workings of time in Euro-modernity, for which we may not have present language or structure. For example, asserting the present-ness of populations divorced from time is not ideal, as such a declaratory move erases the violence that brought about the now and presumes an impartiality of the present (Rifkin 2017: 1). Memory has no compass, and the times of memory have no fixed address. In other words, legal knowledges embedded in the language of the nation state choose to recognise a declared but often merely performative disruption in time over the continuity of ongoing violence. Therefore, the very language that promises justice, through periodisation and fragmentation, erases the harm it has been called upon to heal. By historicising the injury, repair is 'rendered elusive at the very moment of its enunciation into legal language' (Castillejo-Cuéllar 2014: 49). Thus, Leroy argues via Douglass that slavery's drive to perpetuate and thus modify itself for the purposes of enduring teleology, can be understood both through the language of racial capitalism's reading of the continuity of time in the practices of racialised commodification, as well as ongoing evolution of abolition theories and movements (2021: 169–84). In other words, we need to disturb the presumed linearity in legal justice from the perspectives of both state violence and resistances to it. Baldwin uses this unsettling idea of time to collapse the past into the present and unveil the accumulation of time. He states:

> Instead of speaking about the civil rights movement, let us pretend that I stand before you as a witness to, and a survivor of, the latest slave rebellion … we are still governed by the slave codes. When I say a slave rebellion, I mean what is called a civil rights movement was really insurrection. [transcription mine] (Baldwin 1979: 3:36–6:01)

We are still governed by the slave codes, Baldwin tells us. They may not be called slave codes, but their ontology and teleology remain unchanged – hierarchising, extracting, ordering, and annihilating. Therefore, what is required here is a turning away from language that spatialises and periodises reality and consequently obscures space–time continuity in colonial conditions of life. If we are still governed by the ontology of a succession of slave codes, if the slave patrols still run, if colonial dispossession still continues … then slavery abolition and decolonisation are also present work, found in contemporary theories of abolition. 'Modern-day slavery' therefore, unveils itself as a misnomer, that wishes to declare something ended that we are not yet done with. Modern-day slavery also describes nebulously, the present-day and connected expansion of pre-existing logics of unfree labour, that still largely operate along racial and gendered lines (Patterson 2012: 322–59). The values of accumulation stand the test of time. The colonial teleology is ever present. So, it is problematic to cast values temporally (and spatially) when it is the value in accumulation that orders the colonial ever-present. To suggest, for example, that historical figures that were involved in colonial atrocities were just men of their time, acting in keeping with the standards of their time, ignores the embodiedness and coevalness of contingent and entangled temporalities. This argument discounts both the humanity and temporalities of those, in every time, found on the other side of the abyssal line. The enslaved and colonised were also 'men'. They were also of their time. François-Dominique Toussaint L'ouverture was the leader of the Haitian revolution. Nzinga of Ndongo and Matamba fought for freedom for her people against the Portuguese. Mansa Musa's wealth remains incalculable – albeit on the backs of enslaved people. These were embodied people of their time too, who acted in keeping with the complex standards of their time, too. Therefore, to cast values temporally is to deny the humanity of those racialised below the abyssal line and to continue to place them out of time and ever subject to premature death.

So, how do we teach and research law in a world of collapsing ever-present colonial-time? If law does not have the language to read testamentary life, dynamic space, and accumulated time, we may need to look beyond the language of the law. Acknowledging the absences within the law – not just what it does not cover, but what it is not currently structured to do – plays a vital role in effectively transmitting critical legal knowledge. Claudia Rankine's work, for example, compares the ways in which racialised peoples experienced US state power in the aftermath of Hurricane Katrina with the experience of being thrown to the waters out of a slave ship like *Zong*. '[S]till in the difficulty … standing where the deep waters of everything backed up … climbing over bodies … we are drowning here, still in the difficulty', Rankine writes (2014: 83–5). In drawing a shared temporality between Katrina and *Zong*, Rankine's words call on us to imagine that all time was collapsed into a single moment. What if slave ships were sailing right now? … What if disposable bodies are being lost to the waters now? What if colonial land was being accumulated now? What if labour extraction was still racialised? What if indigenous land was still being taken and the bodies of the indigenous were still being forgotten in the ground, now? So, imagination becomes reality. We *are* still in the difficulty. A similar shared temporality can also be drawn between the breathlessness marked by slow violence that enabled the Grenfell fire, racialised disparity in police brutality across the world, vulnerability to COVID-19 including the vaccine apartheid, and the burning of indigenous land and forests (Bhattacharya et al 2021: 173–200). "We cannot breathe." We are still in the difficulty. Water and fire. "We cannot breathe." Actual time is never fractured. Temporality is an unbroken continuum of connected memory … across time, across space. We are still in the difficulty. To think otherwise is to ignore the fact that Euro-modern legal knowledge destroys in itself the capacity within itself to inaugurate the most important part of enquiry – the possible futures that may come to pass for the earth and for humanity (Bluedorn 2002: 20). If we fail to address this, we remain, still and forever in the waters and fires of difficulty. "We cannot breathe."

Towards different times: rebuilding the ruins of time

One of the starkest effects of legal knowledge on Euro-modern temporalities is that legal academics are forced to teach and research through strict prisms of predictability and possibility. Legal education teaches our students to narrow the alternatives open to society in its oscillation through time. Yet this colonial ordering and understanding of time has always been challenged and resisted, through labour strikes, slave rebellions, and similar refusals (Nanni 2017: 19). Though it should be noted that if we read such resistance only through lenses of linearity, we may view them merely as a series of defeats, rather than appreciating them as an accumulated and accumulating commitment to act for the hope of an unpredictable future that understands the concerted power of colonialism (Verges 2020: 5). What is called for within and beyond a decolonial reading of the world, is a more critical approach to interpreting law's relationship to dynamic and interpellated pasts and presents (Crowe and Lee 2015: 260–5). A presumption of linear time often leads to the misconception that decolonisation is a political project of return to a forgotten past, and not a movement for a future that bypasses the confining loop of Euro-modern time and its colonial ever-present.

As both bodies and spaces are co-constitutive and relational, it is possible to parse who and what humanity and its complementary spaces, is and can be, through the spectrum of unsettled time and temporality. This possibility is reflected in Mbiti's argument that African philosophical articulation of time is usually connoted as 'time-for' or 'time-to' or 'time-of' (1990: 16–17). In other words, time subjugated to the subjectivities of human and earth needs, wants, desires, and thus temporalities. This slowing down of time to the rhythm of bio-space, reduces the overexploitation of the earth, as time does not direct the human or the earth. So, non-Euro-modern time is not merely an objective abstraction but can be used to mark bio-spatial orders of existence. This contrasts with the linear trap of modernity, which makes the claim that we can remove ourselves from this bio-spatiality just by waiting on time. Linearity is thus contrasted with time as a cycle, or a spiral, within which humanity's ancestors, present community, and the natural world 'become one' (Ecuador National Planning Council 2009: 18). Cyclical time, it should be noted, does not presume the complete absence of linearity of time or coincidence of temporality. Cyclical time actually predates linear time in European epistemologies (Europe as place not power) (Greenhouse 1989: 1636). By misinterpreting the complexity of time experiences, 'Western understandings of temporality either become fixated with the (guilt and/ or glamour of the) past, or endeavour to escape to the (planning and/or developing of the) future' (Cilliers 2018: 118–19). In other words, Euro-modern time is so pre-occupied with getting rapidly 'post' an imagined past into an unliveable future, that it loses sight of how entrenched the past is in the present, and as such we that live in it are devoid of all will to work for a different future. Decolonisation, thus, also finds its promise and possibility in an urgent and immediate escape from Euro-modern time and temporality. So, time, in the final analysis, is a fundamental spirit of freedom and its fair distribution the ultimate justice (Shippen 2014: 3–7). Not only is the availability of time the counterpoint to unfree labour under the capitalist-colonial-enslavement project, but it also provides the temporal space for critical thought and imagination to break free from the continuous reproduction of the colonial ever-present. Accumulative acceleration is a rapid impetus to get to an uncertain future, so the present is never in view, even if that is the only temporality Euro-modernity allows us to really experience. Thus, St Augustine of Hippo spoke of the need to focus on the contemporaneous, the now, in our understanding of time: 'a time present of things past; a time present of things present; and a time present of things future' (Cilliers 2018: 120).

Being present in time, temporality, and law, therefore requires radical and critical innovation to make the present intelligible. If law 'brews time' as Grabham suggests, then we can brew different times, we can 'remake questions of justice over and over again' (2016: 15). Over and over again, till we are no longer in the difficulty. This re-understanding of time gives new meaning to life as more than a cog in a relentless flow, but asks us to revisit the substance of life itself and the uses of law to preserve life (Greenhouse 1989: 1637). Therefore, to re-embody the legal person to reflect testamentary life, is also to re-order the legal workings of time. Dispossessed populations are narrated as out of time – disappeared, behind, or vanishing (Rifkin 2017: 5). To narrate them back in time is to disrupt the linearity of Euro-modern time and the singularity of Euro-modern temporality. To rethink the future, is to seek legal epistemologies, ontologies, teleologies, and axiologies that break from the past and the present. To understand humanity and the earth as always 'becoming', is not to 'wait on time', but to take hold of it and change the world around us. This requires rethinking the uses of law in the present and future. An engagement with decolonisation requires a strategy to deal with extinction, the future and its pluriversities or multiple universalities.

Afrofuturism may provide one such strategy. 'Afrofuturism', a term coined by Mark Dery, 'studies the appeals that black artists, musicians, critics, and writers have made to the future, in moments where any future was made difficult for them to imagine' (Eshun 2003: 294; Lewis 2008: 139). It finds most expression from the spatial limits of US and 'draws on mythical African pasts in order to envision new black-centered worlds of the future' (Sites 2021: 1). In a certain sense, Afrofuturism borrows its unsettling of normativity from science fiction and magical realism but also seeks to escape the exotification of people of colour that is found in those genres of writing, so assumes that 'race' will continue to be a facet of social existence (Yaszek 2006: 43). Additionally, Afrofuturism categorically asks for a refusal of the racialised disasters that the continuities of time predict (Yaszek 2006: 58–9). Africanfuturism, which emerges as a complementary alternative to the American roots of Afrofuturism, is described as Africans writing, *'from their own roots, rather than imitating what's already out there'* (Bady 2015: webpage). Africanfuturism and Afrofuturism therefore, provide transcendental and ultimately political spaces for Africa and her Diasporas to confront, question, unveil, and reinvent the nature of humanity and Euro-modernity in ways that centre the reality, interests, pasts, and futures of Black people (Yaszek 2006: 47–50, 58; David 2007: 697). This centring involves repudiating the idea that the past is primitive and stereotypically African, and that future modernity must be a uniformity, shorn of supposed African primordiality (Lewis 2008: 140). Thus, Afrofuturism and Africanfuturism confront the unrelenting linearity of Euro-modern organisation of time, because '[t]ime is not linear in this genre. An imagined future can impact the present as it unearths a buried African past' (Peters 2018: webpage). Furthermore, these genres recognise that the law, as part of our social structure, has been used and designed to subjugate and perpetuate global and national structures that have distorted and trapped Blackness into themselves (Schuyler 1991: 14–15). So, these genres are emancipatory devices to imagine and bring forth a different future from what epistemological genocide and contemporary intellectual engagement with Blackness predict (Eshun 2003: 291–3; Yaszek 2006: 58–9). As what is described as the past is often still ongoing, Afrofuturism from an African-American perspective mostly operates with completely lost memories as a referent … reaching back in time. Africanfuturism, in contrast, reaches out from a spatially determinate focus point to concretise memories made primitive. Consequently, both reify the cross-diaspora emancipatory values of Pan-Africanism; they attempt to put imagination and inventiveness to the service of transcending structural limitations.

Nevertheless, some mainstream attempts at using these genres to narrate a counter-factual history do not go far enough to unsettle the structures of power reproduced in hegemonical readings that hierarchise bodies and interwoven space–time. These counterfactual cinematic story-telling forms have attempted to re-envision the world by interposing alternative versions of the past that explore possible future outcomes of changes in accepted timelines (Sandberg 2021: 137). *Black Panther* is a good example: it imagines what the outcome would be if there was a highly advanced African nation hidden from the world (Coogler 2018). However, such mainstream narratives have been unable to imagine a world that departs from strict conceptualisations of Euro-modern readings of the human and space–time. In other words, they rely on the same economic and political imperatives of capital, conquest, governance, and military structures that Euro-modernity asks us to accept as settled (Nyabola 2018: webpage). And so, unable to be truly subversive or disruptive, their narratives often descend into swapped binaries and replacement theory. In opposition to this view, in their clearest and most radical forms, Africanfuturism and Afrofuturism unite Black peoples into a singular yet varied dialogue about the future of being Black, that refuses all the boundaries of Euro-modernity. In his performances, Sun-Ra collapsed the linearity of time. Octavia Butler imagines humans beyond the current definition of the body (2012). Nnedi Okorafor writes about humans who have power to make food grow out of dead land (2011). Thus, Africanfuturism and Afrofuturism provide useful starting points to re-consider the political and intellectual requirements for achieving this collectively imagined future of humanity and the earth. These genres also recognise the relation of those racialised Black to time – always being ahead of time and outside it. Always being alert to the specific dangers of the world specially designed for those who wear Black skin. Always hoping to stay one step ahead while being narrated as backward. Afrofuturism and Africanfuturism recognise that Black temporalities are burdened under the weight of a long history of anti-Blackness, yet still carry within them a different but present promise of forever. This type of contestation is important, as Edkins reminds us that the cycle of contingency means that time and temporality are not only determined by the coloniality of power ... the cycle of contingency also influences and is influenced by responses and contestations (2006: 101). Concerted and invented contestations are designed to and always elicit a response. So, these contestations often appear in forms and ways of remembrance that continue to unsettle what Euro-modern time continues to tell us is settled (Edkins 2006: 108). The challenge of legal knowledge is to make all times and temporalities legible. For example, by using Black-centred science fiction literature as jurisprudential texts (see Adebisi 2022: 24-37). Thus, as academics, we could commit to theorising through the break, to avoid repeating the ongoing violence in our present times. We could take up tools that imagine bodies and space–times beyond this colonial ever-present. This means to live now, to teach now, to research now ... as if the future we wish for already exists ... 'learning from a future we have not yet reached' (Singh 2017: 147). Therefore, I end this chapter with the words of Latour and with hope of escaping Euro-modernity's inescapable robbery of time: 'Modernization has never occurred. There is no tide, long in rising, that would be flowing again today. There has never been such a tide. We can go on to other things – that is, return to the multiple entities that have always passed in a different way' (Latour 1993: 76). Surely, we can go on to other things. Indeed, we must.

6

The Law School: Colonial Ground Zero – a Colonial Convergence in the Human and Space–Time

> What becomes possible when blackness wonders and wanders in the world, heeding the ethical mandate to challenge our thinking, to release the imagination, and to welcome the end of the world as we know it, that is, decolonization, which is the only proper name for justice.
>
> Denise Ferreira da Silva (2018: 22)

Introduction

This chapter starts with the premise taken up in the previous chapters – that decolonisation is a specific anti-colonial political project of justice (as per da Silva), instituted by colonised peoples, including, peoples in what is designated the Global South, racialised peoples, and indigenous peoples. So, decolonisation is the stubborn and enduring refusal of conditions of life imposed by the logics and praxes of colonial domination, through, *inter alia,* Euro-modern legal concepts and meanings of the human and space–time. Therefore, as legal academics attempting to think of legal knowledge through the prisms of decolonisation and anticolonialism, we need to understand what it means, theoretically and practically, to use the phrases 'decolonise the law curriculum/law school'. Here, I must reiterate the point that decolonisation begins as and remains a *political* project. The phrase 'decolonise the law curriculum' and its (mis)use in that sense are somewhat and increasingly mismatched. This is especially so when we detach our work in Global North higher education from the political history and present of ongoing refusal of the capitalist-colonial-enslavement ever-present. Detached from its radical roots, to claim that we are 'decolonising the law curriculum' becomes akin to suggesting that we are 'measuring the yellow' or 'climbing the fragrance'.

To avoid misuse of radical language we must consider the ways in which learning, teaching, research, practice, and other related activity, in law can adopt a position of refusal of colonial logics and praxes. This includes understanding, as Chapter 2 explored, how much colonial code is embedded and reproduced in legal knowledge. So, I suggest that care be taken with the phrase 'decolonising the curriculum,' as it may not be the right phraseology to describe what the marriage of these spheres of knowledge entails within higher education in the Global North, lest we dilute the political nature of the longstanding project of decolonisation. (It may be useful to avoid its use completely.) So, I prefer instead to ask what the political project of decolonisation means for our curricula, research, and related activity in law schools and the practice of law beyond them. Firstly, we must appreciate the impact of colonialism, as 'a structure and not an event', on our work in law schools. This has been the preoccupation of the preceding chapters of this book, with specific emphasis on this in the previous three. Therein, I have discussed, with emphasis on technologies of power, how colonial conditions of life are produced within legal knowledge, through conceptualisation and articulation of the body and space–time. The purpose of those chapters was to trouble Euro-modern legal knowledge and its teleology as a tool of social order. The law school, through its focus on capitalist interests, private law, and foregrounding privilege, has been a key site of imbrication in how this social order has operated, within Euro-modernity, on regulating and maintaining coercive power.

Essentially, I am arguing for a legal knowledge that produces radically different ways of living. In other words, I am asking if it is possible for legal knowledge to oversee a social order that invites, allows, and equips us to live in relation and not possession. That is, living in harmonious relation with others human, the earth, and diverse temporalities, and not living in enclosed and extractive possession of labour, land, and time. So rather than an invitation to decolonise the law school or the law curriculum, this chapter (and indeed this book) poses a different question: *What does it mean to dream of new anticolonial worlds from within the law school?* Consequently, I invite us to look beyond discourse on decolonisation, whose entry points begin only in the Global North. Because to look away from decolonisation as a specific political project that responds, refuses, and seeks to repudiate, a particular structure of life, is to not engage with decolonisation or to mistake it for something else. This approach fails to account for, and often relies on, the technologies by which the colonial matrix of power reifies itself. Therefore, this chapter responds with some theoretical reflection and practical suggestions to the question, 'What does it mean to dream of new anticolonial worlds from within the law school?' The response, (not answer) grounded in detailed appreciation of the ways in which colonial conditions of life are inaugurated and reproduced, queries if and how legal knowledge within the Global North can disrupt and unsettle this cycle of (re)production. Do we follow scripts of indigenous knowledge and of other peoples subjugated by colonialism? What can we do within law schools to rethink the world anew? Therefore, in considering decolonisation within our work, we should not ask, 'how can I decolonise the curriculum that I teach' or 'how can I decolonise my research?' or 'how do we decolonise the law school?', but 'if I was designing, today, a law school for the future world we need, what would it look like?' If we atomise our action, we ignore the logics that continue to produce a law school and world in eternal need of decolonisation.

Decolonisation and the Law School: can we re-imagine legal knowledge with new visions of the human and space–time?

For effective praxis, a good grasp of decolonisation should be coupled with an understanding of what it means to work on decolonisation from within the discipline. In other words, we must begin our work on decolonisation with acute and honest awareness of the place where we are starting from. To begin with the discipline sometimes involves finding new meanings and ways to re-narrate life and space–time from within it. This requires appreciating the multidimensional nature of the discipline to which we belong. In the case of law, that invites us to understand its dual nature as handmaiden of imperialism on the one hand and the hope for liberation from imperialism on the other. Furthermore, this also involves unpacking how law, nationally and internationally, through its alliances with power and its promise of liberating possibility, often operates as 'politics by other means'.

Rutazibwa describes three overlapping frames through which it is possible to (re)engage with decolonisation from within a discipline – ontology, epistemology, and normativity (2018: 158–80). As praxis, we may use these frames as 'lenses through which to read what we are doing ... differently' (Rutazibwa 2018: 162). Ontology is of primary importance to legal knowledge as it invites us to pay attention to and unpack the ways in which Euro-modern legal epistemologies, in particular, have produced the ontology of the world and of the discipline that reproduces the order and normativity of the world (Mignolo and Walsh 2018: 106; Ndlovu-Gatsheni 2021: 884–5). To rethink the ontology of legal knowledge is to demythologise it – to foreclose intellectual tendency to make our texts hagiographies of some of the discipline's key thinkers (Rutazibwa 2018: 163–7). To rethink ontology is to dismantle the borders of the field as epistemic enclosure. Thus, we can engage with questions that uncover the nature of the discipline and its specific entanglement with the capitalist-colonial-enslavement project. What is Euro-modern law? What is the vision of the world and the human that it produces? Are there different concepts of law beyond it with different visions of the human and space–time that we can bring into our work? To do this, we can revisit our points of entry – where we begin to tell our discipline's story. Many law schools begin introductory teaching of law's methods and reasoning from a position of false innocence, colonial amnesia, Eurocentrism, and methodological whiteness. And so, we do not, and cannot explain, from within the discipline, how our discipline has been complicit in producing the current state of the world. We also ignore entire corpuses of indigenous legal knowledges that have existed for many years. Furthermore, this ontological avoidance is illustrated by a tendency to fragmentation in the division of topics and units. In response to this epistemological fragmentation, Bhambra deploys an imitable defragmentation approach within sociology to explore and trace connected histories (2014: 1–17). This approach would aid deconstructive and reconstructive reading of the coincidences of time-space within legal knowledge. Within the legal curriculum, epistemological fragmentation is often evident between a foundational course and a related optional unit. Thereby, detailed explanation for the supposedly objective conditions described in a foundational unit may be later contained in an optional unit. Examples include the core and optional pairings of the following: property law and housing law, public law and immigration law, criminal/contract law and poverty law, and so on. This fragmentation also operates across disciplines – as described using the lens of 'disciplinary decadence' – each discipline, rooted in colonial practices, considers itself complete, self-created, entirely method-dependent, immortal, and omniscient about all other disciplines (Gordon 2015a: 4–5). To remedy this decadence, Gordon suggests transdisciplinarity – disciplines working through each other – as a preliminary antidote; he further suggests a teleological suspension of disciplinarity – a praxis of thinking beyond disciplines to create/cultivate knowledge (2014: 87). Thus, defragmenting legal knowledge to uncover its true ontology, necessitates us relying on knowledge within and outside the discipline as well as beyond the academy.

Secondly, we are asked to problematise questions of how we source knowledge in understanding, teaching, and researching in law – a question of epistemology (Rutazibwa 2018: 168–70). Epistemology is of supreme significance to decolonisation and the law, because decolonisation is a direct response to colonialism's epistemic violence – the use of knowledge to subjugate racialised/indigenous/colonised and otherwise othered populations, with the assistance of law's alliance with coercive power (Spivak 1988: 280–1; Galván-Álvarez 2010: 12). This includes the use of Euro-modern law to delegitimise indigenous jurisprudences. To raise questions of epistemology is to re-engage with how silences have historically and contemporarily been embedded in legal knowledge in determining what gets to be called law, who gets to speak and whose voices are most often heard as legal authority. These questions direct us to unravel how law's ontology was produced through violent erasure of indigenous/racialised/colonised legal knowledges. In other words, silence has been systemised, paradoxically, by the structure provided for seeking equality through (un)protected characteristics. These characteristics, as explained, in Chapter 3, often operate in ways that re-entrench the inequalities they are meant to dismantle. For subaltern voices, the silence is so profound that their silence is silenced (Spivak 1988: 271–313); the cognitive empire so hegemonical and stifling that their speech cannot be heard through it. In response to this structural silencing of certain voices (and also 'making loud' of others), we need to step away from extractivism in our use of 'knowledge production' (Rutazibwa 2018: 170). This term, as often deployed and conceived, mirrors colonial logics of discovery of things that are not actually missing, whose meanings can then be recast for use by the capitalist–colonial machine. 'Knowledge production' is according to Shilliam, 'a process of accumulation and imperial extension so that (post)colonized peoples could only consume or extend someone else's knowledge (of themselves)' (2015: 25). So, Euro-modern legal knowledge systems continue to conceive of colonised, racialised, and indigenous people, as people existing outside the structures of knowledge, who can only enter through doors of conformity. In contrast, 'knowledge cultivation' evokes visions of collaborative growth, grounding, care, and creativity. True dialogue and joint knowledge creation across space–time cannot happen under circumstances that always subjugate the 'other' as inadequate knowers. Other concepts of law should find space within our law schools, as the sort of silence described here is anathema to the use of knowledge for transforming the condition of the oppressed or even the world. Freire recommends dialogue as an antidote to oppressive silencing, but cautions that, 'dialogue cannot occur ... between those who deny others the right to speak their word and those whose right to speak has been denied them' (2005: 88). In other words, we must note and unpick the role that coercive power plays while we adopt a praxis of knowledge cultivation. Therefore, in decolonising legal epistemologies, adequate attention must be paid to the process through which voices have been made absent as well as the intellectual and institutional structures that reproduce those absences. Lest we preside over an incomplete and distorted intellectual domain, whose purposes are cast into confusion and futility.

Consequently, the last frame I want to consider is a combination of 'normativity and teleology' – or a way to imagine our discipline not reproducing the oppressive structures embedded in the status quo (Rutazibwa 2018: 171–3). This frame is probably the most difficult, but also the most important to think through, because the discipline is not just intimately tied to the status quo, it is charged with (re)producing it. I suggest however, that a critical reflection of what the discipline is and whose voices dominate, will almost certainly lead us to question what or who it is for. This question rises most sharply from the disparate space–time experiences of marked bodies within this status quo. As stated in the introduction, many students come to legal education in a quest for social justice. However, in time our students learn, though often not so explicitly, that the coloniser's justice is not justice for the colonised, racialised, and indigenous. Our students learn that 'the claim of the universal translatability of the English word "justice" … is an extraordinarily presumptive one' (Gordon 2013: 70). They learn that peace for the racist is not peace for the anti-racist. Under racialised enslavement, '[t]he slave master finds placid the view of the masses of enslaved people working for him under the whip of the overseer. The enslaved finds peace in a plantation on fire' (Marshall 2020: webpage). Through the eyes of coercive power, peace cannot be universal, as power has been amassed in various ways through the (re)definitions of bodies and space–time. Thinking through the lenses of normativity/teleology allows us to move away from supposedly decolonial praxes which merely diversify the face of coercive power. Rethinking normativity/teleology asks us to confront the coercive accumulations and uses of power within legal knowledge systems in ways which serve the interests of the powerful at the expense of humanity and the earth on which it currently survives. Therefore, we understand that to decolonise is not to change the players in a game, but to question and upturn the very rules upon, and reasons for which, the game is being played. To decolonise is to change the game itself – change the workings of the world for the flourishing survival of humanity, all life, and the earth. Thus, to address normativity/teleology is also to identify and explicitly name the workings of power in selection of curricula content, staff and student recruitment, career progression, research agendas, professional standards, and related structures and processes.

Therefore, to pay closer attention to the historical origins of coercive power, especially in legal knowledge cultivation and use, we need to (re)centre the body in our understanding of ongoing necropolitics. This is because racial injustice, environmental disaster and the global pandemic all make clear the overwhelming yet unequal vulnerability of the body and its contingent vulnerability in its relation to other bodies. Knowledge creation and cultivation, as well as organisational management within the neoliberal university have found it difficult to invite this vulnerable body into its logic of living in possession. To break free from previous modes of knowledge production, and prioritise relationality, requires creativity and innovation as well as transgression and disobedience. So, theories of posthuman education encourage us to include the relational human body within the logic of higher education. Posthumanism recognises that the category 'human' has never really operated as neutral. This category has excluded many across space–time from within its position, by creating narrow limits (racialised, gendered, classed, heteronormative, and so on) of those who are allowed to 'objectively' speak for the 'human'. Posthumanism thus acknowledges the need to think beyond this category of human and realise the variability and extensive breadth of bodies that depart from the normative understanding of the 'human' (Braidotti 2013: 49; MacCormack 2016: 1). By inviting the relational body into the logic of legal academia, we depart from Cartesian dualism and acknowledge that learning and thinking are also bodily affairs. The class and the research field are communal spaces where variable composition of relational bodies influences activities and outcomes. Understanding this means accepting the histories which different bodies bring into law spaces, including the history of the space within which legal thinking happens. Proactively recognising the varying histories of different bodies in the spaces of Euro-modern law, may help to reduce the stress on marginalised members of the community who are forced by the system to contemplate the physical impossibility of the intellectual demand to leave their bodies outside of the room (Crenshaw 1988: 1). By narrating certain bodies as naturally occupying space and others as not, embodied dislocation becomes the norm in legal knowledge production (not cultivation). This dislocation is exacerbated in online and distance learning settings, refusing knowledge cultivation as a communal process. This is evidenced by rewards in academia which are unrelentingly individualistic and egocentric. In contrast to this, de Sousa Santos and Meneses assert that knowledge is born out of struggle, in other words, knowledge is produced with others in rises and falls, victories, and losses (2019: xvii–xliii). Or as Harney and Moten tell us, 'study is what you do with other people. It's talking and walking around with other people, working, dancing, suffering, some irreducible convergence of all three, held under the name of speculative practice' (2013: 10). In terms of legal knowledge in particular, this invites us to think of ourselves and our subject of study more relationally. For example, with more emphasis on obligations that we owe to each other and the earth, rather than the individual rights which we claim.

The foregoing may also inform how we understand disembodiment within Euro-modern legal practices, as evidenced, for example, in punishments required within the legal system that are destructive, confining, and non-restorative, and which also invoke racially disparate allocations of time (Mills 2014b: 27–42; Birhane 2017: webpage). In contrast, movements to abolish prisons and the police acknowledge embodiment in structural and knowledge processes, meaning that beyond and instead of the punitive power of the state, space is created for emotion – joy, grief, mourning, rage, love ... racial trauma. We can thereby recognise that producing knowledge, and not cultivating it, often results in very real impacts from ongoing trauma on the body. Therefore, when we teach about horrific racially traumatic events, it is appropriate to let our students know that it is acceptable to be upset. It is OK to grieve destruction of life and the planet. It is what we do with emotion in the law school that matters. Disregarding the relationship between law, emotion, and society, ignores a vital avenue for understanding the world (Raj 2021: 128–42). Embodied enquiry in research ensures that we work with an ethics of care that does not reproduce logics that prioritise research agendas over testamentary life.

Paying attention to the body in the cultivation of legal knowledge also means paying attention to the spaces the body occupies, within which this knowledge is created. Primarily, this understanding should inform an inclusion in our legal knowledge of the many changing meanings of land, as well as giving us the tools to trace the connections between the dispossession/commodification of land, large-scale geopolitical impoverishment of the 'other' and escalating environmental devastation. Beyond that, our re-understanding of space should also influence our appreciation of the different ways different bodies move through space. Moore and Anderson both explain how academic spaces, including law schools, operate as 'white space'. In other words, law schools operate in ways that make 'organizational and institutional material and ideological resources flow disproportionately' to people who are racialised white (Moore 2020: 1950). This process is implicit and naturalised, such that to mention it or refuse it, is to be disobedient to the system and run the risk of being stopped within it or cast out of it (Anderson 2015: 10–21). Furthermore, the space of the law school operates on continuities of colonial logics of enclosure, whereby knowledge is appropriated, alienated, and commodified. Its decadent boundaries produce further dislocations from reality and the discipline's possible radical futures. Consequently, both time and temporality are implicated in these dislocations. For example, the normativity of enclosing temporality makes itself apparent in the curriculum through the selection of pasts which we choose to study. By refusing the primacy of the body in knowledge-making, in how and what we remember, we ignore memory practices in our study of law. Additionally, learning, teaching, and research are marked by enclosures of time, such that impact and outcomes are often measured by the speed and timeframes within which these endeavours occur, and not in how much of the work is actually done or how much humanity benefits from it. These ways of marking time and labour are diametrically opposed to actual 'academic time' and the realities of embodied knowledge cultivation. Thus, academia in general is characterised by reliance on unpaid labour and disparately experienced wage theft – a continuity of the racially contingent theft of time (Cahill 2020: 28–9). Euro-modern linearity of time and singularity of temporality require knowledge production to occur within fixed times, with achievements written in to reflect Lockean 'improvement' as constant justification. The failure to meet up with these timeframes impacts staff and students from marginalised backgrounds more. So, the racial and gendered and other differentials in success within legal academia and practice suggest a regime that offers disparate allocations of time (Mills 2014b: 27–42). Yet, knowledge cultivation, as well as the actual experience of it, happens in dynamic fashion, beyond linearity and singularity. The foregoing limits the range of futures that we may imagine from within the law school.

In essence, building new worlds using decolonisation's theories and practices signals a 'radical break' from the logics and praxes of colonialism (Rutazibwa 2018: 173). Therefore, while we may start our journey of decolonisation by acknowledging colonial logics in the content our teaching and research, for this journey to lead us anywhere, we must work out how to move on to breaking from colonial logics. So, in recognising the commitment and effort required in decolonising, especially for marginalised students and staff in Global North institutions, Appleton admonishes us to accurately name our endeavours, especially when they fall short of the radical visions of decolonisation (2019: webpage). We must be honest about the limitations of our work and the tensions we operate within. This allows us to pay closer attention to what is possible, what the journey is and where we are in relation to it. So, I invite colleagues and students, to choose within each academic year to do something, personal, provable, and practical toward decolonisation. **Personal** because there is no template for decolonisation, and our unique contribution is a promise to the future. Also, we can act when the institution refuses to. This action must be positive and does not just mean being nice to people. It must make something happen. It must change something – no matter how small. **Practical** because a commitment to act is a deliberate commitment to the outcome of the action, even when we do not know what the outcome itself will be. Practical goals give us more confidence; they make it easier for us to commit to a follow-on action. **Provable** because in this necropolitical deathscape, we all need wins no matter how small. At the end of each year, we can review and reflect and build on what we have done and decide on what needs to come next. Thus, we refrain from naming things as 'decolonised' when there is still a long but hopeful journey ahead of us. These are individual commitments to decolonisation.

However, in seeking to engage in decolonisation in our academic practices, especially as regards disrupting power hierarchies in knowledge cultivation, we also need to remain cognisant of work that is being done in this regard in the Global South and among indigenous populations, both inside and outside of the academy. We must be careful not to appropriate this work as our own or attempt to subsume radical action into the colonial logics within which we work. We must approach this work with a humility guided by a constant reminder that the vast majority of knowledge lies outside of academia … within and beyond disciplines.

Breaking it all down to build it back up again: some specific areas of praxis

To reiterate, decolonisation is not a tick-box exercise that requires academics to complete a set of predetermined tasks. The shape of decolonisation is determined by the shape of the structure it responds to. The purpose of the book has been to explore issues that legal academics should consider when deciding what action they take in this regard. Yet we must accept that most of what we call decolonisation in the academy merely acknowledges colonialism but does little to dismantle it. Despite some progress, we are still bound by colonial logics within the structures of the institutions and the world in which we work and exist. With this caveat, in this section, I want to make some proposals for specific departmental action around three broad areas of practice in legal knowledge, by way of example. These are the curriculum, research, and citations.

The law curriculum

A curriculum is a construct and interpretation ... a way of 'assigning value, a way of discriminating between what we think is important and valuable and what isn't' (Garuba 2015: webpage). Therefore, it is a selection of knowledge that is both contested and constructed. A curriculum also describes, underwrites, and reproduces relations of intersubjectivity, and epistemic power, as well as possibilities opened and foreclosed. This book places itself as a useful starting point in beginning to reflect and unsettle the assumptions legal academics make about the curriculum and the law schools in which they work. For example, on presumptions about the content of the curriculum, one response to the preponderance of white male scholars in teaching and research material is that this is a product of national focus. In other words, the country in which the teaching and research is being done is a 'white country', therefore we must expect that the intellectual material would reflect this. However, as this book has posited, this defence of Eurocentrism ignores the globalisation, superiorisation and universalising of the logics presented in such scholarship as well as the underlying presumptions upon which it is based. It also elides the temporal, factual, and spatial falsity in identifying any country a 'white' country. Thus, in reflecting on how epistemologies of bodies and space–time have produced a particular curricular construction, we should be able to take content and praxis from beyond the field to disrupt that production. For example, we can, relying on indigenous, feminist, and critical pedagogies, disrupt power hierarchies in the classroom and research field, as well as locate teacher, student, researcher and researched as co-learners in the process.

There are many resources made freely available online to aid in this process. Making these resources available online exemplifies the marriage of content and praxis of decolonisation. An example of such a resource, specific to legal education, is a handbook meant to assist law teachers to develop anti-racist pedagogy. The author, Suhraiya Jivraj, is insistent that this handbook is 'not a blueprint for law teachers to forge ahead to decolonise their curriculum' (Jivraj 2020: 15). Rather, understanding that real structural change is often beyond the capacity of individual academics, the handbook provides staff with material for developing critical pedagogical tools that question law's role in producing and maintaining structural inequality through knowledge transmitted in law's foundation units (Jivraj 2020: 16). Similar resources specific to law can be found in the US and UK Guerrilla Guides, which also contain tools to revitalise individual units as well as guiding principles for teaching generally.[1] Morreira and Luckett have also formulated similar, non-law specific questions (2018: webpage). Therefore, a rich vein of activity to explore in this line, especially in achieving democratisation of knowledge through open access practices, is building sector-wide and global repositories for these types of resources – decolonial principles for curricular design, samples of curricula, and so on. Such a repository will encourage overt co-production of knowledge, which repudiates the myth that knowledge can be owned or should be commodifiable. Knowledge cultivation happens in communities of practice – in person or online.

As argued previously, the obvious first candidate for decolonial redesign in legal education is the often-standard introductory unit. This unit's general purpose, broadly, is to provide fresh law students with an overview of legal systems, methods, and theories, as a backdrop to their subsequent study and potential practice of law. Unpicking the entanglement between law and the colonial matrix of power within this unit could be done in myriad ways, including but not limited to: a fuller examination of legal history, encompassing the histories of racialised enslavement and exploitative colonisation; identifying and engaging with legal epistemologies that have been, through colonial logics, reduced to custom or culture; exploring power dynamics that produce disparities in demographic composition of sectors of the profession (from legal education to the judiciary); discussing the differential outcomes of historical and contemporary social power for access to and experience of the legal system; deconstructing the use of language and voice within the content of the legal curriculum; questioning the division between subjects and areas in law – from criminal law and human rights to public and private law, as well as the division between law and other disciplines.

---

[1] Guerrilla Guides UK https://guerillaguidesukllb.wordpress.com/; Guerrilla Guides [USA] https://guerrillaguides.wordpress.com/

Beyond the introductory unit, decolonial disruption can be applied to other broad areas of teaching. Within public law subjects, unsettling the canon could involve: challenging fragmentation by looking beyond the jurisdiction in which legal learning is being done to properly locate said jurisdiction in space–time, thus disrupting the temporal points of entry into the learning material; critically exploring personal investments of legal thinkers in white supremacy; humbly engaging with community activism across space–time – especially in spaces where marginalised populations are the majority; and continually questioning the absence of critical scholarship on 'race' from the curriculum. Another avenue for exploration here, is to examine how the very concept of crime has been produced and developed by histories of racialised enslavement and colonial occupation and the world of racialised capital that emanates therefrom (Moore 2020: 489–502). The contestable core of the legal curriculum is often predominated by private law – essentially the preservation of investments that trace and place themselves in a lineage of capitalist–colonial interest protection. Thus, this area is of primary concern to decolonial disruption. Therefore, in private law subjects, the following is suggested: outlining in critical detail the origins and uses of property and property-making; closer critique of the concept of the 'reasonable man'; exploring and unsettling how differential status of human/bodies within commercial arrangements and agreements is produced; joining the dots and making conceptual connections between seemingly different areas of law that are actually contingent, for example, crime and poverty, homelessness and property, as well as charity and accumulation (Kish and Leroy 2015: 642). These suggestions, it should be remembered, are not endpoint suggestions, they are not meant to achieve a 'decolonised curriculum'. They are meant as entry points that allow us to begin the conversation with current students while we contemplate more radical and continuing transformation that will be embedded in legal education.

Consequently, a concurrent or consecutive step in addressing the curriculum may involve including entire bodies of legal knowledge that law schools do not usually cover. This includes indigenous jurisprudences, some aspects of which have been examined in this book – especially in relation to their epistemologies of the human and space–time. Another example of such bodies of legal knowledge is the study of colonial law. The inclusion of the study of colonial law is important as it would allow the curriculum to engage in fuller explanations and understandings of the nature of current legal ontology and epistemology. This is because there is a close and cyclic connection between the evolution of law in the colonies and the evolution of law in the colonial centres. Legal academics from the metropole were involved in colonial incursion, colonial justification, colonial administration, colonial management as well as in overseeing flag-independence. Thus, in the latter part of territorial colonisation, these legal academics often operated in a dissonant epistemological space – engaging in legal manoeuvres to grant independence to colonies while racialising national law. In other words, they ensured that at independence, the laws, and legal systems of the newly independent or settler states remained resolutely Euro-modern. Ensuring thereby, that colonial legal logics survived the disruption of 'decolonisation'. These academics often occupied significant positions within law schools in the metropole. Therefore, the absence of legal history in general, and colonial law in particular, from the core legal curriculum is a glaring gap that enables Euro-modern law to present itself as a hagiography. Thus, even where legal knowledge attempts to outline its history (for example in human rights law), there is a tendency, in these accounts, to jump from the metropole space–time origins of law to contemporary laws (local and global) in ways that ignore the occurrence and influence of colonial law completely. This avoids an exploration of the inevitable exchanges and inheritances of legal administration subject to those colonial projects and processes.

More broadly, a fundamental engagement with the forgoing will and must inform change in a range of related curricula matters, including how we may perpetuate stereotypes through our use of language or graphics (especially in lectures), classroom activity, assessments, and so on, and what we consider to be settled knowledge or concepts. These changes could also be reflected in the division between core and optional units and the availability of legal clinical work geared towards social justice. This then necessitates taking on decolonisation as a school project that will involve more interaction across the various cohorts within the law school. These moves invite law schools to rethink their place and role in the communities and spaces in which they exist and work. Thus, looking beyond the law school could involve collaboration between itself and law offices which specialise in areas of interest to decolonisation. This could also involve school trips for documentary/film reviews, museum visits, engaging in charity work, attending courtrooms, and so on. It should be noted, however, that some of the more fundamental innovation suggested requires institutional and sector agreement and investment. Not only this, but there is also the consideration of the requirements of the job market into which our students will be going. This is especially true, where funding is required, or where external bodies need to accredit learning processes and content. There are no easy answers to these questions, but we do not know what doors will open till we try to walk through them. To equip our students to understand and change the world, we may have to build new doors.

Research agendas and practices

Another broad area of practice for decolonisation is research. This is especially so for law schools who present their teaching as research-rich, research-led, research-informed or any variation that suggests robust links between teaching and research. A commitment to decolonisation in its fullness must extend beyond the taught curriculum. Nevertheless, in a lot of the discourse on decolonisation, especially in higher education in what is designated the Global North, there is a focus mostly on administrative practice and teaching, to the detriment of theory and research. Yet, in our research, we need to be able to answer the same questions about the entanglements of power that I have suggested we attempt to answer in the cultivation and transmission of legal knowledge. A commitment to decolonisation in research means questioning the theories and epistemologies upon which this research is conducted. This questioning should then have an impact on the research methods we choose as well as the ethics with which we engage. In other words, our research must 'break from ableist, racist, extractive, and settler colonial logics and instead focus on ones that are situated, relational, and ethical' (Springgay and Truman 2022: 172).

Consequently, decolonisation can be considered an ethics for producing a world that operates differently, with a grounded respect for life and the earth. Decolonisation, therefore, is of extreme importance to research ethics as it also helps us to uncover and interrupt research practices that exploit the commodification the body and space–time:

> Ethics of decolonisation reverse or sidestep temporal and spatial forms of punctuation, replacement, and exclusion ... they embrace the coexistence of the peoples who share this place, and embrace the present moment as the time in which all of us share our lives. These ethics expand the present, enabling it to become a real domain of moral action. (Rose 2004: 130)

Therefore, disrupting colonial research ethics and methods is particularly important when our research involves populations in what is designated the Global South or marginalised populations within the Global North. Research with such populations often have had a long history that has been described as 'dirty', 'violating', and 'abusive'. (Smith 2013: xi; Ndlovu-Gatsheni 2017: webpage; Ba 2022: 4), relying on colonial praxis of extraction and enclosure. Here, decolonisation gives us cognitive space to reimagine the realities of these populations who have perennially been either cast out of knowledge or been primarily the object of research. Thus, we can acknowledge and disrupt the role of academia in removing them from the centre of their own lives. Furthermore, publishing research often operates on principles that do not democratise knowledge, by keeping the knowledge produced behind paywalls and thus out of reach of research participants and affected communities in the Global South (Tamale 2020: 281). One of the technologies of temporal displacement that Fabian describes places the researcher and their subject in differing time zones (2014: 94, 173), ensuring that such researched populations are narrated as backward, and the knowledge produced about them is distorted.

Furthermore, the requirement for 'double-blind' peer reviews ignores histories of knowledge appropriation and power differentials, while also relying on presumptions that all participants hold values that are contrary to this history. When proposed research publications are critical of the status quo, through lenses of decolonisation, feminism, antiracism, and so on, these presumptions often result in peer-review processes that are overly critical and confrontational and that also restrict the cultivation of knowledge, through the unwarranted preservation of disciplinary boundaries. Euro-modern legal knowledge as the status quo, thereby reifies itself by being unquestionable … its walls unassailable. This is exacerbated by an absence of either historical or contemporary legal research into race and colonialism in many jurisdictions. In fact, what research there is can sometimes do more harm than good, by mono-methodologically using a restrictive taxonomic conceptualisation of 'race' and a spatial-temporally limited understanding of 'colonialism' to make 'wider' social commentary (Obasogie 2017: 445–64). Such research is often vaunted as courageous, but by detaching the capitalist-colonial-enslavement project from the production of our realities, such research ignores the fundamental salience of race and colonialism to those realities as well as the complicity of legal knowledge in their emergence. This approach to researching racialisation and colonialism within legal knowledge misuses these concepts, prevents a better understanding of them and thus reifies and invisibilises the hegemonic structures and systems that produce them.

I suggest therefore, that the foregoing arises partly because many of the research agendas in Global North universities rely on colonial logics to construct value. Additionally, universities located in what we call the Global South, due to the hegemony of world ranking systems are often compelled to follow the same logics. These ranking systems operate in ways that prioritise historically accumulated reputation and prestige over problem-solving knowledge-making (Altbach and Hazelkorn 2017: webpage). In the UK for example, the Research Excellence Framework (REF) – the standardised system for assessing the quality of research[2] – relies on benchmarking and processes that often do not recognise the power relations behind the origins of most disciplines, including law. Furthermore, by placing more value on individualism, REF does not reward the joint labour actually required to create legal knowledge. In other words, REF does not account for the technologies of power that (re)produce hierarchies of bodies and space–time. In fact, the imbrication between funding, research and REF is so fundamental

---

[2] https://www.ref.ac.uk/

to the running of law schools in universities, that it could rightly be argued that REF operates as a significant hinderance to decolonisation. This it does by leaning on and thus exacerbating power differentials in standard-setting for excellence. Therefore, while academics now exhibit increasing awareness of the hierarchies produced by racialisation and colonialism, they also face increasing pressure to produce research work by taking advantage of these hierarchies. In other words, rather than this awareness leading to legal knowledge being used to overturn these hierarchies, they instead operate as a 'resource, or a technology, on which institutions and organisations rely to achieve production' (Marchais 2020: webpage). This is because, due to the increasing financialisation of universities and the attendant pressure of REF, law schools are more inclined to seek out scholarship that already has the backing of recognised expertise, rather than cultivate new knowledge (Shilliam 2015: 25). This 'means favouring the already privileged, the mainstream, the well regarded by the highly regarded', without acknowledging the violent histories that produced the mainstream (Brown 2016: 42:02–42:24). Sayer's critique of the REF panel system highlights its subjectivity and limited knowledge base, as research is assessed by highly regarded British academics who may, nevertheless, not have the required expertise or originality to evaluate work beyond their knowledge or jurisdiction (2014: 38–45). Consequently, he declares, 'the panels are a crapshoot and the appraisals a farce' (Sayer 2014: 45). This is quite a vehement critique of the method of assessing research knowledge, which is already mainstream, as we know that such knowledge that directly challenges the mainstream can realistically be expected to suffer more through the processes that produce the mainstream. This power and structural imbalance lead many marginalised and/or early career researchers to attempt to tailor their research to the mainstream and dilute their originality, and so, 'the pressure to publish can act as an effective censorship of diversity' (Nolte 2019: 306).

In essence, the structure that validates and rewards legal research impedes certain avenues for producing good knowledge for the benefit of humanity. This is compounded by what types of knowledge formats – textbooks and handbooks, for example – are not considered worthy of REF. All this happens against the backdrop of the 'publishing industrial complex' – a system of knowledge production reliant on the commodification of knowledge and supported by the extraction of free or coerced labour. This labour includes the pressure to publish ongoing work quickly, exploitative use of unpaid reviewers, knowledge extraction from and with unprotected partners in the Global South, as well as the inaccessibility and high cost of research outputs. Legal academics are left with few options in the face of this research edifice. They can attempt to play the research and decolonisation game at the same time – possibly losing both. They can be true to their decolonial aims and accept the often severe economic and career consequences of delayed progress and job insecurity in an already precarious sector. They could also hope that their law schools would disinvest from REF – a decidedly long shot. Ultimately, it is more important than ever, in our decolonial work to pay closer attention to how institutional research practices hinder that work.

Citationality

A smaller step that can be taken, in the face of these almighty institutional pressures, could be to ensure that our citational practices in law do not reproduce logics of silence and extractivism (Mott and Cockayne 2017: 954–73). Critical practices of citationality invite us to reflect on the dominance of certain bodies in citation and how that predominance preserves patterns of power (Ahmed 2016: 15–16, 148–58; 2013: webpage). Here, I use 'citation' or 'citationality' to describe a broad range of ways of academic acknowledgement of prior and existing intellectual labour. Citations, in this sense, extend beyond who we cite in our research, but also who regularly appears in our teaching, in our reading lists, in which research areas are of concern, in who we partner with in research, in how we acknowledge research labour, who is included and who is missing, who has contributed and who is taking part. Paying closer attention to citationality, in this way, allows us to uncover how it 'connects temporalities, joins past, present, and future discourses, documents, and performance practices … plays a pivotal role in linking particular articulations of subjectivity to wider formations of cultural knowledge and authority' (Goodman et al 2014: 449). This goes beyond merely referencing marginal academics in ways that may only serve to grant them access to colonial structures and rewards (Last Positivist 2021: webpage). The instrumentalisation of citation as criteria for excellence coupled with performative diversity, often foster a culture of extractivist citationality – where the research of marginalised researchers is mined for quotes. In response, Liboiron invites academia into reading relations and practices that are slowed down, reciprocal, and humble, that do not repeat the histories of dispossessive extraction (2021b: webpage).

Thus, critical citationality includes thinking differently about how we track knowledge sources and the effects that flow from selectivity. By constantly citing bodies already granted profligate life and not others, we fragment knowledge across space–time. We continue to place marginalised bodies in close proximity to silence and as far as possible from normativity. We make those bodies, spaces, and times always in transgression of legal knowledge. Citing normative bodies only is an investment in a vision of the world that cannot produce testamentary life. Morrison implicates the violence in the continuity of the colonial in the nation state, within the ambit of citational practices that preserve the content of a disciplinary core. She notes that '[c]anon building is empire building. Canon defense is national defense'

(Morrison 1994: 374). Thus, critical, decolonial, and anti-racist citationality is also an invitation for us to turn away from producing knowledge that protects empires and structures at the expense of life and the planet. In addition to departmental and sector commitments to transgressive and critical citationality, editorial boards can also adopt active mission statements. This could involve engaging in practices to boost citations from a diverse selection of the Global South scholars and marginalised populations in the Global North. For example, *Policy Studies Journal* (PSJ), recognising that word count limits often lead scholars to jettison citations from newer and marginal researchers, changed their policy such that references would no longer be included in word limits for submissions.[3] The sorts of practices recommended in this section turn away from restrictive and individualised extractivist citational practices, to relations that respect and grant credence to the field from which citations are so often exploitatively 'mined', fields such as decolonisation and anti-racist scholarship, but also queer studies and Black feminist studies, as well as unnamed fields that lie beyond the purview of the ivory tower.

To build new worlds: making new bodies, spaces, and temporalities out of the Euro-modern law school

As I come to the end of this chapter, I return to the question of legal knowledge and its purposes: What/who are law schools for? Decolonisation in law invites us to confront reality and reclaim transformational purposes of legal knowledge, to engage in 'teleological suspension of disciplinarity' … going beyond the discipline, to revitalise the study and practice of law by generating new fields of legal knowledge within and without it (Gordon 2014: 87). Otherwise, we leave the discipline to decay, while engaging in performative representationalism. The desire to have a representative cohort of students and staff often suggests that the law school should have a representative purpose. In other words, it is notionally accepted that law schools are meant for a diverse set of staff and students representing a diverse set of ideas and aims. But all that diversity is often still subjugated to the normativity of Euro-modern legal knowledge. In thinking through why certain bodies carrying certain types of knowledge are easier to subsume into law schools, we must pay closer attention to how power reproduces the status quo, and how unsettling it is to disrupt that reproduction from a position of marginalisation. Otherwise, we run the risk of: conflating

---

[3] 'PSJ Commitment to Just and Equitable Citation'. https://onlinelibrary.wiley.com/pb-assets/assets/15410072/PSJ%20References%20and%20Diversity%20082021%20typo%20corrected-1629920526.pdf (Accessed 10 December 2021).

embodied difference with epistemic difference; using diversity as a goal to be reached rather than a measure of the malaise in a structure; and hoping that othered bodies come into powerful institutions to change those structures unwilling and resistant to change. This type of diversity often turns out to be harmful to marginalised people and a hinderance to cultivating new strands of enquiry. Marginalised students and staff must constantly narrate themselves as harmed in the face of refusals to listen, minimising of harm, and even threats of violence. Consequently, rather than such a law school being honest about its unwillingness to change, it expends a lot of financial and human resources to pretend to change. This it does to profess transformation from a position it already realises is untenable. Therefore, insistence on adhering to untenability, especially in law schools, exposes harmful alliances with power while simultaneously exposing staff and students to harm. All this narrows the purposes to which legal knowledge can aspire. And so, while a lack of diversity in a staff and student body in a law school is indicative of structural processes that produce this lack, caution is important in addressing it, especially in the care and value necessary for those willing to engage in the work. Ultimately, committing to positive change is an act of honesty, not just about what our discipline is, but what it has been and what it can be.

So, for one last time, I want to take us back to the deck of the *Zong*, to revisit once more the effect of producing legal knowledge that respects and preserves commodities and capital over testamentary life. Imagine the scene, this deck of a slave ship. Screams in unremembered languages rent the night sky, from bodies whose names the slave traders had not deigned to know or record. Precious cargo held in vulnerable bodies. Which of these is intelligible to Euro-modern law? Their life or their value as property (Krikler 2007: 37)? What story and which principles of the *Zong* survive into law schools? Which bodies, which spaces, which times, which legal knowledge survive the *Zong*? The fact that the slavers were in possession of those bodies, that space, and in that time, meant that their actions served to make the most of those bodies, that space, and that time, hoping that legal knowledge will be on their side. So overboard the bodies must go. For the cargo may mean more in death than in life in the eyes of the law. These actions and presumptions lean heavily on the divergences allowed by Euro-modern legal knowledge, within the category 'human', within the hierarchisation of spaces, and in the devastation of time. Scream. Splash. Silence. Whose body is being made inhuman? Which spaces are really desolation? Whose times are no more? Scream. Splash. Silence. And then the bodies were all gone. And off to the law the 'humans' go to claim insurance for the lost cargo made unhuman. And so, the bodies, spaces, and times of the *Zong* expand into the present and the future. Decolonisation invites us to, within our law schools, disrupt a body of knowledge that allows this and the many other exploitations that continue into the present, leaning heavily on the divergences allowed by

Euro-modern legal knowledge, within the category 'human', within the hierarchisation of spaces, and in the devastation of time. Decolonisation for us, therefore, means to upend the illusion that the present teleology of Euro-modern law and the law school are a departure not a continuation from the past. To survive this present darkness, the world needs a body of legal knowledge that gives us a way 'to see, to hurt, to feel, but also a way to dream, to move, to sit still. To live in relation and not possession' (Davies 2021: 1:15:23–1:15:48). Understanding and disrupting the ways in which Euro-modern legal knowledge forces us into modalities of possession and not relation, means that we recognise that what happened on the *Zong* was not an aberration, but the logical conclusion of a colonial legal knowledge that underwrites living in possession and domination … as was Amritsar, Sharpeville, the murder of Stephen Lawrence, the Grenfell fire, the killing of George Floyd, the bodies in the waters of the Mediterranean, the fires of the Amazon, and the earth's perdition in rising waters. Scream. Splash. Silence. Until the bodies are no more.

Conclusion: Another University Is Necessary to Take Us towards Pluriversal Worlds

> Our strategy should be not only to confront Empire, but to lay siege to it. To deprive it of oxygen. To shame it. To mock it. With our art, our music, our literature, our stubbornness, our joy, our brilliance, our sheer relentlessness—and our ability to tell our own stories.
>
> Arundhati Roy (2003: 112)

> To oppression, plundering and abandonment, we respond with life.
>
> Gabriel García Márquez (1982)

Decolonisation within disciplines must be driven by its much wider utility to the flourishing of life in all its dynamism, thus Márquez and Roy ask us to lay siege and respond to colonial conditions with everything we are. So, I want to conclude this book by briefly reflecting on the context of the overarching structures within which law schools find themselves – the university and the world. I reiterate here my earlier suggestion that it may be impossible to effectively 'decolonise our teaching/research', if this ambition fails to acknowledge how colonial logics have ordered the university sector and the world in which we live. Understanding the limitations of the structures within which we work allows us to be simultaneously intentional and honest about our endeavours. So, we must ask ourselves from within the law school, what outcomes we want our actions in decolonisation to produce, not just in our schools, but in the university and the world beyond. What does it mean to work in a university and live in a world where colonial logics are ceased?

Decolonisation for law schools, as I have argued in the previous chapters, is a means to produce a jurisprudence for a different future, a different university, and a different world, that breaks from the logics of the past. Consequently, it should be noted that this future cannot be attained without addressing and repairing the wider harms introduced by the intellectual misuse of bodies, life, and space–time. In other words, actualising decolonisation as the complete cessation of the operation of colonial logics, envisions other meanings of justice, which would include, for example, reparative justice. 'Reparative justice' in this sense, entails the repair of the colonial conditions of the past 500 years – including the devaluing of life, the commodification of everything and the destruction of the planet. This articulation of reparation departs from how it is often framed, in public and political discourse, as a project that only legislates individual or group financial compensation within state organs, language and structure of hetero-patriarchal racial capitalism (that is, colonialism). This framing ignores decolonial demands for repair and restoration as well as for the cessation of destruction, that are at the heart of reparative justice (Kelley 2002: chapter 4). Reparation that has decolonisation as a guiding logic seeks 'a change in global power relations' and not merely diversification of the face of power or inclusion of members of marginalised populations in the workings of colonialism (Wittman 2016: 200). Thus, group or individual monetary compensation only makes sense as reparative justice if accompanied by a cessation of the orders of power that continue to produce the colonial conditions being complained of, the restitution of unjust accumulations, as well as a process for performing environmental, cultural, social, and psychological repair (Stanford-Xosei 2019: 182; Táíwò 2021: 108–112; Táíwò 2022: chapter 5). The question for law schools in this, is if it is possible or even desirable to achieve this form of anticolonial reconstruction from within the language and conceptualisation of Euro-modern legal knowledge, from within the structures of the university, and from within the current global order. Thus, decolonisation reveals itself as an apocalyptic endeavour. Apocalyptic in this sense does not mean the end of the world, but the end of *a* world that emerges from colonialism, which has narrated itself as *the world*, but is destructive to many people on earth and the earth itself. The truth is that we quite possibly cannot know if we will be able to decolonise our university and the world from within the law school, even if we changed all of our colonially inherited logics. However, we can work it out as we are working it out. Because, despite the potential impossibility of decolonisation, the alternative is the perdition that the world exists in due to global living proceeding on logics that destroy relations of solidarity between all life on the planet … logics which place all life and the planet in almost inescapable danger. Thus, decolonisation may be impossible, but we have no choice but to go ahead with it. I have written this book in the hope that all of us (inside and outside the law school) may develop the tools necessary to imagine and bring into existence a more beautiful world than the one which we have now … 'a world of freedom, real justice, balance, and shared abundance, a world woven in a new design' (Starhawk 2008: 8).

The Euro-modern university as colonial export ... and the universe beyond

The capacity of universities to become spaces where new worlds are imagined is hindered by their past and present alliances with the capitalist-colonial-enslavement project. In the present, institutions of higher education continue to be increasingly drawn into the logic of racialised capital, and so their role as bastions of transformational knowledge is progressively revealed as uncertain. This is exemplified particularly by the commodification of knowledge, the consumerisation of the student class and the acute deterioration of working conditions. Financialisation is made apparent by the various standardisation measures across higher education, for example, in the UK, the Research Excellence Framework (REF) and the National Student Survey (NSS). Financialisation is further exemplified by rising tuition fees, growing casualisation of academic staff, unmanageable workloads, discriminatory pay gaps, incongruous funding models, and unequal access to higher education. Therefore, the alliance of the university with the logics of the capitalist-colonial-enslavement project and the world it has produced, means that its aims, processes, and objectives can never be fully divorced from the maintenance of this project, no matter how it desires and attempts to narrate itself otherwise. Furthermore, the university seems to be suffering an identity crisis – holding itself out as both a public and a consumer good.

These crises place the university at odds with movements for decolonisation within and outside the academy. Decolonisation that unsettles the status quo and the reproduction of epistemic violence and continuing epistemicide seeks to disrupt the colonial logics of commodification of body–space–time. Yet it seems that the neoliberal university can only survive through colonial logics of commodification of body–space–time. This dependency is demonstrated by the university's reliance on logics of financialiszation, improvement, and hierarchisation, in ways that do not significantly break from colonial logics of global commodification of space, nature, life, humanity, and variably valued labour (Rustin 2016: 154–9). The neo-liberalisation of universities is also characterised by: fees and migratory structures that keep out citizens of the Global South, except for the extremely advantaged; empty promises of social mobility to internal disadvantaged populations; and unequally competitive research frameworks that privilege research ratings over flourishing planetary liveability as a core value of the research.

The reverberations of these features of higher education are extended across space–time, as through processes of colonisation, flag independence, and expansion, the nature of the Euro-modern university has been globalised, thus supplanting, and subjugating all other forms of knowledge exchange (Grosfoguel 2012: 83). The ideal of the Euro-modern university was constructed along with the superiorisation of Euro-modernity over all other knowledge systems. Accordingly, universities in the Global North developed under logics of hierarchies of knowledge, their rise enabling educational disenfranchisement and colonial destruction of indigenous places of learning – for example, the 13th century university at Sankoré in Timbuktu (Nawangwe 2021: 215–19). Thus, Euro-modern knowledge was often weaponised to subordinate, with its champions often conflating 'adequately high' entrance standards with the 'standards of academic performance as those achieved by the European' (Colonial Office 1945: 81, 58). And so, the current ontology of the university finds a prominent place for itself, within a long history of colonial knowledge production that has often been harmful to populations objectified by research, from whom knowledge has been extracted without their consent. Within the colonial–enslavement project, knowledge was repeatedly used to justify dispossession, as well as to facilitate administration of this project. Consequently, not only was the Euro-modern university complicit in all this, but it also (in many cases, materially) benefited from these processes (Grosfoguel et al 2016: ix–xi).

Faced with its own ontology and history, when confronted with the prospect of decolonisation, neoliberal universities are more likely to ignore it completely. Statues of prominent architects of colonial dispossession inexplicably remain standing on university grounds, neither is colonial loot acknowledged or returned (Stemplowska 2021: 626). Alternatively, universities may performatively engage in very 'soft-reform' tokenistic inclusivity, rather than radical and beyond-reform actions that centre body–space–time and so disrupt the long history of reproducing colonial logics in Global North universities (de Oliveira et al 2015: 31–7). The former approach uses a deficit model to persistently narrate the already-harmed as inherently inadequate and in need of help, while paying no attention to those who are granted profligate life within the academy. Yet, those already privileged within the academy sometimes perceive the slightest infringement on their favoured position as unbearable afront and their wrath is often visited on marginal students and staff as they bring the weight of their networks and esteem to crush again those who have persistently been made 'wretched of the earth'. Thus, the academy's often limited claims to reparative justice are exposed as window dressings to be blown away by the institution's torrential power. Status quo is king. Long live the status quo. For effective engagement with decolonisation, the university must be honest about its past and present. This includes its complicity with colonialism, racism, patriarchy, capitalism, and the destruction of the planet: 'It will not be enough to change the practices of research, reading, writing, and teaching' (Lipsitz 2019: 47). More fundamental change is needed … in other words, another university.

Colonial logics and praxes carried into the present have produced a distinct, seemingly intractable version of the university. Curricula, research, and other university activity invariably unevenly reflect particular global relations and serve specific and privileged interests. These produce the absences and over-representations that have been complained about by students in their demands to decolonise. However, even our well-meaning responses to these demands often ignore the histories and nature of universities and their role in producing and upholding the structures that we are trying to reform. Thus, we underestimate the scale and the nature of the problem we are dealing with. This is especially the case in relation to understanding how global power dynamics are reproduced in curricula, research activities and university processes. This is exemplified by North–South academic partnerships that rely on the subjugation of racialised, formerly colonised and indigenous peoples and their knowledges. So, these partnerships often engage in 'rehashing simplistic outdated arguments that were discredited by scholars in the global South decades ago' (Tamale 2020: 4). How then do we build this new university?

Mostly, universities have left the job of imagining a new structure of knowledge to members of the university who are already marginalised within the structure of the university. For those who take up the mantle, they encounter harm, pushback, delay, and retribution when working to decolonise or liberalise the university. For them, it is difficult and maybe misguided to continue to conceive of the university as a liberatory space. Considering this harm, the university can be re-understood, not as a safe space for social elevation and public impact, but a place to engage in paid labour while planning the abolition of the university. 'In the face of these conditions one can only sneak into the university and steal what one can' (Harney and Moten 2013: 26). If the academy cannot provide safety, then safety will be constructed without it. For marginalised peoples, to remain in the academy is to cultivate ground and fields ripe for conversations about constructing liberatory epistemologies and politics beyond the strictures of the university's confines. To remain is also to turn the spotlight inwards. To pay more attention to power structures inside and outside the classroom and how we are complicit with them. To be honest with ourselves and others about what we are willing to give up in the present for a future world that we will never see, and which may never come to pass.

Therefore, despite the role played by the academy in creating the inequalities of this present world, its space can be transformed into a revolutionary site for 'a pedagogy of liberation' (hooks 1989: 64). This requires us to reimagine the ideal role of institutions of knowledge cultivation as help and not hindrance to achieving decolonisation beyond them. Knowledge should not have been enclosed, should not have been made property, should not have been commodified. Knowledge is produced by intersubjective relations, in the classroom, and in research ... but also on the battlefield, in the struggle, in the market, on the dance floor, in homes, in places of worship and mourning and grief and joy and laughter ... in spaces and times to which the university cannot reach. So, we must understand and accept that there are some knowledges that the university is not entitled to, not just as a matter of politics, but because the logics of the neoliberal university have demonstrated its inability to handle these knowledges and the bodies that carry them with the necessary respect and care. These are knowledges that require communality to cultivate them for the purposes of liberation. The capitalist–colonial–enslavement project has made knowledge co-terminous with property, thus allowing the university to falsely lay claim to universality … allowing Euro-modernity to lay claim to the universe. To break free from this, for a different world, another knowledge, another university is necessary.

The world in which we teach the world we teach: finding the power for repair

One constant in the history of humanity is continued underclass resistance to the coercive power of the state/sovereign and its interrelated colonial–capitalist structures. From slave uprisings to labour unions, from anticolonial protests and the global movement for Black lives … power from below has always resisted the meanings that coercive power has imposed on being and thinking. Consequently, Cabral reminds us, that it is the masses who are the true source of power to which we must return (Cabral 1974: 61). One of the most striking images from the South African anti-apartheid movement was the defiant single fist raised against the immeasurable might of the apartheid government and their equally powerful international supporters … often accompanied by a loud cry of *"Amandla!"* – power. And the response is *"Awethu"* (to us, to the people). This counterintuitive image of a single fist raised up against the immense edifice of amassed state/colonial power often belies its true significance, which is an ever-present reminder of the continuous existence of a multi-ethnic, multi-peopled, multi-temporal, multi-spatial underclass resistance (made underclass by the coercive power of hetero-patriarchal racial capitalism) crying out in many languages and none, *"Amandla!"* – power. This resistance has always worked like an ant in the trunk of an elephant as is persistently refuses colonial–capitalism's coercive power the ability to completely consolidate its dominance. *Amandla* (power). *Awethu* (to us, to the people).

This call-and-response acknowledges where true liberatory power lies – in the active communality of collective power. It also signals what this power may be able to achieve. In the context of imagining decolonisation, of imagining new worlds, it should be noted that this underclass, by entering into the university, has severely unsettled the university's claim to its universe. The law school's/university's failure to confront histories of racialised capital and planetary destruction as well as their complicity in structurally, epistemologically, ontologically, and axiologically enabling the reproduction of these harms, has hindered the development of alternatives to colonial–capitalism's way of assigning value at the expense of humanity and the planet upon which we survive. 'It seems to be easier for us today to imagine the thoroughgoing deterioration of the earth and of nature than the breakdown of late capitalism' (Jameson 1994: xii). Current practices of value assignation have been imbricated in the covenant between coercive power, commodification, and violence, but the power of underclass solidarity can be harnessed for liberation and building new worlds. hooks argues that our global value system is based on violence and domination (hooks 2004: 115), which essentially describes the use of social and political power to dictate how 'some may live and some must die' (Mbembé 2019: 66). Essentially, freedom is narrated as access to profligate life at the expense of others and the earth. Consequently, violent dominator culture can never achieve community. It is a culture aimed for destruction. Yet, this world order is built, not only on dispossession of things that can be quantified and touched, like land, property, and museum artefacts, but also the dispossession of ideas and ways of being and knowing. One of those ways of knowing is the knowledge that some things cannot and should not be quantified, like land, and life and time. No bookkeeping can really re-order and restore the catastrophe, the epistemicide, this hollowing out of the world and its spirit. Quantifying damage invites marginalised peoples to constantly narrate themselves as harmed without receiving care or reciprocal narration (Tuck 2009: 409–28). In trying to make the intangible quantifiable, we lose the beauty of the intangible and cannot account for its loss.

So, to reverse the future dangers of climate change and continuing planetary injustice, law schools, universities, and global structures of power are encouraged to, in conversation with the multi-people underclass, inside and outside of the university, devise other ways of assigning value, beyond the merely financial, that also account for economic, environmental, epistemic, and societal damage (Gudynas 2013: 177–81). Thus, within our knowledge-making, we need to find ways to ensure that the complexity of testamentary life on the planet is not just intelligible to each other, but also equally valuable as life. This invites a disruption of the colonial logics that have ordered the world. The terms of reference upon which this order is built are not able to carry humanity much further – we have come thus far *despite* them, not because of them. And the earth and waters bear witness to the bodies and lives and land that colonialism has used, swallowed, and destroyed. And so, to revisit Cabral and find room for repairing the world, we must return to the source of communal collective power, to the people, so that we may in community, imagine new ways of being and valuing being. And to colonialism and its dominating logics we defiantly say once more: *"Amandla"* (power). And the response is *"Awethu"* (to us, to the people).

The final scene and why we have never needed permission to dream it

I have written this book as a very long suggestion to say that there is hope in decolonisation to build a different world, university, and law school, even considering, the uphill task as has been described in the preceding pages. Decolonial work and other emancipatory politics in this valley is a 'relaunch of an ongoing promise, a "not yet," a "what is coming," which – always – separates hope from utopia' (Mbembé 2001: 206). However, as the modalities of life in the aftermath of truth and reconciliation programmes in South Africa, New Zealand, and Canada demonstrate … without complete truth, there can be no genuine reconciliation. No true way forward. No liberation. No source to return to. This is not a binary game of saints and sinners, a fairy-tale of darkness and light, but a desperate quest to build a flourishing world together with imperfect humans. The law holds within itself a promise for justice and survival of the earth and those who live on it … if we can unpack its role as part of a societal continuum that is always infused with contemporary populist anxieties, political considerations, personal prejudices, and a product/producer of horrendous histories. We must also recognise the inequalities of power wrought with the law and how they have brought us all here. We live in yesterday's memories of law and order. And even if there were two sides to these histories, often one is a mountain, and the other is a speck of dust. Therefore, we must bravely confront the question of what form of order the coercive power of the state and global structures require and have required for so long. In response we must be clear on what needs to be abolished and what must replace it. This question is radical, because it goes to the root of the world we have built and the values it has been built on, and how legal knowledge can be used to build a better future. This opens the door to possibility of a world where destruction is neither normalised nor inevitable, and so Hartman asks, 'Is abolition a synonym for love?' (2020: webpage). Because to want to build a world of flourishing futures is to love the one we have now, and those that live on it, and everything in it, so that we are willing to risk our comfort today, that the world may survive tomorrow.

I bring this book to an end with a final lesson, this time from August Wilson's stage play, *Ma Rainey's Black Bottom* (Wilson and Stewart 1985), immortalised in film in 2020 (Wolfe). On the surface, this is the story of Ma Rainey's band – Cutler, Toledo, Slow Drag, and Levee – waiting to record a new album in a South Side Chicago recording studio owned by a white man – Sturdyvant. The band members banter, tell stories, joke, reflect, and argue as they wait for Ma Rainey to turn up for the recording. These conversations uncover tensions between Levee, the young ambitious trumpeter, and Cutler and Toledo, who are older and more accepting of the world in which they live and its inequalities. Set in 1927, it is inevitable that the discussions among the band members turn to the realities of living with particular temporal markers of racial injustice – including the fear of lynching, as well as Levee's horrific backstory … witnessing his mother's rape, his father killed for avenging her, Levee brutally injured – his family violently dispossessed and traumatised by a gang of white men covetous of their land. This alludes very strongly to the true story of the 1921 Tulsa Race Massacre in which a thriving community of Black people was completely destroyed – 1500 buildings, '10,000 people homeless, 183 hospitalised with gunshot wounds or burns, 222 families with the father "missing or dead" and 87 now "with no mother"' (Foner 2021: 11). Such is Levee's backstory and fuel for his ambition for the independence and economic security that would come from having his own band.

However, in the penultimate scenes, Ma Rainey fires him for daring to try to encroach on her territory, both professionally and personally. Apart from challenging Ma's authority, Levee has taken a liking to Ma Rainey's lover – Dussie Mae. Levee tries to sell his compositions to Sturdyvant, who buys them for a pittance. So, in frustration, Levee stabs Toledo to death because Toledo steps on Levee's new shoes. The last scene of the movie (but not the play) shows about a dozen white men recording Levee's song for Sturdyvant in a perfect example of appropriation (Wolfe 2020: 1:22:25–1:26:22). In the last scene of the play, Levee's trumpet can be heard playing a subdued note 'struggling for the highest of possibilities and blowing pain and warning' (Wilson and Stewart 1985: 111). But this final scene (play or movie) makes no sense without the first scene, and so, we go back. We go back to Levee witnessing his mother's rape. But this is not the first scene either. And so, we go back. … The first scene – colonialism's first scene – is the real crime scene. Stolen land, stolen labour, stolen riches … stolen life, devalued life, misused life, on a plundered earth made wretched. Those final scenes make no sense without this first scene.

However, for us, the good news, the hopeful news, is that this present world is not humanity's final scene, and it is up to us to write our next scene. And so, we must write colonialism's final scene so that the earth and our time on its stage may not be brought to an untimely end. However, in writing its final scene, we also cannot ignore colonialism's first scenes. We must write the final scene with the first scene in mind, because it will make no sense without the first scene. Colonialism cannot be written out, if we do not acknowledge the truth of how it was written in, kept in play and made the major actor in the theatre of abused life. The final scene must be written, narrated, and performed in a way that opens the door to possibility of a world where destruction is neither normalised nor inevitable. We must figure out how to get there from the reality of where we are now, and where we have come from. Not from an imagined past and a non-existent present.

This departure will take a magnitude of effort and all our collective subversive power. To build the world's future in a radical rupture from the past, new visions, new dreams, new imaginations are needed. As Sankara tells us:

> You cannot carry out fundamental change without a certain amount of madness. In this case, it comes from nonconformity, the courage to turn your back on the old formulas, the courage to invent the future … it took the madmen of yesterday for us to be able to act with extreme clarity today. (Sankara 1988: 144)

Sankara exemplifies here an anticolonial spirit of 'disobedient relationality that always questions, and thus is not beholden to, normative academic logics' (McKittrick 2021: 45). In this, Sankara also reminds us that methods and praxis which challenge colonial thought have often been narrated as 'madness'. For example, enslaved Africans who escaped and sought freedom were clinically diagnosed with 'drapetomania', because their minds and bodies stubbornly refused the conditions of colonialism imposed as the natural order of life (Willoughby 2018: 579). This is why theory and thought from the other side of the abyssal line matter – to articulate what is hidden, to bring to light experiences for which there is no language within the Euro-modern academy. This book is a defiant love letter to the world to come, for law students, teachers, researchers, practitioners – anyone willing to imagine a new world woven in a new design. That, we the people – in this place, in this time – may in community have the courage, despite this current darkness, to act with extreme clarity today, and invent a future that does not repeat the logics from colonialism's first scene.

Amandla (power). And the response is *Awethu* (to us, to the people). We *are* the possibility.

References

Abazi, Enika and Albert Doja. (2018). 'Time and Narrative: Temporality, Memory, and Instant History of Balkan Wars'. *Time & Society* 27(2): 239–72.

Abraham, Arthur. (1974). 'Bai Bureh, the British, and the Hut Tax War'. *The International Journal of African Historical Studies* 7(1): 99–106.

Achiume, E. Tendayi. (2021). 'Digital Racial Borders'. *American Journal of International Law* 115: 333–8.

Adebisi, Foluke Ifejola. (2016). 'Decolonising Education in Africa: Implementing the Right to Education by Re-Appropriating Culture and Indigeneity Special Issue: The Right to Education'. *Northern Ireland Legal Quarterly* 67(4): 433–52.

Adebisi, Foluke. (2021). 'Should We Rethink the Purposes of the Law School? A case for decolonial thought in legal pedagogy'. *The Journal of the Society for Advanced Legal Studies* 2(3): 428–49.

Adebisi, Foluke. (2022) 'Black/African Science Fiction and the Quest for Racial Justice through Legal Knowledge: How Can We Unsettle Euromodern Time and Temporality in Our Teaching?'. *Law, Technology and Humans* 4(2): 24–37.

Ahmed, Sara. (2006). *Queer Phenomenology*. Duke University Press.

Ahmed, Sara. (2012). *On Being Included: Racism and Diversity in Institutional Life*. Duke University Press.

Ahmed, Sara. (2013). 'Making Feminist Points'. *Feminist Killjoys*. 11 September. https://feministkilljoys.com/2013/09/11/making-feminist-points/ (Accessed 17 February 2022).

Ahmed, Sara. (2016). *Living a Feminist Life*. Duke University Press.

Ahmed, Sara. (2019). *What's the Use?* Duke University Press.

Akbar, Amna A. (2015). 'Law's Exposure: The Movement and the Legal Academy'. *Journal of Legal Education* 65(2): 352–73.

Akurang-Parry and Kwabena Opare. (2000). 'Colonial Forced Labor Policies for Road-Building in Southern Ghana and International Anti-Forced Labor Pressures, 1900–1940'. *African Economic History* 28: 1–25.

Al-Bulushi, Yousuf (2020) 'Thinking Racial Capitalism and Black Radicalism from Africa: An Intellectual Geography of Cedric Robinson's World-System'. *Geoforum* 132: 252–62.

REFERENCES

Alcoff, Linda Martín. (2007). 'Mignolo's Epistemology of Coloniality'. *CR: The New Centennial Review* 7(3): 79–101.

Allen, Richard B. (2017). 'Asian Indentured Labor in the 19th and Early 20th Century Colonial Plantation World'. *Oxford Research Encyclopedia of Asian History*. 29 March. https://doi.org/10.1093/acrefore/9780190277727.013.33 (Accessed 17 February 2022).

Allen, Richard. (2018). 'Slavery in a Remote but Global Place: The British East India Company and Bencoolen, 1685–1825'. *Historia Social y de la Educación* 7(2): 151–76.

Allen, Robert C. (2020). 'Poverty and the Labor Market: Today and Yesterday'. *Annual Review of Economics* 12(1): 107–34.

Altbach, Philip G. and Ellen Hazelkorn. (2017). 'Why Most Universities Should Quit the Rankings Game'. *University World News*. 8 January. https://www.universityworldnews.com/post.php?story=20170105122700949 (Accessed 17 February 2022).

American Medical Association Press Release. (2020). 16 November. https://www.ama-assn.org/press-center/press-releases/new-ama-policy-recognizes-racism-public-health-threat (Accessed 17 February 2022).

Anderson, Benedict. (2006). *Imagined Communities: Reflections on the Origin and Spread of Nationalism*. Verso Books.

Anderson, Elijah. (2015). 'The White Space'. *Sociology of Race and Ethnicity* 1(1): 10–21.

Andrews, Kehinde. (2018). *Back to Black: Retelling the Politics of Black Radicalism for the 21st Century*. Zed Books.

Anghie, Antony. (2006). 'The Evolution of International Law: Colonial and Postcolonial Realities'. *Third World Quarterly* 27(5): 739–53.

Anghie, Antony. (2007). *Imperialism, Sovereignty and the Making of International Law*. Vol. 37. Cambridge University Press.

Anghie, Antony. (2014). 'Towards a Postcolonial International Law'. In Singh, Prabhakar and Benoît Mayer (eds). *Critical International Law: Postrealism, Postcolonialism, and Transnationalism*. 121–42. Oxford University Press.

Anzaldúa, Gloria. (1987). *Borderlands/La Frontera*. Aunt Lute Books.

Aoki, Keith. (1998). 'Neocolonialism, Anticommons Property, and Biopiracy in the (Not-So-Brave) New World Order of International Intellectual Property Protection'. *Indiana Journal of Global Legal Studies* 6(1): 11–58.

Apple, Michael W. (1993). 'The Politics of Official Knowledge: Does a National Curriculum Make Sense?' *Discourse* 14(1): 1–16.

Appleton, Nayantara Sheoran. (2019). 'Do Not "Decolonize"… if You Are Not Decolonizing: Progressive Language and Planning Beyond a Hollow Academic Rebranding'. *Critical Ethnic Studies* 4 (no pagination). http://www.criticalethnicstudiesjournal.org/blog/2019/1/21/do-not-decolonize-if-you-are-not-decolonizing-alternate-language-to-navigate-desires-for-progressive-academia-6y5sg [Accessed 17 February 2022].

Arendt, Hannah. (1973). *The Origins of Totalitarianism*. Harcourt Brace Jovanovich.
Aristotle. (350 BCE). 'Politics, Book 1'. http://www.perseus.tufts.edu/hopper/text?doc=Perseus%3Atext%3A1999.01.0058%3Abook%3D1 (Accessed 17 February 2022).
Aronin, Scott. (2016). 'One in Four Students Suffer from Mental Health Problems'. YouGov Report. 9 August. https://yougov.co.uk/news/2016/08/09/quarter-britains-students-are-afflicted-mental-hea/ (Accessed 17 February 2022).
Ba, Oumar. (2022). '"The Europeans and Americans Don't Know Africa": Of Translation, Interpretation, and Extraction'. *Millennium*. 28 January. https://doi.org/10.1177/03058298211063927 [Accessed 17 February 2022].
Baars, Grietje. (2019). *The Corporation, Law and Capitalism: A Radical Perspective on the Role of Law in the Global Political Economy*. Brill.
Bady, A. (2015). 'Things to Come'. *The New Inquiry*. 6 March. https://thenewinquiry.com/things-to-come/ [Accessed 17 February 2022].
Baird, Ian G. (2020). 'Thinking about Indigeneity with Respect to Time and Space: Reflections from Southeast Asia'. *Espace Populations Sociétés* (Space Populations Societies). 2020/1–2. https://doi.org/10.4000/eps.9628 (Accessed 17 February 2022).
Baldwin, James. (1979). 'James Baldwin Speech at Berkeley'. 5 January. https://www.youtube.com/watch?v=qcjSoakCuIk&t=583s (Accessed 17 February 2022).
Basu, Anustup. (2020). *Hindutva as Political Monotheism*. Duke University Press.
Bell, Duncan. (2020). *Dreamworlds of Race: Empire and the Utopian Destiny of Anglo-America*. Princeton University Press.
Benjamin, Ruha, (2019). 'Introduction'. In Benjamin, Ruha (ed). *Captivating Technology: Race, Carceral Technoscience, And Liberatory Imagination in Everyday Life*. Duke University Press.
Benjamin, Walter. (2009). *On the Concept of History*. New York: CreateSpace Independent Publishing Platform.
Best, L.A. (1968). 'Outlines of a Model of Pure Plantation Economy'. *Social and Economic Studies* 17(3): 283–326.
Bevernage, Berber. (2016). 'Tales of Pastness and Contemporaneity: On the Politics of Time in History and Anthropology'. *Rethinking History* 20(3): 352–74.
Bhabha, Homi K. (2012). *The Location of Culture*. Routledge.
Bhambra, Gurminder K. (2014). *Connected Sociologies*. Bloomsbury Publishing.
Bhambra, Gurminder K. (2017). 'Why are the White Working Classes Still Being Held Responsible for Brexit and Trump?' *LSE Blog*. https://blogs.lse.ac.uk/brexit/2017/11/10/why-are-the-white-working-classes-still-being-held-responsible-for-brexit-and-trump/ (Accessed 17 February 2022).
Bhambra, Gurminder K. (2020). 'Colonial Global Economy: Towards a Theoretical Reorientation of Political Economy'. *Review of International Political Economy* 28(2): 307–22.

Bhandar, Brenna. (2014). 'Property, Law, and Race: Modes of Abstraction'. *UC Irvine Law Review* 4(1): 203–18.

Bhandar, Brenna. (2018). *Colonial Lives of Property*. Duke University Press.

Bhattacharyya, Gargi, Adam Elliott-Cooper, Sita Balani, Kerem Nişancıoğlu, Kojo Koram, Dalia Gebrial, Nadine El-Enany, and Luke de Noronha. (2021). *Empire's Endgame: Racism and the British State*. London: Pluto Press.

Biko, Steve. (1981). 'Black Consciousness and the Quest for a True Humanity'. *Ufahamu* 11(1): 133–42.

Birhane, Abeba. (2017). 'Descartes Was Wrong: "A Person Is a Person through Other Persons"'. *Aeon Ideas*. 7 April. https://aeon.co/ideas/descartes-was-wrong-a-person-is-a-person-through-other-persons (Accessed 17 February 2022).

Birhane, Abeba. (2021). 'Algorithmic Injustice: A Relational Ethics Approach'. *Patterns* 2(2): 1–9.

Birth, Kevin. (2012). *Objects of Time: How Things Shape Temporality*. Springer.

Black, Christine. (2009). 'A Timely Jurisprudence for a Changing World'. *International Journal for the Semiotics of Law – Revue Internationale de Sémiotique Juridique* 22(2): 197–208.

Bluedorn, Allen C. (2002). *The Human Organization of Time: Temporal Realities and Experience*. Stanford University Press.

Boatcă, Manuela. (2013). 'The Eastern Margins of Empire: Coloniality in 19th century Romania'. In Mignolo, Walter D., and Arturo Escobar (eds). *Globalization and the Decolonial Option*. 222–38. Routledge.

Bonair-Agard, Roger. (nd). 'Letters to the Revolution'. http://letterstotherevolution.com/roger-bonair-agard (Accessed 17 February 2022).

Bourdieu, Pierre. (2000). *Pascalian Meditations*. Stanford University Press.

Braidotti, Rosi. (2013). *The Posthuman*. John Wiley & Sons.

Brandt, Allan M. (1978). 'Racism and Research: The Case of the Tuskegee Syphilis Study'. *The Hastings Center Report* 8(6): 21–9.

Bravo, Karen E. (2013). 'Black Female "Things" in International Law: A Meditation on Saartjie Baartman and Truganini'. In Levitt Jeremy (ed). *Black Women and International Law: New Theory, Old Praxis*. 289–326. Cambridge University Press.

Brogden, Mike. (1987). 'The Emergence of the Police: The Colonial Dimension'. *The British Journal of Criminology* 27(1): 4–14.

Brown, Wendy. (2016). The University and its Worlds Panel, 7 June. https://www.youtube.com/watch?v=s07xFdD-ivQ&t=2647s (Accessed 17 February 2022).

Burridge, Roger and Julian Webb. (2008). 'The Values of Common Law Legal Education Reprised'. *The Law Teacher* 42(3): 263–9.

Burton, Antoinette. (2020). 'Accounting for Colonial Legal Personhood: New Intersectional Histories from the British Empire'. *Law and History Review* 38(1): 143–50.

Butler, Octavia E. (2012). *Bloodchild: And Other Stories*. Open Road Media.

Byrd, Rudolph P., Johnnetta Betsch Cole, and Beverly Guy-Sheftall. (2009). *I Am Your Sister: Collected and Unpublished Writings of Audre Lorde*. Oxford University Press.

Cabral, Amílcar, and Africa Information Service Staff. (1974). *Return to the Source*. NYU Press.

Cabral, Amílcar. (2016). *Resistance and Decolonization*. Rowman & Littlefield.

Cabral, Amílcar Lopes and Richard Handyside. (1969). *Revolution in Guinea: An African People's Struggle: Selected Texts by Amilcar Cabral*. Stagel.

Cahill, Damien. (2020). 'Wage Theft Is Core University Business'. *Advocate: Journal of the National Tertiary Education Union* 27(3): 28–9.

Caldwell, John, Bruce Missingham, and Jeff Marck. (2001). 'The Population of Oceania in the Second Millennium'. Paper presented at the IUSSP Conference on the History of World Population in the Second Millennium, Florence, 27–30 June.

Carlos, Yasmin Paula. (2011). 'Race-Ing to Justice: Gendered Justice Paves the Way for Adopting the Reasonable Black Man Standard into Fourth Amendment Jurisprudence'. *Widener Journal of Law, Economics, and Race* 2(1): 1–37.

Castillejo-Cuéllar, Alejandro. (2014). 'Historical Injuries, Temporality and the Law: Articulations of a Violent Past in Two Transitional Scenarios'. *Law and Critique* 25(1): 47–66.

Certeau, Michel. (1984). *The Practice of Everyday Life: Vol. 1*. Berkeley: University of California Press.

Césaire, Aimé. (2001). *Discourse on Colonialism*. NYU Press.

Chatterjee, Partha. (2003). 'The Nation in Heterogeneous Time'. In Özkırımlı, Umut (ed). *Nationalism and Its Futures*. 33–58. London: Palgrave Macmillan.

Chigudu, Simukai. (2021). '"Colonialism Had Never Really Ended": My Life in the Shadow of Cecil Rhodes'. *The Guardian*. 14 January. https://www.theguardian.com/news/2021/jan/14/rhodes-must-fall-oxford-colonialism-zimbabwe-simukai-chigudu [Accessed 17 February 2022].

Chowdhury, Tanzil. (2020). *Time, Temporality and Legal Judgment*. Routledge.

Cilliers, Johan. (2018). 'The Kairos of Karos: Revisiting Notions of Temporality in Africa'. *Stellenbosch Theological Journal* 4(1): 113–32.

Clarence-Smith, William G. (1990). 'The Hidden Costs of Labour on the Cocoa Plantations of São Tomé and Príncipe, 1875–1914'. *Portuguese Studies* 6: 152–72.

Cleve, George Van. (2006). 'Somerset's Case and Its Antecedents in Imperial Perspective'. *Law and History Review* 24(3): 601–46.

REFERENCES

Coates, Ta-Nehisi. (2015). *Between the World and Me*. Text Publishing.

Cobain, Ian. (2016). *The History Thieves: Secrets, Lies and the Shaping of a Modern Nation*. Portobello Books.

Cohen, Felix S. (1935). 'Transcendental Nonsense and the Functional Approach'. *Columbia Law Review* 35(6): 809–49.

Colonial Office. (1945). *Report of the Commission on Higher Education in the Colonies* (Cmd 6647).

Combahee River Collective. (1983). 'The Combahee River Collective Statement'. In Smith, Barbara (ed). *Home Girls: A Black Feminist Anthology*. 264–74. Rutgers University Press.

Conaghan, Joanne. (1996). 'Tort Law and the Feminist Critique of Reason'. Anne Bottomley (ed). *Feminist Perspectives on the Foundational Subjects of Law*. 47–68. Routledge Cavendish.

Coogler, Ryan, director. (2018) *Black Panther*. Marvel Studios. 2 hours 14 minutes.

Coronil, Fernando. (2015). 'Latin American Postcolonial Studies and Global Decolonization'. *Postcolonial Studies: An Anthology*: 175–92.

Crenshaw, Kimberlé Williams. (1987). 'Race, Reform, and Retrenchment: Transformation and Legitimation in Antidiscrimination Law'. *Harvard Law Review* 101(7): 1331–87.

Crenshaw, Kimberlé Williams. (1988). 'Toward a Race-Conscious Pedagogy in Legal Education Foreword'. *National Black Law Journal* 11(1): 1–14.

Crenshaw, Kimberlé. (1990). 'Mapping the Margins: Intersectionality, Identity Politics, and Violence against Women of Color'. *Stanford Law Review* 43(6): 1241–300.

Crowe, Jonathan and Constance Youngwon Lee. (2015). 'Law as Memory'. *Law and Critique* 26(3): 251–66.

Cuestas-Caza, Javier. (2018). 'Sumak Kawsay is not Buen Vivir'. *Alternautas* 5(1): 49–63.

Cunningham, Vinson. (2020). 'The Argument of "Afropessimism"' *The New Yorker*. 20 July. https://www.newyorker.com/magazine/2020/07/20/the-argument-of-afropessimism (Accessed 17 February 2022).

Cusicanqui, Silvia Rivera. (2012). 'Ch'ixinakax utxiwa: A Reflection on the Practices and Discourses of Decolonization'. *South Atlantic Quarterly* 111(1): 95–109.

d'Aspremont, Jean. (2018). 'Statehood and Recognition in International Law: A Post-Colonial Invention'. In Capaldo, Giuliana Ziccardi (general editor). *The Global Community Yearbook of International Law and Jurisprudence 2018*. 139–52. Oxford University Press.

Da Silva, Denise Ferreira. (2015). 'Before Man: Sylvia Wynter's Rewriting of the Modern Episteme'. In McKittrick, Katherine (ed). *Sylvia Wynter: On Being Human as Praxis*. 90–105. Duke University Press.

Dalrymple, William. (2015). 'The East India Company: The Original Corporate Raiders'. *The Guardian*. 4 March. https://www.theguardian.com/world/2015/mar/04/east-india-company-original-corporate-raiders (Accessed 17 February 2022).

Dalrymple, William. (2019). *The Anarchy: The East India Company, Corporate Violence, and the Pillage of an Empire*. Bloomsbury Publishing.

Darian-Smith, Eve. (2013). 'Postcolonial Theories of Law'. In Banakar, Reza and Max Travers (eds). *Law and Social Theory*. 247–64. Hart Publishing.

Darian-Smith, Eve. (2015). Postcolonial Law. In James D. Wright (editor-in-chief). *International Encyclopedia of the Social & Behavioral Sciences*. 2nd edition. Vol 18. 647–51. Elsevier.

Daughton, James Patrick. (2021). *In the Forest of No Joy: The Congo-Océan Railroad and the Tragedy of French Colonialism*. W.W. Norton & Company.

David, Marlo. (2007). 'Afrofuturism and Post-Soul Possibility in Black Popular Music'. *African American Review* 41(4): 695–707.

Davies, Andrea A. [(2021)]. 'Day 4: Closing Conversation. A Map to the Door of No Return at 20: A Gathering'. https://www.youtube.com/watch?v=nVaEzhHSow4&t=4550s (Accessed 17 February 2022).

Davies, Margaret. (1994). *Asking the Law Question*. Law Book Co.

Davies, Thom, Arshad Isakjee, and Surindar Dhesi. (2017). 'Violent Inaction: The Necropolitical Experience of Refugees in Europe'. *Antipode* 49(5): 1263–84.

Davis, Mike. (2002). *Late Victorian Holocausts: El Niño Famines and the Making of the Third World*. Verso Books.

de Oliveira Andreotti, Vanessa, Sharon Stein, Cash Ahenakew, and Dallas Hunt. (2015). 'Mapping Interpretations of Decolonization in the Context of Higher Education'. *Decolonization: Indigeneity, Education & Society* 4(1) (2015): 31–7.

de Sousa Santos, Boaventura. (2016). *Epistemologies of the South: Justice against Epistemicide*. Routledge.

de Sousa Santos, Boaventura. (2018). *The End of the Cognitive Empire: The Coming of Age of Epistemologies of the South*. Duke University Press.

Degnen, Cathrine. (2018). *Cross-Cultural Perspectives on Personhood and the Life Course*. Palgrave Macmillan.

Delgado, Richard, and Jean Stefancic. (2017). *Critical Race Theory: An Introduction*. (Third edition). New York University Press.

Derrida, Jacques and Francis Charles Timothy Moore. (1974). 'White Mythology: Metaphor in the Text of Philosophy'. *New Literary History* 6(1): 5–74.

Devenney, Mark. (2011). 'Property, Propriety and Democracy'. *Studies in Social Justice* 5(2): 149–65.

Diop, Cheikh Anta and Mercer Cook. (2012). *The African Origin of Civilization: Myth or Reality*. Chicago Review Press.

Dolhare, María Itatí and Sol Rojas-Lizana. (2018). 'The Indigenous Concept of Vivir Bien in the Bolivian Legal Field: A Decolonial Proposal'. *The Australian Journal of Indigenous Education* 47(1): 19–29.

Douglass, Frederick. (2018). *Lessons of the Hour*. Yale University Press.

Douzinas, Costas. (2000). *The End of Human Rights: Critical Thought at the Turn of the Century*. Bloomsbury Publishing.

Drescher, Seymour. (2009). *Abolition: A History of Slavery and Antislavery*. Cambridge University Press.

DuBois, William Edward Burghardt. (1897). 'Strivings of the Negro People'. *The Atlantic*. 1 August. https://www.theatlantic.com/magazine/archive/1897/08/strivings-of-the-negro-people/305446/ (Accessed 17 February 2022).

Dussel, Enrique D, Javier Krauel, and Virginia C Tuma. (2000). 'Europe, Modernity, and Eurocentrism'. *Nepantla: Views from South* 1(3): 465–78.

Dyer, Richard. (1988). 'White'. *Screen* 29(4): 44–65.

Edelstein, Dan. Stefanos Geroulanos, and Natasha Wheatley. (2020). 'Chronocenosis: An Introduction to Power and Time'. In Edelstein, Dan, Stefanos Geroulanos and Natasha Wheatley (eds). *Power and Time: Temporalities in Conflict and the Making of History*. 1–50. University of Chicago Press.

Edkins, Jenny. (2006). 'Remembering Relationality'. In Bell, D. (ed). *Memory, Trauma and World Politics: Reflections on the Relationship Between Past and Present*. 99–115. Palgrave Macmillan.

Eduardo Gudynas, (2013). *Transitions to Post-Extractivism: Directions, Options, Areas of Action*. In Lang, Miriam and Dunia Mokrani (eds). *Beyond Development: Alternative Visions from Latin America*. 165–88. Amsterdam: Rosa Luxemburg Foundation and Transnational Institute.

Eichhorn, Stephen J. (2020). 'How the West Was Won: A Deconstruction of Politicised Colonial Engineering'. *The Political Quarterly* 91(1): 204–9.

El-Enany, Nadine. (2020). *(B)ordering Britain: Law, Race and Empire*. Manchester University Press.

Elkins, Caroline. (2005). *Britain's Gulag: The Brutal End of Empire in Kenya*. Random House.

Eltis, David. (2001). 'The Volume and Structure of the Transatlantic Slave Trade: A Reassessment'. *The William and Mary Quarterly* 58(1): 17–46.

Escobar, Arturo. (2008). *Territories of Difference: Place, Movements, Life, Redes*. Duke University Press.

Escobar, Arturo. (2011). 'Sustainability: Design for the Pluriverse'. *Development* 54(2): 137–40.

Escobar, Arturo. (2013). 'Worlds and Knowledges Otherwise'. In Mignolo, Walter D. and Arturo Escobar. *Globalization and the Decolonial Option*. 33–64. Routledge.

Eshun, Kodwo. (2003). 'Further Considerations of Afrofuturism'. *CR: The New Centennial Review* 3(2): 287–302.

Eslava, Luis and Sundhya Pahuja. (2020). 'The State and International Law: A Reading from the Global South'. *Humanity: An International Journal of Human Rights, Humanitarianism, and Development* 11(1): 118–38.

Eze, Emmanuel Chukwudi (ed). (1997). *Race and the Enlightenment: A Reader*. Wiley-Blackwell.

Fabian, Johannes. (2014). *Time and the Other: How Anthropology Makes Its Object*. Columbia University Press.

Fanon, Frantz. (2007). *The Wretched of the Earth*. Grove/Atlantic, Inc.

Fanon, Frantz. (2008). *Black Skin, White Masks*. Grove Press.

Faubert, Michelle. (2018). *Granville Sharp's Uncovered Letter and the Zong Massacre*. Springer.

Fayemi, Ademola Kazeem. (2009). 'Human Personality and the Yoruba Worldview: An Ethico-Sociological Interpretation'. *The Journal of Pan African Studies* 9(2): 166–76.

Feintrenie, Laurène. (2014). 'Agro-industrial Plantations in Central Africa, Risks and Opportunities'. *Biodiversity and Conservation* 23(6): 1577–89.

Fernández-Armesto, Felipe. (2013). *1492: The Year Our World Began*. Bloomsbury Publishing.

Ferreira da Silva, Denise. (2018). 'Hacking the Subject: Black Feminism and Refusal beyond the Limits of Critique'. *PhiloSOPHIA* 8(1): 19–41.

Fields, Karen E. and Barbara Jeanne Fields. (2014). *Racecraft: The Soul of Inequality in American Life*. Verso Trade.

Finnis, John. (2011). 'Revolutions and Continuity of Law'. In AWB Simpson (ed). *Philosophy of Law: Collected Essays Volume IV*. 407–35. Oxford University Press.

Fitzmaurice, Andrew. (2007). 'The Genealogy of Terra Nullius'. *Australian Historical Studies* 38(129): 1–15.

Foner, Eric. (2021). 'United States of Amnesia' *The London Review of Books* 43(17): 11–13. https://www.lrb.co.uk/the-paper/v43/n17/eric-foner/united-states-of-amnesia (Accessed 17 February 2022).

Ford, Lisa and Naomi Parkinson. (2021). 'Legislating Liberty: Liberated Africans and the Abolition Act, 1806–1824'. *Slavery & Abolition* 42(4): 827–46.

Foucault, Michel. (1987). *The Thought from Outside*. Zone Books; MIT Press.

Foucault, Michel. (1995). *Discipline and Punish: The Birth of the Prison*. Vintage.

Foucault, Michel. (2013a). 'Right of Death and Power Over Life'. In Campbell, Timothy and Adam Sitze (eds). *Biopolitics: A Reader*. 41–60. Duke University Press.

Foucault, Michel. (2013b). 'Society Must Be Defended: Lecture at the Collège de France'. In Campbell, Timothy and Adam Sitze (eds). *Biopolitics: A Reader*. 61–81. Duke University Press.

Foucault, Michel. (2021). 'Nietzsche, Genealogy, History'. In Bouchard, Donald (ed). *Language, Counter-Memory, Practice: Selected Essays and Interviews.* 139–64. Cornell University Press.

Fox, Adam. (2009). 'Sir William Petty, Ireland, and the Making of a Political Economist, 1653–87'. *The Economic History Review* 62(2): 388–404.

Franco, Rébecca and Nawal Mustafa. (2019). 'Invalidating the Archive: Interpreting Silences and Inconsistencies'. *Sentio* 1(1): 42–8.

Franks, C.E.S. (2002). 'In Search of the Savage *Sauvage*: An Exploration into North America's Political Cultures'. *American Review of Canadian Studies* 32(4): 547–80.

Freire, Paulo. (2005). *Pedagogy of the Oppressed.* Continuum.

Galván-Álvarez, Enrique. (2010). 'Epistemic Violence and Retaliation: The Issue of Knowledges in "Mother India"/Violencia y Venganza Epistemológica: La Cuestión de Las Formas de Conocimiento En Mother India'. *Atlantis* 32(2): 11–26.

Gandhi, Leela. (2019). *Postcolonial Theory: A Critical Introduction.* Columbia University Press.

Gaonkar, Dilip Parameshwar. (2001). 'On Alternative Modernities'. In Gaonkar, Dilip Parameshwar (ed). *Alternative Modernities.* 1–23. Duke University Press.

Garner, Steve. (2007). *Whiteness: An Introduction.* Routledge.

Garner, Steve. (2017). *Racisms: An Introduction.* Sage.

Garuba, Harry. (2015). 'What is an African Curriculum'. *Mail & Guardian.* 17 April. https://mg.co.za/article/2015-04-17-what-is-an-african-curriculum/ (Accessed 17 February 2022).

Gershoni, Yekutiel. (1987). 'The Drawing of Liberian Boundaries in the Nineteenth Century: Treaties with African Chiefs versus Effective Occupation'. *The International Journal of African Historical Studies* 20(2): 293–307.

Getachew, Adom. (2019). *Worldmaking after Empire: The Rise and Fall of Self-Determination.* Princeton University Press.

Gillman, Susan. (2015). 'Remembering Slavery, Again'. *Caribbean Quarterly.* 61(4): 1–19.

Gilmore, Ruth Wilson. (2007). *Golden Gulag: Prisons, Surplus, Crisis, and Opposition in Globalizing California.* University of California Press.

Gilroy, Paul. (2013). *There Ain't No Black in the Union Jack.* 2nd edition. London: Routledge.

Glissant, Edouard. (1992). *Caribbean Discourse: Selected Essays.* University of Virginia Press.

Goldberg, David Theo. (2008). 'Racial States'. In Goldberg D.T. and Solomos J. (eds). *A Companion to Racial and Ethnic Studies.* 233–58. John Wiley & Sons.

González, Aitor Jimenez. (2018). 'Decolonizing Legal Studies: A Latin Americanist Perspective'. In Cupples, Julie and Ramón Grosfoguel (eds). *Unsettling Eurocentrism in the Westernized University.* 131–44. Routledge.

Goodman, Jane E., Matt Tomlinson, and Justin B. Richland. (2014). 'Citational Practices: Knowledge, Personhood, and Subjectivity'. *Annual Review of Anthropology* 43(1): 449–63.

Gopal, Priyamvada. (2019). *Insurgent Empire: Anticolonial Resistance and British Dissent.* Verso Books.

Gopal, Priyamvada. (2021). 'On Decolonisation and the University'. *Textual Practice* 35:6: 873–99.

Gordon, Lewis R. (2011). 'Shifting the Geography of Reason in An Age of Disciplinary Decadence'. *Transmodernity: Journal of Peripheral Cultural Production of the Luso-Hispanic World* 1(2): 95–103.

Gordon, Lewis R. (2013). 'Thoughts on Dussel's "Anti-Cartesian Meditations"'. *Human Architecture: Journal of the Sociology of Self-Knowledge* 11(1): 67–72.

Gordon, L.R. (2014). 'Disciplinary Decadence and the Decolonisation of Knowledge'. *Africa Development* 39(1): 81–92.

Gordon, Lewis R. (2015a). *Disciplinary Decadence: Living Thought in Trying Times.* Routledge.

Gordon, Lewis R. (2015b). *What Fanon Said: A Philosophical Introduction to His Life and Thought.* Fordham University Press.

Gordon, Lewis R. (2018). 'Disciplining as a Human Science'. In Gržinić, Marina and Aneta Stojnić (eds). *Shifting Corporealities in Contemporary Performance: Danger, Im/Mobility and Politics.* 233–250. Springer.

Gordon, Lewis R. (2020). *Freedom, Justice, and Decolonization.* Routledge.

Gordon, Lewis R., Annie Menzel, George Shulman, and Jasmine Syedullah. (2018). 'Afro pessimism'. *Contemporary Political Theory* 17(1): 105–37.

Gordon, Robert W. (1984). 'Critical Legal Histories'. *Stanford Law Review* 36(1/2): 57–125.

Grabham, Emily. (2016). *Brewing Legal Times: Things, Form, and the Enactment of Law.* University of Toronto Press.

Graham, Mary. (1999). 'Some Thoughts About the Philosophical Underpinnings of Aboriginal Worldviews'. *Worldviews: Global Religions, Culture, and Ecology* 3(2): 105–18.

Graham, Nicole. (2010). *Lawscape: Property, Environment, Law.* Routledge.

Grear, Anna. (2003). 'A Tale of the Land, The Insider, The Outsider and Human Rights (An Exploration of Some Problems and Possibilities in The Relationship Between the English Common Law Property Concept, Human Rights Law, And Discourses of Exclusion and Inclusion)'. *Legal Studies* 23(1): 33–65.

Grear, Anna. (2007). 'Challenging Corporate "Humanity": Legal Disembodiment, Embodiment and Human Rights'. *Human Rights Law Review* 7(3): 511–43.

Grear, Anna. (2015). 'Deconstructing Anthropos: A Critical Legal Reflection on "Anthropocentric" Law and Anthropocene "Humanity"'. *Law and Critique* 26(3): 225–49.

Greenhouse, Carol J. (1989). 'Just in Time: Temporality and the Cultural Legitimation of Law'. *The Yale Law Journal* 98(8): 1631–51.
Greenhouse, Carol J. (2018). *A Moment's Notice*. Cornell University Press.
Grimes, Katie Walker. (2017). *Christ Divided: Antiblackness as Corporate Vice*. Fortress Press.
Grosfoguel, Ramón. (2012). 'The Dilemmas of Ethnic Studies in the United States: Between Liberal Multiculturalism, Identity Politics, Disciplinary Colonization, and Decolonial Epistemologies'. *Human Architecture: Journal of the Sociology of Self-Knowledge* 10(1): 81–9.
Grosfoguel, Ramon. (2016). 'What is Racism?'. *Journal of World-Systems Research* 22(1): 9–15.
Grosfoguel, Ramón, Roberto Hernández, and Ernesto Rosen Velásquez. (2016). *Decolonizing the Westernized University: Interventions in Philosophy of Education from Within and Without*. Lexington Books.
Gudynas, Eduardo. (2011). 'Buen Vivir: Today's Tomorrow'. *Development* 54(4): 441–7.
Hadden, Sally E. (2003). *Slave Patrols: Law and Violence in Virginia and the Carolinas*. Harvard University Press.
Hall, Catherine, Nicholas Draper, Keith McClelland, Katie Donington, and Rachel Lang. (2014). *Legacies of British Slave-Ownership: Colonial Slavery and the Formation of Victorian Britain*. Cambridge University Press.
Hall, Stuart. (2017). *Familiar Stranger*. Duke University Press.
Handler, Jerome S. (2016). 'Custom and Law: The Status of Enslaved Africans in Seventeenth-Century Barbados'. *Slavery and Abolition* 37(2): 233–55.
Handler, Jerome S. and Matthew C. Reilly. (2017). 'Contesting "White Slavery" in the Caribbean: Enslaved Africans and European Indentured Servants in Seventeenth-Century Barbados'. *New West Indian Guide/Nieuwe West-Indische Gids* 91(1–2): 30–55.
Haraway, Donna. (1988). 'Situated Knowledges: The Science Question in Feminism and the Privilege of Partial Perspective'. *Feminist Studies* 14(3): 575–99.
Harlow, Barbara and Mia Carter. (2003). *Archives of Empire: Volume 2. The Scramble for Africa*. Duke University Press.
Harney, Stefano and Fred Moten. (2013). *The Undercommons: Fugitive Planning and Black Study*. https://www.minorcompositions.info/wp-content/uploads/2013/04/undercommons-web.pdf (Accessed 17 February 2022).
Harrington, John. (2012). 'Time as a Dimension of Medical Law'. *Medical Law Review* 20(4): 491–515.
Harris, Cheryl I. (1993). 'Whiteness as Property'. *Harvard Law Review* 106(8): 1707–91.
Hartman, Saidiya V. (1997). *Scenes of Subjection: Terror, Slavery, and Self-Making in Nineteenth-Century America*. Oxford University Press.

Hartman, Saidiya V. (2002). 'The Time of Slavery'. *The South Atlantic Quarterly* 101(4): 757–77.

Hartman, Saidiya V. (2020). 'The End of White Supremacy: An American Romance'. *Bomb Magazine* 152. 5 June. https://bombmagazine.org/articles/the-end-of-white-supremacy-an-american-romance/ [Accessed 17 February 2022].

Hasani, Enver. (2003). 'Uti Possidetis Juris: From Rome to Kosovo International Law under Fire'. *Fletcher Forum of World Affairs* 27(2): 85–98.

Heuman, Gad. (2010). 'Slave Rebellions'. In Heuman, Gad and Trevor Burnard (eds). *The Routledge History of Slavery*. 220–33. Routledge.

Hickel, Jason. (2017). *The Divide: A Brief Guide to Global Inequality and Its Solutions*. Random House.

Hickel, Jason, Dylan Sullivan, and Huzaifa Zoomkawala. (2021). 'Plunder in the Post-Colonial Era: Quantifying Drain from the Global South through Unequal Exchange, 1960–2018'. *New Political Economy* 26(6): 1030–47.

Hicks, Dan. (2016). 'The Temporality of The Landscape Revisited'. *Norwegian Archaeological Review* 49(1): 5–22.

Hicks, Dan. (2020). *The Brutish Museums*. Pluto Press.

Hochschild, Adam. (1999). *King Leopold's Ghost: A Story of Greed, Terror, and Heroism in Colonial Africa*. Houghton Mifflin Harcourt.

Holmes, Oliver W. (1923). *The Common Law*. Little, Brown and Company.

Hom, Andrew R. (2010). 'Hegemonic Metronome: The Ascendancy of Western Standard Time'. *Review of International Studies* 36(4): 1145–70.

hooks, bell. (1989). *Talking Back: Thinking Feminist, Thinking Black*. Vol. 10. South End Press.

hooks, bell. (2003). *Teaching Community: A Pedagogy of Hope*. Psychology Press.

hooks, bell. (2004). *The Will to Change: Men, Masculinity, and Love*. Atria Books.

Hoy, David Couzens. (2012). *The Time of Our Lives: A Critical History of Temporality*. MIT Press.

Humes, Brian D., Elaine K. Swift, Richard M. Valelly, Kenneth Finegold, and Evelyn C. Fink. (2002). 'Representation of the Antebellum South in the House of Representatives: Measuring the Impact of the Three-Fifths Clause'. In Brady, David W. and Mathew D. McCubbins (eds). *Party, Process, and Political Change in Congress: New Perspectives on the History of Congress*. 452–66. Stanford University Press.

Humphreys, David. (2017). 'Rights of Pachamama: The Emergence of an Earth Jurisprudence in the Americas'. *Journal of International Relations and Development* 20(3): 459–84.

Ibhawoh, Bonny and Jeremiah I. Dibua. (2003). 'Deconstructing Ujamaa: The Legacy of Julius Nyerere in the Quest for Social and Economic Development in Africa'. *African Journal of Political Science* 8(1): 59–83.

Icaza, Rosalba. (2017). 'Decolonial Feminism and Global Politics: Border Thinking and Vulnerability as a Knowing Otherwise'. In Woons, Marc and Sebastian Weier (eds). *Critical Epistemologies of Global Politics*. 26–45. E-International Relations.

Icaza, Rosalba. (2018). 'Social Struggles and The Coloniality of Gender'. In Rutazibwa, Olivia U. and Robbie Shilliam (eds). *Routledge Handbook of Postcolonial Politics*. 58–71. Routledge.

Iliffe, John. (1979). *A Modern History of Tanganyika*. Cambridge University Press.

IMF. (2021). 'WORLD ECONOMIC OUTLOOK: Recovery During a Pandemic Health Concerns, Supply Disruptions, and Price Pressures'. October. https://www.imf.org/en/Publications/WEO/Issues/2021/10/12/world-economic-outlook-october-2021 [Accessed 17 February 2022].

Ipinyomi, Foluke. (2012). 'Is Côte d'Ivoire a Test Case for R2P? Democratization as Fulfilment of the International Community's Responsibility to Prevent'. *Journal of African Law* 56(2): 151–74.

Ipinyomi, Foluke Ifejola. (2015). 'A Right to a Project of (African) Life: Boko Haram, ESC Classification of the Right to Education, and the Unjustifiability of Generationalising Human Rights'. *Journal of Academic Perspectives* 2015(4): 1–21.

Ireland, Paddy. (2018). 'Making Sense of Contemporary Capitalism Using Company Law'. *Australian Journal of Corporate Law* 33: 379–401.

Irwin, Graham W. (1975). 'Precolonial African Diplomacy: The Example of Asante'. *The International Journal of African Historical Studies* 8(1): 81–96.

Jackson, Mark. (2017). 'For New Ecologies of Thought: Towards Decolonising Critique'. In Jackson, Mark (ed). *Coloniality, Ontology, and the Question of the Posthuman*. 19–62. Routledge.

Jackson, Mark. (2020). 'On Decolonizing the Anthropocene: Disobedience via Plural Constitutions'. *Annals of the American Association of Geographers*: 1–11.

Jackson, Ronald L. (2006) *Scripting the Black Masculine Body: Identity, Discourse, And Racial Politics in Popular Media*. Suny Press.

Jackson, Zakiyyah Iman. (2020). *Becoming Human: Matter and Meaning in an Antiblack World*. Vol. 53. NYU Press.

James, C.L.R. (1989). *The Black Jacobins: Toussaint L'ouverture and the San Domingo Revolution*. Vintage Books. Second edition revised.

Jameson, Fredric. (1994) *The Seeds of Time*. Columbia University Press.

Jenkins, Katy. (2015). 'Unearthing Women's Anti-Mining Activism in the Andes: Pachamama and the "Mad Old Women"'. *Antipode* 47(2): 442–60.

Jensen, Steffen and Olaf Zenker. (2015). 'Homelands as Frontiers: Apartheid's Loose Ends – An Introduction'. *Journal of Southern African Studies* 41(5): 937–52.

Jivraj, Suhraiya. (2020). 'Towards Anti-racist Legal Pedagogy: A Resource'. https://research.kent.ac.uk/decolonising-law-schools/wp-content/uploads/sites/866/2020/09/Towards-Anti-racist-Legal-Pedagogy-A-Resource.pdf (Accessed 17 February 2022).

Johnson, Samuel. (2010). *The History of the Yorubas: From the Earliest Times to the Beginning of the British Protectorate*. Cambridge University Press.

Jones, David Ivon. (1921). *Communism in South Africa: Presented to the Executive of the Third International on Behalf of the International Socialist League South Africa*. LSL Press.

Juif, Dácil and Ewout Frankema. (2018). 'From Coercion to Compensation: Institutional Responses to Labour Scarcity in the Central African Copperbelt'. *Journal of Institutional Economics* 14(2): 313–43.

Jung, Moon-Kie and João H. Costa Vargas (eds). (2021). *Antiblackness*. Duke University Press.

Kantai, Parselelo. (2007). 'In the Grip of The Vampire State: Maasai Land Struggles in Kenyan Politics'. *Journal of Eastern African Studies* 1(1): 107–22.

Kedar, Alexandre Sandy. (2014). 'Expanding Legal Geographies: A Call for a Critical Comparative Approach'. In Braverman, Irus, Nicholas Blomley, David Delaney, and Alexandre Kedar (eds). *The Expanding Spaces of Law: A Timely Legal Geography*. 95–119. Stanford University Press.

Keenan, Sarah. (2010). 'Subversive Property: Reshaping Malleable Spaces of Belonging'. *Social & Legal Studies* 19(4): 423–39.

Keenan, Sarah. (2019). 'From Historical Chains to Derivative Futures: Title Registries as Time Machines'. *Social & Cultural Geography* 20(3): 283–303.

Kelley, Robin D.G. (2002). *Freedom Dreams: The Black Radical Imagination*. Beacon Press.

Kelley, Robin D.G. (2017). 'What Did Cedric Robinson Mean by Racial Capitalism?' *Boston Review*. 12 January. https://bostonreview.net/articles/robin-d-g-kelley-introduction-race-capitalism-justice/ (Accessed 17 February 2022).

Kendi, Ibram X. (2016). *Stamped from the Beginning: The Definitive History of Racist Ideas in America*. Hachette UK.

Kennedy, Duncan. (1976). 'Form and Substance in Private Law Adjudication'. *Harvard Law Review* 89(8): 1685.

Killingray, David. (1986). 'The Maintenance of Law and Order in British Colonial Africa'. *African Affairs* 85(340): 411–37.

Kimmerer, Robin Wall. (2013). *Braiding Sweetgrass: Indigenous Wisdom, Scientific Knowledge and the Teachings of Plants*. Milkweed Editions.

Kincheloe, Joe L. (2011). 'Critical Ontology and Indigenous Ways of Being: Forging a Postcolonial Curriculum'. In Hayes, Kecia, Shirley R. Steinberg, and Kenneth Tobin (eds). *Key Works in Critical Pedagogy*. 333–49. Brill Sense.

King, Tiffany Lethabo, Jenell Navarro, and Andrea Smith (eds). (2020). *Otherwise Worlds: Against Settler Colonialism and Anti-Blackness*. Duke University Press.

Kinouani, Guilaine. (2021) *Living While Black: The Essential Guide to Overcoming Racial Trauma*. Random House.

Kish, Zenia and Justin Leroy. (2015). 'Bonded Life: Technologies of Racial Finance from Slave Insurance to Philanthrocapital'. *Cultural Studies* 29(5–6): 630–51.

Koch, Alexander, Chris Brierley, Mark M. Maslin, and Simon L. Lewis. (2019). 'Earth System Impacts of the European Arrival and Great Dying in the Americas after 1492'. *Quaternary Science Reviews* 207: 13–36.

Kreijen, Gérard. (2004). *State Failure, Sovereignty and Effectiveness: Legal Lessons from the Decolonization of Sub-Saharan Africa*. Vol. 50. Martinus Nijhoff Publishers.

Krikler, Jeremy. (2007). 'The Zong and the Lord Chief Justice'. *History Workshop Journal* 64(1): 29–47.

Kundnani, Arun. (2021). 'The Racial Constitution of Neoliberalism'. *Race & Class* 63(1): 51–69.

Lacey, Nicola. (2014). '"Legal Education as Training for Hierarchy" Revisited'. *Transnational Legal Theory* 5(4): 596–600.

Lamble, Sarah, Sarah Keenan, Davina Cooper, and Margaret Davies. (2017). *Law Unlimited: Materialism, Pluralism, and Legal Theory*. Routledge.

Large, Donald W. (1973). 'This Land Is Whose Land: Changing Concepts of Land as Property'. *Wisconsin Law Review* 1973(4): 1039–83.

Last Positivist. (2021). 'Citational Justice'. *Sooty Empiric*. 23 November. http://sootyempiric.blogspot.com/2019/12/citational-justice.html (Accessed 17 February 2022).

Latour, Bruno. (1993). *We Have Never Been Modern*. Harvard University Press.

Lefebvre, Henri. (2009). *State, Space, World: Selected Essays*. University of Minnesota Press.

Lefebvre, Henri and Donald Nicholson-Smith. (1991). *The Production of Space*. Vol. 142. Oxford: Blackwell.

Leonardo, Zeus. (2009). *Race, Whiteness, and Education*. Routledge.

Leroy, Justin and Destin Jenkins. (2021). 'Introduction: The Old History of Capitalism'. In Leroy, Justin and Destin Jenkins (eds). *Histories of Racial Capitalism*. 1–26. Columbia University Press.

Leroy, Justin. (2021). 'Racial Capitalism and Black Philosophies of History'. In Leroy, Justin and Destin Jenkins (eds). *Histories of Racial Capitalism*, 169–84. Columbia University Press.

Letseka, Moeketsi. (2012). 'In Defence of Ubuntu'. *Studies in Philosophy and Education* 31(1): 47–60.

Levin, Richard and Daniel Weiner. (1996). 'The Politics of Land Reform in South Africa After Apartheid: Perspectives, Problems, Prospects'. *The Journal of Peasant Studies* 23(2–3): 93–119.

Lewis, George E. (2008) 'Foreword: After Afrofuturism'. *Journal of the Society for American Music* 2(2): 139–53.

Liboiron, Max. (2021a). *Pollution is Colonialism*. Duke University Press.

Libroron, Max. (2021b). '#Collabrary: A Methodological Experiment for Reading with Reciprocity – How Can We Change Academic Reading Relations that Tend to be Extractive into Something More Reciprocal, Humble, Generous, and Accountable?' 3 January. https://civiclaboratory.nl/2021/01/03/collabrary-a-methodological-experiment-for-reading-with-reciprocity/ (Accessed 17 February 2022).

Lima, Mendelson, Joine Cariele Evangelista do Vale, Gerlane de Medeiros Costa, Reginaldo Carvalho dos Santos, Washington Luiz Félix Correia Filho, Givanildo Gois, et al. (2020). 'The Forests in the Indigenous Lands in Brazil in Peril'. *Land Use Policy* 90: 104258.

Linarelli, John, Margot E. Salomon, and Muthucumaraswamy Sornarajah. (2018). *The Misery of International Law: Confrontations with Injustice in the Global Economy*. Oxford University Press.

Lipsitz, George. (2019). 'The Sounds of Silence: How Race Neutrality Preserves White Supremacy'. In Crenshaw, Kimberlé Williams (ed). *Seeing Race Again: Countering Colorblindness across the Disciplines*. 23–51. University of California Press.

Locke, John. (1999). *Two Treatises of Government*. McMaster University Archive of the History of Economic Thought.

Lopez, Ian F. Haney. (1994). 'The Social Construction of Race: Some Observations on Illusion, Fabrication, and Choice'. *Harvard Civil Rights-Civil Liberties Law Review* 29(1): 1–62.

Lorimer, Douglas A. (1984). 'Black Slaves and English Liberty: A Re-Examination of Racial Slavery in England'. *Immigrants & Minorities* 3(2): 121–50.

Lowe, Chris, Tunde Brimah, Peal-Alice Marsh, William Minter, and Monde Muyangwa. (1997). 'Talking About "Tribe": Moving from Stereotypes to Analysis'. *Africa Policy E-Journal*: 1–8.

Lowe, Lisa. (2015). *The Intimacies of Four Continents*. Duke University Press.

Lugones, Maria. (2013). 'The Coloniality of Gender'. In Mignolo, Walter D., and Arturo Escobar (eds). *Globalization and the Decolonial Option*. 369–90. Routledge.

Lundström, Markus and Paola Sartoretto. (2021). 'The Temporal Nexus of Collective Memory Mediation: Print and Digital Media in Brazil's Landless Movement 1984–2019'. *Social Movement Studies*: 1–16.

MacCormack, Patricia. (2016). *Posthuman Ethics: Embodiment and Cultural Theory*. Routledge.

MacEachern, Scott. (2000). 'Genes, Tribes, and African History'. *Current Anthropology* 41(3): 357–84.

Macharia, Keguro. (2021). 'From Repair to Pessimism'. *Brick* 106. 11 May. https://brickmag.com/from-repair-to-pessimism/ (Accessed 17 February 2022).

Maeso, Silvia Rodríguez and Marta Araújo. (2015). 'Eurocentrism, Political Struggles and the Entrenched Will-to-Ignorance: An Introduction'. In Araújo, Marta and Silvia R. Maeso (eds). *Eurocentrism, Racism and Knowledge: Debates on History and Power in Europe and the Americas*. 1–22. Springer.

Maldonado-Torres, Nelson. (2007). 'On the Coloniality of Being: Contributions to the Development of a Concept'. *Cultural Studies* 21(2–3): 240–70.

Maldonado-Torres, Nelson. (2020). 'Latin American and Caribbean Colonial Studies and/in the Decolonial Turn'. In Martínez-San Miguel, Yolanda and Santa Arias (eds). *The Routledge Hispanic Studies Companion to Colonial Latin America and the Caribbean (1492–1898)*. 117–31. Routledge.

Mamdani, Mahmood. (2012). *Define and Rule: Native as Political Identity*. Harvard University Press.

Manji, Ambreena S. (2006). *The Politics of Land Reform in Africa: From Communal Tenure to Free Markets*. Zed Books.

Manji, Ambreena. (2019). 'Land Reform in Kenya: The History of an Idea'. *The Platform*. 4 January. https://theplatform.co.ke/land-reform-in-kenya-the-history-of-an-idea/ (Accessed 17 February 2022).

Mapokgole, Reshoketswe B. (2014) 'There Is No Black in the Rainbow (Nation): A Bikoist and Fanonian Approach to Understanding "Xenophobic" Violence in South Africa'. Senior Theses, Trinity College, Hartford. Trinity College Digital Repository. https://digitalrepository.trincoll.edu/theses/425 (Accessed 17 February 2022).

Marchais, Gauthier. (2020) 'Contemporary Research Must Stop Relying on Racial Inequalities'. *Africa at LSE*. https://blogs.lse.ac.uk/africaatlse/2020/01/30/research-must-stop-racial-inequalities-colonialism/ (Accessed 17 February 2022).

Márquez, Gabriel García. (2022). 'Acceptance Speech: The Nobel Prize in Literature 1982'. https://www.nobelprize.org/prizes/literature/1982/marquez/lecture/ (Accessed 17 February 2022).

Marshall, Yannick Giovanni. (2020). 'The Racists' Peace'. *Aljazeera*. 7 June. https://www.aljazeera.com/opinions/2020/6/7/the-racists-peace (Accessed 17 February 2022).

Martin, R.M. (1994). 'A Feminist View of The Reasonable Man: An Alternative Approach to Liability in Negligence for Personal Injury'. *Anglo-American Law Review* 23: 334–74.

Martínez-Cobo, José R. (1986). 'Study of the Problem of Discrimination against Indigenous Populations'. *New York: United Nations* 87. https://www.un.org/esa/socdev/unpfii/documents/MCS_v_en.pdf (Accessed 17 February 2022).

Mason, Ernest D. (1979). 'Alain Locke on Race and Race Relations'. *Phylon (1960–)* 40(4): 342–50.

Massey, Doreen. (2005). *For Space*. Sage.

Mawani, Renisa. (2014). 'Law as Temporality: Colonial Politics and Indian'. *UC Irvine Law Review* 4(1): 65–96.

Maybury-Lewis, David. (2002). 'Genocide against Indigenous Peoples'. In Hinton A.L. (ed). *Annihilating Difference: The Anthropology of Genocide.* 43–53. University of California Press.

Mayo, Peter. (2012). 'Nyerere's Postcolonial Approach to Education'. In Abdi, Ali, A. (ed). *Decolonizing Philosophies of Education*, 43–57. SensePublishers.

Mbembé, Achille. (2018). 'The Idea of a Borderless World'. *Africa Is a Country.* 11 November. https://africasacountry.com/2018/11/the-idea-of-a-borderless-world (Accessed 17 February 2022).

Mbembe, Achille. (2019). *Necropolitics.* Duke University Press.

Mbembé, J-A. (2001). *On the Postcolony.* Vol. 41. University of California Press.

Mbiti, John S. (1990). *African Religions and Philosophy.* Heinemann.

McCarthy, Thomas. (2009). *Race, Empire, and the Idea of Human Development.* Cambridge University Press.

McIntyre, Michael and Heidi J. Nast. (2011). 'Bio(necro) Polis: Marx, Surplus Populations, and the Spatial Dialectics of Reproduction and "Race"'. *Antipode* 43(5): 1465–88.

McKittrick, Katherine. (2006). *Demonic Grounds: Black Women and the Cartographies of Struggle.* University of Minnesota Press.

McKittrick, Katherine. (2015). 'Yours in the Intellectual Struggle: Sylvia Wynter and the Realization of the Living'. In McKittrick, Katherine (ed). *Sylvia Wynter: On Being Human as Praxis.* 1–8. Duke University Press.

McKittrick, Katherine. (2021). *Dear Science and Other Stories.* Duke University Press.

Meghji, Ali. (2020). 'Towards a Theoretical Synergy: Critical Race Theory and Decolonial Thought in Trumpamerica and Brexit Britain'. *Current Sociology*, 70(5). 1–18.

Melamed, Jodi. (2015). 'Racial Capitalism'. *Critical Ethnic Studies* 1(1): 76–85.

Memmi, Albert. (2006). *Decolonization and the Decolonized.* University of Minnesota Press.

Menkiti, Ifeanyi A. (1984). 'Person and Community in African Traditional Thought'. In Wright, Richard A. (ed). *African Philosophy: An Introduction.* 171–82. 3rd edition. University Press of America.

Mignolo, Walter D. (2009). 'Epistemic Disobedience, Independent Thought and Decolonial Freedom'. *Theory, Culture & Society* 26(7–8): 159–81.

Mignolo, Walter D. (2011). *The Darker Side of Western Modernity.* Duke University Press.

Mignolo, Walter D. (2013a). 'Delinking: The Rhetoric of Modernity, the Logic of Coloniality and the Grammar of De-Coloniality'. In Mignolo, Walter D. and Arturo Escobar (eds). *Globalization and the Decolonial Option.* 303–68. Routledge.

Mignolo, Walter D. (2013b). 'Introduction: Coloniality of Power and De-Colonial Thinking'. In Mignolo, Walter D. and Arturo Escobar (eds). *Globalization and the Decolonial Option*. 1–21. Routledge.

Mignolo, Walter D. and Arturo Escobar (eds). (2013). *Globalization and the Decolonial Option*. Routledge.

Mignolo, Walter D., and Catherine E. Walsh. (2018). *On Decoloniality: Concepts, Analytics, Praxis*. Duke University Press.

Mignolo, Walter, Luisa Elena Delgado, and Rolando J. Romero. (2000). 'Local Histories and Global Designs: An Interview with Walter Mignolo'. *Discourse* 22(3): 7–33.

Miller, Robert J., Jacinta Ruru, Larissa Behrendt, and Tracey Lindberg. (2010). *Discovering Indigenous Lands: The Doctrine of Discovery in the English Colonies*. Oxford University Press.

Mills, Charles W. (2007). 'White Ignorance'. In Sullivan, Shannon and Nancy Tuana (eds). *Race and Epistemologies of Ignorance*. 13–38. SUNY Press.

Mills, Charles W. (2013). 'An Illuminating Blackness'. *The Black Scholar* 43(4): 32–7.

Mills, Charles W. (2014a). *The Racial Contract*. Cornell University Press.

Mills, Charles W. (2014b). 'White Time: The Chronic Injustice of Ideal Theory'. *Du Bois Review: Social Science Research on Race* 11(1): 27–42.

Mills, Charles W. (2015). 'Global White Ignorance'. In Gross, Matthias and Linsey McGoey (eds). *Routledge International Handbook of Ignorance Studies*. 217–27. Routledge.

Mirza, Heidi Safia. (2018). 'Racism in Higher Education: "What Then, Can Be Done?"'. In Arday, Jason and Heidi Safia Mirza (eds). *Dismantling Race in Higher Education: Racism, Whiteness and Decolonising the Academy*. 3–23. Palgrave Macmillan.

Mitter, Siddhartha. (2018). 'The River Site'. *Popula*, 25 July. https://popula.com/2018/07/25/the-river-site/ (Accessed 17 February 2022).

Modiri, Joel M. (2015). 'Law's Poverty'. *Potchefstroom Electronic Law Journal/Potchefstroomse Elektroniese Regsblad* 18(2): 223–73.

Modiri, Joel M. (2016). 'The "Event" of Racism'. *Daily Maverick*. 16 November. https://www.dailymaverick.co.za/opinionista/2016-11-17-the-event-of-racism/ (Accessed 17 February 2022).

Modiri, Joel M. (2018). 'Conquest and Constitutionalism: First Thoughts on an Alternative Jurisprudence'. *South African Journal on Human Rights* 34(3): 300–25.

Modiri, Joel M. (2020). 'The Aporias of Decolonisation in the South African Academy'. In Oluwaseun Tella and Shireen Motala (eds). *From Ivory Towers to Ebony Towers: Transforming Humanities Curricula in South Africa, Africa and African-American Studies*. 157–73. Jacana.

Moore, J.M. (2020). '"Law", "Order", "Justice", "Crime": Disrupting Key Concepts in Criminology through the Study of Colonial History'. *The Law Teacher* 54(4): 489–502.

Moore, John. (2021). 'Protecting the Property of Slavers: London's First State Funded Police Force'. *Abolitionist Futures*. 11 August. https://abolitionistfutures.com/latest-news/protecting-the-property-of-slavers-londons-first-state-funded-police-force (Accessed 17 February 2022).

Moore, Wendy Leo. (2020). 'The Mechanisms of White Space(s)'. *American Behavioral Scientist* 64(14): 1946–60.

Moore, Wilbert E. (1941). 'Slave Law and the Social Structure'. *The Journal of Negro History* 26(2): 171–202.

Moosavi, Leon. (2020). 'The Decolonial Bandwagon and the Dangers of Intellectual Decolonisation'. *International Review of Sociology* 30(2): 332–54.

Moreton-Robinson, Aileen. (2015). *The White Possessive: Property, Power, and Indigenous Sovereignty*. University of Minnesota Press.

Morgan, Jennifer L. (2018). 'Partus Sequitur Ventrem: Law, Race, and Reproduction in Colonial Slavery'. *Small Axe: A Caribbean Journal of Criticism* 22(1): 1–17.

Morreira, Shannon and Kathy Luckett. (2018). 'Questions Academics Can Ask to Decolonise Their Classrooms'. *The Conversation*. 17 October. https://theconversation.com/questions-academics-can-ask-to-decolonise-their-classrooms-103251 (Accessed 17 February 2022).

Morrison, Toni. (1994). 'Unspeakable Things Unspoken: The Afro-American Presence in American Literature'. In Mitchell, Angelyn (ed). *Within the Circle: An Anthology of African American Literary Criticism from the Harlem Renaissance to the Present*. 368–98. Duke University Press.

Mott, Carrie and Daniel Cockayne. (2017). 'Citation Matters: Mobilizing the Politics of Citation toward a Practice of "Conscientious Engagement"'. *Gender, Place & Culture* 24(7): 954–73.

Mudimbé, Vumbi Yoka. (1991). *Parables and Fables: Exegesis, Textuality, and Politics in Central Africa*. University of Wisconsin Press.

Munshi, Sherally. (2020). 'Unsettling the Border'. *UCLA Law Review* 67(6): 1720–67.

Naffine, Ngaire. (2009). Law's Meaning of Life: Philosophy, Religion, Darwin and the Legal Person. Bloomsbury Publishing.

Naffine, Ngaire. (2011). 'Women and the Cast of Legal Persons'. In Jones, Jackie, Anna Grear, Rachel Anne Fenton, and Kim Stevenson (eds). *Gender, Sexualities and Law*. 15–25. Routledge.

Naldi, Nerio. (1989). 'Petty's Labour Theory of Prices'. *Quaderni Di Storia Dell'economia Politica* 7(1): 3–36.

Nanni, Giordano. (2017). *The Colonisation of Time: Ritual, Routine and Resistance in the British Empire*. Manchester University Press.

Napoleon, Val. (2007). 'Thinking About Indigenous Legal Orders'. Research Paper for the National Centre for First Nations Governance. http://fngovernance.org/ncfng_research/val_napoleon.pdf (Accessed 17 February 2022).

Napoleon, Val and Hadley Friedland. (2014). 'Indigenous Legal Traditions: Roots to Renaissance'. In Dubber, Markus D. and Tatjana Hörnle (eds). *The Oxford Handbook of Criminal Law*. 225–47. Oxford: Oxford University Press.

Narayan, John. (2019). 'British Black Power: The Anti-Imperialism of Political Blackness and the Problem of Nativist Socialism'. *The Sociological Review* 67(5): 945–67.

Nawangwe, Barnabas. (2021). 'Africa's Destiny and Higher Education Transformation'. In Land, Hilligje van't, Andreas Corcoran, and Diana-Camelia Iancu (eds.) *The Promise of Higher Education: Essays in Honour of 70 Years of IAU*. 215–19. Springer Nature.

Ndlovu-Gatsheni, Sabelo J. (2017). 'Decolonising Research Methodology Must Include Undoing Its Dirty History'. *The Conversation*. 26 September. http://theconversation.com/decolonising-research-methodology-must-include-undoing-its-dirty-history-83912 (Accessed 17 February 2022).

Ndlovu-Gatsheni, Sabelo J. (2018). *Epistemic Freedom in Africa: Deprovincialization and Decolonization*. Routledge.

Ndlovu-Gatsheni, Sabelo J. (2021). 'The Cognitive Empire, Politics of Knowledge and African Intellectual Productions: Reflections on Struggles for Epistemic Freedom and Resurgence of Decolonisation in the Twenty-First Century'. *Third World Quarterly* 42(5): 882–901.

Neves, Jonathan and Hillman, Nick. (2016). 'The 2016 Student Academic Experience Survey'. Report for the Higher Education Academy. https://www.hepi.ac.uk/2016/06/09/hepi-hea-2016-student-academic-experience-survey/ (Accessed 17 February 2022).

Niane, Djibril Tamsir (ed). (1984). *Africa from the Twelfth to the Sixteenth Century*. UNESCO.

Nichols, Robert Lee. (2005). 'Realizing the Social Contract: The Case of Colonialism and Indigenous Peoples'. *Contemporary Political Theory* 4(1): 42–62.

Nkrumah, Kwame. (1966). *Neo-Colonialism: The Last Stage of Imperialism*. International Publishers.

Nolte, Insa. (2019). 'The Future of African Studies: What We Can Do to Keep Africa at the Heart of Our Research'. *Journal of African Cultural Studies* 31(3): 296–313.

Núñez-Parra, Lorena, Constanza López-Radrigán, Nicole Mazzucchelli, and Carolina Pérez. (2021). 'Necropolitics and the Bodies That Do Not Matter in Pandemic Times'. *Alter* 15(2): 190–7.

Nunn, Kenneth B. (1997). 'Law as a Eurocentric Enterprise'. *Law and Inequality: A Journal of Theory and Practice* 15(2): 323–72.

NUS. (2012). *Race for Equality: A Report on the Experiences of Black Students in Further and Higher Education*. National Union of Students.

Nyabola, Nanjala. (2018). 'Wakanda Is Not African, and That's OK'. *Aljazeera Opinions*. 3 March. https://www.aljazeera.com/opinions/2018/3/13/wakanda-is-not-african-and-thats-ok (Accessed 17 February 2022).

Obama, Barack. (2004). *Dreams from My Father: A Story of Race and Inheritance*. Crown Publishing.

Obasogie, Osagie K. (2015). 'The Constitution of Identity: Law and Race'. In Sarat, Austin and Patricia Ewick (eds). *The Handbook of Law and Society*. 337–50. John Wiley and Sons.

Obasogie, Osagie K. (2017). 'Race in Law and Society: A Critique'. In López, Ian Haney (ed). *Race, Law and Society*. 445–64. Routledge.

Ohline, Howard A. (1971). 'Republicanism and Slavery: Origins of the Three-Fifths Clause in the United States Constitution'. *The William and Mary Quarterly: A Magazine of Early American History*: 563–84.

Okorafor, Nnedi. (2011). *Who Fears Death*. Penguin.

Okoro, N. Kingsley. (2010). 'African Traditional Education: A Viable Alternative for Peace Building Process in Modern Africa'. *Journal of Alternative Perspectives in the Social Sciences* 2(1): 136–59.

Olaniyan, Tejumola. (2014). 'The Misconception of Modernity, a Conversation with European Attraction Limited'. 6 February. https://www.youtube.com/watch?v=N0yKhmpTpG4 (Accessed 17 February 2022).

Olusoga, David. (2018). 'The Treasury's Tweet Shows Slavery Is Still Misunderstood'. *The Guardian*. 12 February. https://www.theguardian.com/commentisfree/2018/feb/12/treasury-tweet-slavery-compensate-slave-owners (Accessed 17 February 2022).

Onwuachi-Willig, Angela. (2005) 'This Bridge Called Our Backs: An Introduction to the Future of Critical Race Feminism Symposium'. *U.C. Davis Law Review* 39(3): 733–42.

Onyebuchi, Michael. (2018). 'Menkiti, Gyekye and Beyond: Towards A Decolonization of African Political Philosophy'. *Filosofia Theoretica: Journal of African Philosophy, Culture and Religions* 7(2): 1–18.

Orukpe, Williams Ehizuwa. (2019). 'Diplomatic Machinery in Pre-Colonial Nigeria: A Study of the Benin Royal Court as an Instrument of Diplomacy (1180–897)'. *Port Harcourt Journal of History & Diplomatic Studies*: 37–57.

Oshin, Olasiji. (1988). 'Developing Infrastructure of Exploitation: The Example of Colonial Transport on The Bauchi Tin Fields, 1902–1914'. *Transafrican Journal of History* 17: 123–38.

Oswald, Michael (director). (2017). *The Spider's Web: Britain's Second Empire*. 1 hour 20 minutes.

Oyěwùmí, Oyèrónkẹ́. (1997). *The Invention of Women: Making an African Sense of Western Gender Discourses*. University of Minnesota Press.

Palan, Ronen and Jamie Stern-Weiner. (2012). 'Britain's Second Empire'. *New Left Review*. http://www.newleftproject.org/index.php/site/article_comments/britains_second_empire (Accessed 17 February 2022).

REFERENCES

Palmer, Robin. (1986). 'Working Conditions and Worker Responses on Nyasaland Tea Estates, 1930–1953'. *The Journal of African History* 27(1): 105–26.

Palmer, Vernon Valentine. (1995). 'The Origins and Authors of the Code Noir'. *Louisiana Law Review* 56(2): 363–408.

Parsons, Timothy. (2012). 'Being Kikuyu in Meru: Challenging the Tribal Geography of Colonial Kenya'. *The Journal of African History* 53(1): 65–86.

Patterson, Orlando. (2012). 'Trafficking, Gender and Slavery: Past and Present'. In Allain, Jean (eds). *The Legal Understanding of Slavery: From the Historical to the Contemporary*. 322–59. Oxford: Oxford University Press.

Peters, Bolanle Austen. (2018). 'This is Afrofuturism'. *African Arguments*. 6 March. https://africanarguments.org/2018/03/this-is-afrofuturism/ (Accessed 17 February 2022).

Peters, Timothy D., Roshan de Silva-Wijeyeratne, and John Flood. (2017). 'Disruption, Temporality, Law: The Future of Law and Society Scholarship?' *Griffith Law Review* 26(4): 459–68.

Pettigrew, William A. (2013). *Freedom's Debt: The Royal African Company and the Politics of the Atlantic Slave Trade, 1672–1752*. UNC Press Books.

Petty, William. (1899). *The Economic Writings of Sir William Petty*. Volume 1. The University Press. https://oll.libertyfund.org/title/hull-the-economic-writings-of-sir-william-petty-vol-1 (Accessed 17 February 2022).

Pfister, Gertrud. (2006). 'Colonialism and the Enactment of German Identity: Turnen in South-West Africa'. *Journal of Sport History* 33(1): 59–83.

Philippopoulos-Mihalopoulos, Andreas. (2014). *Spatial Justice: Body, Lawscape, Atmosphere*. Routledge.

Phiri, Madalitso Zililo. (2020). 'History of Racial Capitalism in Africa: Violence, Ideology, and Practice'. In Oloruntoba, Samuel Ojo and Toyin Falola (eds). *The Palgrave Handbook of African Political Economy*. 63–81. Palgrave Macmillan.

Pimblott, Kerry. (2020). 'Decolonising the University: The Origins and Meaning of a Movement'. *The Political Quarterly* 91(1): 210–16.

Pirie, Fernanda. (2013). *The Anthropology of Law*. Oxford University Press.

Plessis, W.J. du. (2011). 'African Indigenous Land Rights in a Private Ownership Paradigm'. *Potchefstroom Electronic Law Journal/Potchefstroomse Elektroniese Regsblad* 14(7): 45–69.

Powell, H. Jefferson. (2005). *A Community Built on Words: The Constitution in History and Politics*. University of Chicago Press.

Quiggin, John. (2015). 'John Locke against Freedom'. *Jacobin*. 28 June. https://jacobinmag.com/2015/06/locke-treatise-slavery-private-property (Accessed 17 February 2022).

Quijano, A. (2000a). 'Coloniality of Power, Eurocentrism, and Latin America'. *Nepantla: Views from the South* 1(3): 533–80.

Quijano, Anibal. (2000b). 'Coloniality of Power and Eurocentrism in Latin America'. *International Sociology* 15(2): 215–32.

Quijano, Aníbal. (2013). 'Coloniality and Modernity/Rationality'. In Mignolo, Walter D. and Arturo Escobar (eds). *Globalization and the Decolonial Option*. 22–32. Routledge.

Quijano, Aníbal. (2016). 'Bien Vivir–Between Development and the De/Coloniality of Power'. *Alternautas–Vol. 3–Issue 1–July 2016*: 1–23.

Rahmatian, Andreas. (2009). 'Neo-colonial Aspects of Global Intellectual Property Protection'. *The Journal of World Intellectual Property* 12(1): 40–74.

Raj, Senthorun. (2021). 'Teaching Feeling: Bringing Emotion into the Law School'. *The Law Teacher* 55(2): 128–42.

Rankine, Claudia. (2014). *Citizen: An American Lyric*. Graywolf Press.

Ranta, Eija Maria. (2016). 'Toward a Decolonial Alternative to Development? The Emergence and Shortcomings of Vivir Bien as State Policy in Bolivia in The Era of Globalization'. *Globalizations* 13(4): 425–39.

Rawley, James A. and Stephen D. Behrendt. (2005). *The Transatlantic Slave Trade: A History*. University of Nebraska Press.

Razack, Sherene H. (2018). 'When Place Becomes Race'. In Gupta, Tania Das, Carl E. James, Chris Andersen, Grace-Edward Galabuzi, and Roger C.A. Maaka (eds). *Race and Racialization, 2E: Essential Readings*. 74–82. Canadian Scholars' Press.

Razack, Sherene. (2002). 'Introduction'. In Razack Sherene (ed). *Unmapping a White Settler Society*. 1–20. Between the Lines.

Reichel, Philip L. (1988). 'Southern Slave Patrols as a Transitional Police Type'. *American Journal of Police* 7(2): 51–78.

Reisman, W. Michael. (1995). 'Protecting Indigenous Rights in International Adjudication'. *American Journal of International Law* 89(2): 350–62.

Ress, David. (2020). *Deeds, Titles, and Changing Concepts of Land Rights: Colonial Innovations and Their Impact on Social Thought*. Springer Nature.

Rifkin, Mark. (2017). *Beyond Settler Time: Temporal Sovereignty and Indigenous Self-Determination*. Duke University Press.

Roberts, Dorothy. (2011). *Fatal Invention: How Science, Politics, and Big Business Re-create Race in the Twenty-First Century*. New Press/ORIM.

Roberts, John Morris and Odd Arne Westad. (2013). *The History of the World*. Oxford University Press.

Robinson, Cedric J. (2000). *Black Marxism: The Making of The Black Radical Tradition*. University of North Carolina Press.

Rodney, Walter. (2018). *How Europe Underdeveloped Africa*. Verso Trade.

Rose, Deborah Bird. (2004). *Reports from a Wild Country: Ethics for Decolonisation*. UNSW Press.

Rothberg, Michael. (2020). *The Implicated Subject*. Stanford University Press.

Roy, Arundhati. (2003). *War Talk*. South End Press.

Rupprecht, Anita. (2008). '"A Limited Sort of Property": History, Memory and the Slave Ship Zong'. *Slavery and Abolition* 29(2): 265–77.

Rustin, Michael. (2016). 'The Neoliberal University and Its Alternatives'. *Soundings* 63(63): 147–76.

Rutazibwa, Olivia U. (2018). 'On Babies and Bathwater: Decolonizing International Development Studies'. In Jong, Sara de, Rosalba Icaza, and Olivia U. Rutazibwa (eds). *Decolonization and Feminisms in Global Teaching and Learning*. 158–80. Routledge.

Said, Edward W. (1994). *Culture and Imperialism*. Vintage.

Said, Edward W. (2003). *Orientalism*. London: Penguin Books.

Saldívar, José David. (2013). 'Unsettling Race, Coloniality, and Caste: Anzaldúa's Borderlands/La Frontera, Martinez's Parrot in the Oven, and Roy's The God of Small Things'. In Mignolo, Walter D. and Arturo Escobar (eds). *Globalization and the Decolonial Option*. 193–221. Routledge.

Saldívar-Hull, Sonia and Ranajit Guha. (2001). *The Latin American Subaltern Studies Reader*. Duke University Press.

Sandberg, Russell. (2021). *Subversive Legal History: A Manifesto for the Future of Legal Education*. Routledge.

Sanjinés, Javier. (2013). 'The Nation: An Imagined Community?' In Mignolo, Walter D. and Arturo Escobar (eds). *Globalization and the Decolonial Option*. 149–62. Routledge.

Sankara, Thomas. (1988). *Thomas Sankara Speaks: The Burkina Faso Revolution, 1983–87*. Pathfinder Press.

Santos, Boaventura de Sousa and Maria Paula Meneses. (2019). 'Introduction: Epistemologies of the South—Giving Voice to the Diversity of the South'. In Santos, Boaventura de Sousa and Maria Paula Meneses (eds). *Knowledges Born in the Struggle: Constructing the Epistemologies of the Global South*. xvii–xliii. Routledge.

Santos, Milton. (2021). *The Nature of Space*. Duke University Press.

Sato, Shohei. (2017). '"Operation Legacy": Britain's Destruction and Concealment of Colonial Records Worldwide'. *The Journal of Imperial and Commonwealth History* 45(4): 697–719.

Sayer, Derek. (2014). *Rank Hypocrisies: The Insult of the REF*. Sage.

Schroeder, Doris, Julie Cook, François Hirsch, Solveig Fenet, and Vasantha Muthuswamy (eds). (2018). *Ethics Dumping: Case Studies from North-South Research Collaborations*. SpringerBriefs in Research and Innovation Governance. Springer International Publishing.

Schuyler, George Samuel. (1991). *Black Empire*. UPNE.

Seed, Patricia. (2015). 'How Globalization Invented Indians in the Caribbean'. In Sansavior, Eva and Richard Scholar (eds). *Caribbean Globalizations, 1492 to the Present Day*. 58–82. Oxford University Press.

Sen, Amartya. (1982). *Poverty and Famines: An Essay on Entitlement and Deprivation*. Oxford University Press.

Shaull, Richard. (2018) Foreword. In Freire, Paulo. *Pedagogy of the Oppressed*. Bloomsbury Publishing.

Shaw, Joshua David Michael. (2021). 'The Spatio-Legal Production of Bodies Through the Legal Fiction of Death'. *Law and Critique* 32(1): 69–90.

Shaw, Malcolm N. (1997). 'Peoples, Territorialism and Boundaries'. *European Journal of International Law* 8(3): 478–507.

Shepherd, Christopher J. and Andrew McWilliam. (2013). 'Cultivating Plantations and Subjects in East Timor: A Genealogy'. *Journal of the Humanities and Social Sciences of Southeast Asia* 169(2–3): 326–61.

Shilliam, Robbie. (2015). *The Black Pacific: Anti-colonial Struggles and Oceanic Connections*. Bloomsbury Publishing.

Shilliam, Robbie. (2018). *Race and the Undeserving Poor: From Abolition to Brexit*. Agenda Publishing.

Shippen, Nichole. (2014). *Decolonizing Time: Work, Leisure, and Freedom*. Springer.

Shringarpure, Bhakti. (2019). *Cold War Assemblages: Decolonization to Digital*. Routledge.

Sian, Katy P. (2019). *Navigating Institutional Racism in British Universities*. Springer.

Siddiqui, Kalim. (2020). 'The Political Economy of the Slave Trade, Capital Accumulation and the Rise of Britain'. *World Financial Review*. 6 February. https://www.researchgate.net/publication/339458064_2020_The_Political_Economy_of_the_Slave_Trade_-_Capital_Accumulation_and_the_Rise_of_Britain_WFR (Accessed 17 February 2022).

Simpson, Audra. (2007). 'On Ethnographic Refusal: Indigeneity, "Voice" and Colonial Citizenship'. *Junctures: The Journal for Thematic Dialogue* 9: 67–80.

Singh, Juliette. (2017). *Unthinking Mastery: Dehumanism and Decolonial Entanglements*. Duke University Press.

Sirmans, M. Eugene. (1962). 'The Legal Status of the Slave in South Carolina, 1670–1740'. *The Journal of Southern History* 28(4): 462–73.

Sites, William. (2021). *Sun Ra's Chicago: Afrofuturism and the City*. University of Chicago Press.

Skloot, Rebecca. (2017). *The Immortal Life of Henrietta Lacks*. Broadway Paperbacks.

Smith, Linda Tuhiwai. (2013). *Decolonizing Methodologies: Research and Indigenous Peoples*. Zed Books Ltd.

Solarz, Marcin Wojciech and Małgorzata Wojtaszczyk. (2015). 'Population Pressures and the North–South Divide between the First Century and 2100'. *Third World Quarterly* 36(4): 802–16.

Solón, Pablo. (2018). 'Vivir Bien: Old Cosmovisions and New Paradigms'. *Great Transition Initiative* (February). http://greattransition.org/publication/vivir-bien (Accessed 17 February 2022).

Spillers, Hortense J. (1987). 'Mama's Baby, Papa's Maybe: An American Grammar Book'. *Diacritics* 17(2): 65–81.

Spivak, Chakravorty Gayatri. (1988). 'Can the Subaltern Speak?' In Nelson, Cary and Lawrence Grossberg (eds). *Marxism and the Interpretation of Culture*. 271–313. University of Illinois Press.

Springgay, Stephanie and Sarah E. Truman. (2022). 'Critical Walking Methodologies and Oblique Agitations of Place'. *Qualitative Inquiry* 28(2): 171–6.

Stanford-Xosei, Esther. (2019). 'The Long Road of Pan-African Liberation to Reparatory Justice'. In Adi, Hakim (ed). *Black British History: New Perspectives*. 176–98. Zed Books Ltd.

Stanley, Christopher. (1988). 'Training for the Hierarchy? Reflections on the British Experience of Legal Education'. *The Law Teacher* 22(2): 78–86.

Starhawk. (2008). *Webs of Power: Notes from the Global Uprising*. New Catalyst Books.

Stemplowska, Zofia. (2021). 'The Rhodes Statue: Honour, Shame and Responsibility'. *The Political Quarterly* 92(4): 629–37.

Stewart, Brian M. (2012). 'Chronolawgy: A Study of Law and Temporal Perception Note'. *University of Miami Law Review* 67(1): 303–28.

Stewart, Lynn. (1995). 'Louisiana Subjects: Power, Space and the Slave Body'. *Ecumene* 2(3): 227–45.

Stokely Carmichael (Kwame Ture). (2007). *Stokely Speaks: From Black Power to Pan-Africanism*. Chicago Review Press.

Stolker, Carel. (2015). *Rethinking the Law School: Education, Research, Outreach and Governance*. Cambridge University Press.

Sundiata, Ibrahim K. (1974). 'Prelude to Scandal: Liberia and Fernando Po, 1880–1930'. *The Journal of African History* 15(1): 97–112.

Sundiata, Ibrahim K. (1996). *From Slaving to Neoslavery: The Bight of Biafra and Fernando Po in the Era of Abolition, 1827–1930*. University of Wisconsin Press.

Tafira, Kenneth. (2015). 'Why Land Evokes Such Deep Emotions in Africa'. *The Conversation*. 27 May. https://theconversation.com/why-land-evokes-such-deep-emotions-in-africa-42125 (Accessed 17 February 2022).

Táíwò, Olúfẹmi O. (2019). 'States Are Not Basic Structures: Against State-Centric Political Theory'. *Philosophical Papers* 48(1): 59–82.

Táíwò, Olúfẹmi O. (2021). 'Reconsidering Reparations: The Movement for Black Lives and Self-Determination'. In Hogan, Brandon, Michael Cholbi, Alex Madva, and Benjamin S. Yost (eds). *The Movement for Black Lives: Philosophical Perspectives*. 93–115. Oxford University Press.

Táíwò, Olúfẹmi O. (2022). *Reconsidering Reparations*. Oxford University Press.

Tamale, Sylvia. (2020). *Decolonization and Afro-feminism*. Daraja Press.

Tatour, Lana. (2019). 'The Culturalisation of Indigeneity: The Palestinian-Bedouin of the Naqab and Indigenous Rights'. *The International Journal of Human Rights* 23(10): 1569–93.

Taylor, Charlotte. (2020). 'Representing the Windrush Generation: Metaphor in Discourses Then and Now'. *Critical Discourse Studies* 17(1): 1–21.

Tella, Oluwaseun. (2016). 'Understanding Xenophobia in South Africa: The Individual, the State and the International System'. *Insight on Africa* 8(2): 142–58.

Tharoor, Shashi. (2017). '"But What About the Railways … ?" The Myth of Britain's Gifts to India'. *The Guardian*. 8 March. https://www.theguardian.com/world/2017/mar/08/india-britain-empire-railways-myths-gift (Accessed 17 February 2022).

Tharoor, Shashi. (2018). *Inglorious Empire: What the British did to India*. Penguin UK.

The Republic of Ecuador National Planning Council. (2009). *National Plan for Good Living 2009–2013: Building a Plurinational and Intercultural State (Summarized Version)*. https://www.planificacion.gob.ec/wp-content/uploads/downloads/2016/03/Plan-Nacional-Buen-Vivir-2009-2013-Ingles.pdf (Accessed 17 February 2022).

Thomas, Keith. (1973). *Religion and the Decline of Magic: Studies in Popular Beliefs in Sixteenth and Seventeenth-Century England*. Penguin UK.

Thomson, Alan. (1987). 'Critical Legal Education in Britain'. *Journal of Law and Society* 14(1): 183–97.

Thornton, Margaret. (1998). 'Technocentrism in the Law School: Why the Gender and Colour of Law Remain the Same'. *Osgoode Hall Law Journal* 36(2): 369–98.

Todd, Zoe. (2020). '(An Answer)'. *Anthrodendum* (blog). https://anthrodendum.org/2020/01/27/an-answer/ (Accessed 17 February 2022).

Traber, Daniel. (2007). *Whiteness, Otherness and The Individualism Paradox from Huck to Punk*. Springer.

Travis, Mitchell. (2015). 'We're All Infected: Legal Personhood, Bare Life and The Walking Dead'. *International Journal for the Semiotics of Law-Revue internationale de Sémiotique juridique* 28(4): 787–800.

Tsosie, Rebecca. (2000). 'Land, Culture, and Community: Reflections on Native Sovereignty and Property in America Property, Wealth, and Inequality'. *Indiana Law Review* 34(4): 1291–312.

Tuck, Eve. (2009). 'Suspending Damage: A Letter to Communities'. *Harvard Educational Review* 79(3): 409–28.

Tuck, Eve and K. Wayne Yang. (2012). 'Decolonization Is Not a Metaphor'. *Decolonization: Indigeneity, Education & Society* 1(1): 1–40.

Tuck, Eve and Marcia McKenzie. (2014). *Place in Research: Theory, Methodology, and Methods*. Routledge.

Turner, K.B., David Giacopassi, and Margaret Vandiver. (2006). 'Ignoring the Past: Coverage of Slavery and Slave Patrols in Criminal Justice Texts'. *Journal of Criminal Justice Education* 17(1): 181–95.

Twining, William L. (1994). *Blackstone's Tower: The English Law School*. Stevens.

Tzouvala, Ntina. (2019). 'A False Promise? Regulating Land-Grabbing and the Post-Colonial State'. *Leiden Journal of International Law* 32(2): 235–53.

Tzouvala, Ntina. (2020). *Capitalism as Civilisation: A History of International Law*. Vol. 142. Cambridge University Press.

Uchendu, Egodi and Uche Okonkwo. (2021). 'The Aba Women's War of 1929 in Eastern Nigeria as Anti-Colonial Protest'. In Hobson, Janell (ed). *The Routledge Companion to Black Women's Cultural Histories*. 245–54. Routledge.

UN General Assembly. (2007). 'United Nations Declaration on the Rights of Indigenous Peoples'. *UN Wash* 12: 1–18.

Van Deusen, Nancy E. (2015). *Global Indios: The Indigenous Struggle for Justice in Sixteenth-Century Spain*. Duke University Press.

Varela, Raquel, and João Louçã. (2020). 'African Forced Labour and Anti-colonial Struggles in the Portuguese Revolution: A Global Labour History Perspective'. In Brandon, Pepijn, Peyman Jafari, and Stefan Müller (eds). *Worlds of Labour Turned Upside Down: Revolutions and Labour Relations in Global Historical Perspective*. 199–223. Brill.

Vázquez, Rolando. (2012). 'Towards a Decolonial Critique of Modernity: Buen Vivir, Relationality and The Task of Listening'. *Capital, Poverty, Development, Denktraditionen im Dialog: Studien zur Befreiung und interkulturalität* 33: 241–52.

Vázquez, Rolando. (2017). 'Precedence, Earth and the Anthropocene: Decolonizing Design'. *Design Philosophy Papers* 15(1): 77–91.

Veracini, Lorenzo. (2011). 'Introducing Settler Colonial Studies'. *Settler Colonial Studies* 1(1): 1–12.

Veracini, Lorenzo. (2014). 'Understanding Colonialism and Settler Colonialism as Distinct Formations'. *Interventions* 16(5): 615–33

Verges, Françoise. (2020). *A Decolonial Feminism*. Ubu Publisher.

Wa Thiong'o, Ngugi. (1992). *Decolonising the Mind: The Politics of Language in African Literature*. East African Publishers.

Waites, Bernard. (1999). *Europe and the Third World: From Colonisation to Decolonisation c.1500–1998*. Macmillan International Higher Education.

Walcott, Rinaldo. (2015). 'Genres of Human: Multiculturalism, Cosmopolitics, and the Caribbean Basin'. In McKittrick, Katherine (ed). *Sylvia Wynter: On Being Human as Praxis*. 183–202. Duke University Press.

Walker, Timothy. (2007). 'Slave Labor and Chocolate in Brazil: The Culture of Cacao Plantations in Amazonia and Bahia (17th–19th Centuries)'. *Food and Foodways* 15(1–2): 75–106.

Wallman, Diane. (2014). 'Slave Community Food Ways on a French Colonial Plantation'. In Bérard, Benoît (ed). *Bitasion: Archéologie des Habitations-Plantations des Petites Antilles* (*Lesser Antilles Plantation Archaeology*). Sidestone Press Academics. 45–68.

Walters, Wendy W. (2017). '"Still in the Difficulty": The Afterlives of Archives'. In Johnson, Erica L. and Éloïse Brezault (eds). *Memory as Colonial Capital: Cross-Cultural Encounters in French and English*. 179–98. Palgrave Macmillan.

Ward, Ian. (2019). 'A Painted Ship and a Painted Ocean: Gregson v Gilbert Revisited'. In Battisti, Chiara and Fiorato, Sidia (eds). *Law and the Humanities: Cultural Perspectives*. 233–48. De Gruyter.

Warmington, Paul. (2015). 'Dystopian Social Theory and Education'. *Educational Theory* 65(3): 265–81.

Webb, Derek A. (2014). 'The Somerset Effect: Parsing Lord Mansfield's Words on Slavery in Nineteenth Century America'. *Law and History Review* 32(3): 455–90.

Weheliye, Alexander G. (2014). *Habeas Viscus: Racializing Assemblages, Biopolitics, and Black Feminist Theories of the Human*. Duke University Press.

Welzel, Christian. (2011). 'The Asian Values Thesis Revisited: Evidence from the World Values Surveys'. *Japanese Journal of Political Science* 12(1): 1–31.

Wickramasinghe, D.W. Ananda and Donald C. Cameron. (2005). 'British Capital, Ceylonese Land, Indian Labour: The Imperialism and Colonialism of Evolution of Tea Plantations in Sri Lanka'. *Proceedings of the 4th International Critical Management Studies Conference, New Zealand*, 4–6.

Wilde, Oscar. (1969). *The Soul of Man under Socialism*. Floating Press.

Wilderson III, Frank B. (2015). *Incognegro: A Memoir of Exile and Apartheid*. Duke University Press.

Wilderson III, Frank B. (2020). *Afropessimism*. Liveright Publishing.

Williams, Damien Patrick. (2020). 'Fitting the Description: Historical and Sociotechnical Elements of Facial Recognition and Anti-Black Surveillance'. *Journal of Responsible Innovation* 7(sup1): 74–83.

Williams, Eric. (2014). *Capitalism and Slavery*. UNC Press Books.

Williams, Patricia J. (1988). 'On Being the Object of Property'. *Signs: Journal of Women in Culture and Society* 14(1): 5–24.

Willis, Anne-Marie. (2006). 'Ontological Designing'. *Design Philosophy Papers* 4(2): 69–92.

Willoughby, Christopher D.E. (2018). 'Running Away from Drapetomania: Samuel A. Cartwright, Medicine, and Race in the Antebellum South'. *Journal of Southern History* 84(3): 579–614.

Wilson, August and Michael Stewart. (1985). *Ma Rainey's Black Bottom*. Concord Theatricals.

Wilson, Francis. (2011). 'Historical Roots of Inequality in South Africa'. *Economic History of Developing Regions* 26(1): 1–15.

Wing, Adrien Katherine (ed). (2000). *Global Critical Race Feminism: An International Reader*. NYU Press.

Wittmann, Nora. (2016). 'Reparations: Legally Justified and Sine qua Non for Global Justice, Peace and Security'. *Global Justice: Theory Practice Rhetoric* 9(2): 199–219.

Wolfe, George C. (director). (2020). *Ma Rainey's Black Bottom*. Escape Artists, Mundy Lane Entertainment, Netflix. 1 hour 34 minutes.

Wolfe, Patrick. (2006). 'Settler Colonialism and the Elimination of the Native'. *Journal of Genocide Research* 8(4): 387–409.

Wolfe, Patrick. (2007). 'Corpus Nullius: The Exception of Indians and Other Aliens in US Constitutional Discourse'. *Postcolonial Studies* 10(2): 127–51.

Wolfe, Patrick. (2016). *Traces of History: Elementary Structures of Race*. Verso Books.

Wood, Ellen Meiksins. (1997). 'Modernity, Postmodernity or Capitalism?' *Review of International Political Economy* 4(3): 539–60.

World Bank. (2013). *Growing Africa: Unlocking the Potential of Agribusiness*. World Bank. https://doi.org/10.1596/26082 (Accessed 17 February 2022).

Wright, Shelley. (2001). *International Human Rights, Decolonisation and Globalisation: Becoming Human*. Vol. 3. Psychology Press.

Wynter, Sylvia. (1995). 'The Pope Must Have Been Drunk, the King of Castile a Madman: Culture as Actuality, and the Caribbean Rethinking Modernity'. In Ruprecht, Alvina Roberta and Cecilia Taiana (eds). *The Reordering of Culture: Latin America, the Caribbean and Canada in the Hood*. 17–41. McGill-Queen's Press.

Wynter, Sylvia. (2003). 'Unsettling the Coloniality of Being/Power/Truth/Freedom: Towards the Human, After Man, Its Overrepresentation – an Argument'. *CR: The New Centennial Review* 3(3): 257–337.

Wynter, Sylvia. (2013). 'Towards the Sociogenic Principle: Fanon, Identity, the Puzzle of Conscious Experience, and What It Is Like to Be "Black"'. In Gomez-Moriana, Antonio and Mercedes Duran-Cogan (eds). *National Identities and Sociopolitical Changes in Latin America*. 30–66. Routledge.

Yanagihara, Hanya. (2016). *A Little Life*. Pan Macmillan.

Yang, K. Wayne (writing as la paperson). (2017). *A Third University Is Possible*. University of Minnesota Press.

Yaszek, Lisa. (2006). 'Afrofuturism, Science Fiction, and the History of the Future'. *Socialism and Democracy* 20(3): 41–60.

Zook, George Frederick. (1919). 'Chapter II: The Royal Adventurers in England'. *The Journal of Negro History* 4(2): 143–62.

Cases Cited

Butts v Penny (1677) 2 Lev. 201, 83 E.R. 518.
Cooper v Stuart (1889) 14 App Cas 286.
Donoghue v Stevenson (1932) A.C. 562.
Gelly v Cleve (1694) 1 Ld. Raym. 147, 91 E.R. 994.
Gregson v Gilbert (1783) 99 ER 629.
Hall v Brooklands Auto Racing Club (1933) 1 K.B. 205.
Hudgins v Wrights (1806) 11 Va. (1 Hen. & Mun.) 134. https://lawlibrary.wm.edu/wythepedia/images/e/eb/HeningHudginsVWrights1808.pdf (Accessed 17 February 2022).
Milirrpum v Nabalco Pty Ltd (1971) 17 FLR 141.
Re Southern Rhodesia (1919) A.C. 211.
Smith v Gould (1706) 92 ER 338.
Somerset v Stewart (1772) 98 ER 499.
Southern Pacific Co v Jensen (1916) 244 US 205.
Vaughan v Menlove (1837) 132 Eng. Rep. 490.
Wi Parata v The Bishop of Wellington (1877) 3 NZ Jur (NS) 72.
William Cooper v The Honourable Alexander Stuart (New South Wales) (1889) UKPC 1.

Index

A

abolition 12, 15, 53, 55–6
  theories of 121–2
academic objectivity, claims to 6
academic scholarship 40–1
academic staff 4–5, 150
accumulation 18, 71, 94, 109, 119–20
  through dispossession 33
  logics of 98
  purposes of 72
  values of 122
Africanfuturism 125–6
Afrofuturism 125–6
Afropessimism 111
Ahmed, Sara 39
Anderson, Elijah 115
Anghie, Antony 48
annihilation 101
  intellectual tools of 41–2
anti-Blackness 18–19, 60, 82–4
anticolonialism
  movements 20, 29, 32, 40
  politics 33
antiracism
  scholarship 145
Anzaldua, Gloria 101
Appleton, Nayantara Sheoran 136
Aristotle 72
articulation, politics of 96–7
atrocity 61–2
authoritative power 8

B

Baars, Grietje 11
Baldwin, James 15, 121
Bar Standards Board (BSB) 2
belonging, technologies of 101
Benjamin, Ruha 36
Bhabha, Homi K. 23
Bhambra, Gurminder K. 131
Bhandar, Brenna 75–6
biological race 51
biopolis 80
  emergence of 80

Black Lives Matter 33–4
Black lives movement 120
Black Marxism 31
Black people 31, 51, 156
Black Radical Tradition (BRT) 30–1
bodies, marking of 79
body-politics 88
borderisation 21, 83
Bravo, Karen E. 75
BRT *see* Black Radical Tradition (BRT)
BSB *see* Bar Standards Board (BSB)

C

Cabral, Amilcar 23–4, 108–9, 153
canon 3, 15, 29, 144–5
capital accumulation 10–11, 54, 62, 78, 114
capital appropriation 66
capitalism 33, 151
  way of assigning value 154
capitalist-colonial-enslavement project 39–40, 45, 49–50, 105, 150
capitalist-colonial interest protection 139
capitalist-colonial machine 132
capitalist-colonial power 76
Cartesian dualism 71–2, 85–6, 88, 112, 134
cartographical logics 102
categorisation, modes of 69
Cesaire, Aime 14–15
citationality 144–5
civilisation 21
classroom activity 140
climate change 154
closed thinking 36–7
Coates, Ta-Nehisi 108–9, 120
coerced labour 17
coercive power 8, 74, 103, 131, 153
  Euro-modern law's 39–40
  historical origins of 133
  structures of 33
Cohen, Felix S. 7–8
collaborative growth, visions of 132
collective power, active communality of 153–4

colonial/colonialism 9–10, 15–16, 20–1, 24, 26, 33, 38–40, 47, 68, 81–2, 106, 130, 142–3, 151, 156
  administration 139
  borders 99
  critiques of 25, 29–30
  definition of 10
  design and spirit of 65
  dispossession 119, 121–2
  economic and political emancipation from 23
  emergence and maintenance of 35
  epistemologies 46, 73, 107
  incursion 139
  infectability of 75
  intellectual labour of 41
  interaction, diverse nature of 26
  justification 139
  lands, Euro-modern law ventures into 57–62
  languages 28–9
  law 140
  logics of 25, 62, 74, 157
  management 139
  mapping 92
  material and structural benefits of 22
  matrix of power 72
  micro and macro analysis of 32
  operations 80
  possessions 98
  power 22, 35, 123
  practices of 74
  product of 49
  repudiation of 24
  responses to 27
  sacrifice zones of 92–3
    land 93–101
    legal spaces 105–7
    reproduction of commodification 101–5
  stage of 43
  state's emergence with 74–5
  technologies 69
  teleology 122
  time and temporalities of 116
  transformation of 22
  violence 114
  workings of 149
coloniality of power 68
colonial knowledge
  enfoldment of 72–3
  production of 69, 151
  systems 67
colonial logics 28–30, 40, 48–9, 74, 81–3, 90, 111, 120–1, 129, 136, 138, 148, 151
  application of 60
  disruption of 154
  dominance of 32
  influences of 92–3
  intractability of 115
  operation of 149
  survival of 82
colonisation 18, 43, 70, 94
  designation for 19
  exploitative 94
  logics and praxes of 103
  processes of 150
colonised territory 19
Columbus, Christopher 16
commercial affluence 19–20
commodification 66
  colonial logics of 150
  reproduction of 101–5
communal collective power 154
communal process 134
community, definition in 107
constriction 66
consumerisation of higher education 4
contingency, operations of 115
corporate power, value of 49
corporate violence 60
Crenshaw, Kimberlé Williams 6
CRF *see* Critical Race Feminism (CRF)
Critical Race Feminism (CRF) 74
Critical Race Theory (CRT) 30, 32, 74
curriculum 129, 137–9, 152
cyclical time 123–4

D

Dakota Access Pipeline protests 104–5
Darian-Smith, Eve 9–10
d'Aspremont, Jean 48
decolonial disruption 139
decolonial work 155
decolonisation 16, 65, 88, 98, 106, 121–2, 124, 145–6, 150
  in academic practices 136
  analogy on colonial table 21–33
  areas of interest to 140
  citationality 144–5
  contemporary demands for 21
  critical adoption of 11
  definition of 15
  demands of 12, 30
  description of 14–16
  within disciplines 148
  discourse on 141
  eternal need of 130
  failure of 24
  for higher education 33–7
  and law schools 130–6, 148
  and legal knowledge 39
  movements 30
  political moves for 20
  potential impossibility of 149
  project of 129
  promise of 9–10
  prospect of 151

INDEX

radical language of 16
radical visions of 136
research agendas and practices 142–4
strategies 12
template for 136
theories of 12, 14–15, 32, 35, 136
voyage of colonial discovery 16–21
decolonised curriculum 139
defragmentation approach 131
dehumanisation 70–1, 74
demarcation, governance and legitimation of 51
Dery, Mark 125
de Sousa Santos, Boaventura 44–5, 134
disciplinarity, suspension of 28
disciplinary decadence 44, 131
discrimination, structural teleology of 40–1
discriminatory scholarship 42–3
disembodiment 134
disobedient relationality 157
dispossession 71, 94, 109, 119–20
  logics of 98
  technologies of 62
diversity 1, 4, 9, 146
Donoghue, May 116
'double-blind' peer reviews 142
Douglass, Frederick 121
drapetomania 157
DuBois, W.E.B. 31, 70

E

earth
  deterioration of 154
  justice and survival of 155
economic vulnerability 57–8
Edkins, Jenny 126
El-Enany, Nadine 49
Elkins, Caroline 60
Eltis, David 18
enclosure, colonial logics of 135
English common law 52
enslavement 18, 55, 120
  abolition of 55
  African labour for 43, 50
  Euro-modern legal journeys in 49–57
  practices of 96
epistemic dispossession 66
epistemicides 41
epistemic violence 150
epistemologies 44, 68–9, 130–1
Equality Act (2010) 71
equality, motives of 79
ethnicity, use of 70
ethnocentrism, natural tendency for 19
Eurocentrism 18–19, 40, 44, 137
Euro-modern academy 157
Euro-modernity 29, 72, 105–6, 113–14, 129
  boundaries of 126
  globalisation of 110
  legal 61, 103–4, 109, 134, 145

linearity 110
objectivity 9
recognition by 48–9
selective destructiveness of 67
temporality 124
time in 121
university 150
Euro-modern law 4, 6, 8, 15–16, 47, 65, 117
  colonial ontology 46–9
  entanglement of 65
  nature of 39
  school 145–7
  spaces of 134
European trading companies 60
exploitative colonisation 94, 97, 138
extractivism 132
Eze, Emmanuel Chukwudi 42

F

Fabian, Johannes 141–2
famines, colonial maladministration of 17
Fanon, Frantz 82, 89–90, 108–9
financialisation 150
flag independence 150
Foucault, Michel 1, 79–80
  analysis 81
  biopolitical ascription 80
fragmentation 66
Freire, Paulo 132
French Code Noir 50

G

Gandhi, Mahatma 23
Garvey, Marcus 31
gender, mathematical conjunction of 73
geopolitical inter-dynamics 20–1
Getachew, Adom 26
Gilmore, Ruth Wilson 31–2, 81–2, 112
Gladstone, William 18
global abyssal thinking 47
global colonial economy 17
global inequality 18
globalisation 16
  of Euromodernity 110
Global North 21, 78, 99–101, 141
  decolonising movements in 34
  higher education in 10, 128–9
  institutions 136
  ivory towers 29
  legal knowledge within 130
  racial state in 49
  universities in 34, 142, 151
global power structures 20
Global South 10, 78, 100–1, 128, 143
  communities in 141–2
  land and labour in 99
  resources 21

scholars and marginalised populations 145
Goldberg, David Theo 49, 115
Gordon, Lewis R. 37, 44, 82, 131
Grabham, Emily 117, 124
Grenfell fire 122–3
Grosfoguel, Ramon 45

H

Haraway, Donna 85–6
Harris, Cheryl I. 76
Hartman, Saidiya V. 88–9, 155
hermeneutical injustice 73
hetero-patriarchal racial capitalism 149
Hickel, Jason 102
Hicks, Dan 58
hierarchisation 65
  legitimation of 40
higher education
  consumerisation of 4
  features of 150
  in Global North 10, 128–9
  institutions of 150
  standardisation measures across 150
historical injustices 119
Holmes, Oliver W. 38–9
human/body 76, 128–30
  closure, settlement, and negation of 45
  colonialism 76–84
  concepts of 67
  conceptualisations of 88
  contours of 84–5
  decolonisation 130–6
  definition of 66
  epistemologies of 139
  Euro-modern law school 145–7
  labour 93–4
  law curriculum 137–40
  praxis 137
  as property 53
  research agendas and practices 140–4
  status, generated differences in 52
  visions of 130–6
humanity 11, 38–9, 92–3, 119–21
  classifications of 47, 69
  and earth 2
  expense of 133
  hierarchisation and delegitimisation of 44–5
  importance and essence of 87
  micro-regulation of 64
  structural hierarchisation of 43
Hurricane Katrina 122
Hut Tax War of 1898 60

I

Icaza, Rosalba 12
IKS *see* indigenous knowledge systems (IKS)
imperial capital 79
imperialism 20

imperial power, technology of 67
indigenous dispossession 7
indigenous jurisprudences 26, 62–3
indigenous knowledge systems (IKS) 7, 86–7
indigenous land 47, 100
  dispossession of 31
  unfree labour and appropriation of 45
indigenous population 16, 25–6, 43
individual racism 31
institutionalised racism 79
intellectual knowledge systems 44
international law 47
  antiquity of 48
  colonialism and immiseration of 48
  coloniality of 48–9
international legal order 47
intersubjectivity, relations of 137
intra-European conflict 59
Ireland, landlords in 95

J

Jivraj, Suhraiya 138
judicial precedent 116
jurisdictions 139
  borders of 8
jurisprudence 40, 62–4, 66
  for future 148
  indigenous 26, 62–3
  legal 47
justice 9–10
  anti-colonial political project of 128
  through legal knowledge 45–6
  motives of 79

K

Kimmerer, Robin Wall 93
knowledge 152–3
  and colonialism 108–9
  commodification of 143, 150
  coproduction of 138
  creation and cultivation 133
  cultivation 135–6, 138, 152
  formats 143
  production 132, 134
  structures of 132
  systems 150–1
Kreijen, Gerard 48

L

labour
  Lockean division of 111
  mathematical valuation of 96
LACDS *see* Latin American and Caribbean decolonial school of thought (LACDS)
land 93
  actual acquisition of 97
  anti-colonial meanings of 106–7
  appropriation 95

INDEX

colonisation of 98
dispossession/commodification of 27, 102, 135
Euro-modern epistemologies of 101
form of acquisition of 96–7
global appropriation of 94–5
improvement of 97
legal alienation of 94
legal epistemology of 98
legal ontology 95
as private property 97–8
profitable use of 101
and space 104
ways of thinking of 99
Latin American and Caribbean decolonial school of thought (LACDS) 26
Latour, Bruno 117
law 1–4
classrooms 116
diversity 4–9
justice 9–10
liberation 9–10
methods and reasoning 131
law curriculum 66, 129
specific areas of 137–40
law schools 5, 10–13, 140, 145–6
cohorts within 140
content and research aims of 3
curricular and research aims 3
decolonisation for 148
institutions of 9
legal knowledge in 7
research in 4
in UK 2, 4–5
law's colonial ontology 38–46
Euro-modern law 46–64
Lefebvre, Henri 75
legal academics 143
legal curriculum 138, 140
legal education 76–7, 123, 138
legal epistemology 99
legal jurisprudences 47
legal knowledge 46, 67, 76–84, 105–7, 109, 113, 115–17, 130–6
claims of 5
cultivation of 135
decolonisation within 39, 64
on Euro-modern temporalities 123
expressions of 117
re-imagining of 49
testamentary life within 84–91
time-space within 131
uninterrogated 79
legal language, imprecision in 52–3
legal learning 139
legal logics, equivocation within 58
legal person, definition of 85–6
legal personality 85
Leroy, Justin 121

liberalism, Euro-modern claims to 89–90
liberal social attitudes 40
liberation 9–10, 153
Liboiron, Max 144
life
dichotomy 79
within legal knowledge 84–91
teleological co-optation of 65
linearity 123–4
Locke, Alain 70, 75, 96–7, 135–6
labour theory of property 96–7
loss, legal principle of 53–4
Luckett, Kathy 138

M

Maldonado-Torres, Nelson 82–3
Manicheanism 28
Manji, Ambreena S. 101
Ma Rainey's band 155
marginalisation 145–6
Martinez-Cobo, Jose R. 86
Marx's critique of capitalism 81
Mau Mau uprisings 60
Mbembe, Achille 40, 80
McIntyre, Michael 80
Mignolo, Walter D. 88
Mills, Charles W. 43
modern-day slavery 122
modernity 102, 113, 123–4
Moreton-Robinson, Aileen 76
Morreira, Shannon 138

N

Naffine, Ngaire 85
Nast, Heidi J. 80
nationalism 23–4
National Student Survey (NSS) 150
necropolis 80
necropolitical–colonial world 40
necropolitics 39–40
Negro 42, 65, 89
neo-colonialism 43
neoliberal universities 151
neutrality 2, 4, 6, 30, 41, 45, 51, 54
Ngatitoa tribe 117
nobody's land 100
non-belonging, technologies of 101
normativity 76, 130, 132–3
North–South academic partnerships 152
NSS *see* National Student Survey (NSS)

O

Obama, Barack 38–9
objectivity 54
universality and 39
Olaniyan, Tejumola 114
ontology 130
Operation Legacy 114

oppressive silencing 132
Oyewumi, Oyeronke 73

P

Palmer, Vernon Valentine 51
Pan-Africanism 125
parochialism, dominant imposition of 40
partus sequitur ventrem 52
patriarchism 33
patriarchy 151
performative duality 55
Petty, William 95–7
place 105
  conceive of 107
  definition of 103
planet, destruction of 151
pluriversity 4–9
political decolonisation 89
political power 154
population loss 17
postcolonialism 22, 27
posthumanism 133–4
Powell, H. Jefferson 51
power
  colonial matrix of 28, 129, 138
  epistemic coloniality of 36
  maldistribution of 39
  mechanisms of 28
  necropolitical structures of 89
  for repair 153–4
  of state/sovereign 153
  structures of 54, 61, 115
  technologies of 77, 115, 129
praxis/praxes 111, 129, 130–1
  dominance of 32
  influences of 92–3
  survival of 82
  specific areas of 137
pre-existing praxis 95
premature death 112
private property 54, 100
Privy Council 41
profitable labour 97
property, definition of 105
public discourse 56–7

Q

QLD *see* qualifying law degree (QLD)
qualifying law degree (QLD) 2
Quijano, Anibal 20

R

racial/race/racialisation/racism 28, 51, 68, 71, 77–8, 81, 88–9, 139, 142–3, 151
  biopolitical function of 81
  capitalism 78, 93
  classification by 69–70

commodification 121
contract 43–4
definition of 31–2, 70–1
enslavement 83, 97, 119, 133, 138
fundamental significance of 115
injustice 70, 156
making 19
mathematical conjunction of 73
modalities of 71
socio-legal operation of 51–2
violence 32
radical break 136
radical language 15, 24, 129
Rankine, Claudia 122
REF *see* Research Excellence Framework (REF)
repair, decolonial demands for 149
reparative justice 149
reproduction, technology of 44
research agendas 142–4
Research Excellence Framework (REF) 142–3, 150
research labour 144
restoration, decolonial demands for 149
Robinson, Cedric 31
Rutazibwa, Olivia U. 130

S

sacrifice zones 102
Said, Edward W. 92
Sankara, Thomas 157
Scotland, landlords in 95
settler colonialism 25–7
shared temporality 122–3
Shilliam, Robbie 132
slave/slavery 54–5
  abolition 121–2
  codes 121–2
  economy 51
  plantations 17
  race 83–4
  rebellions 15
  traders 146
  uprisings 153
slow-violence 61
social constructionism 70
social injustices 2
social power 154
Solicitors Qualifying Examination (SQE) 2, 4
sovereignty 58–9
space 105
  conceive of 107
  definition of 66, 103
  global commodification of 150
  history of 134
space-time 33–4, 141
  commodification of 20
  definition of 66
  distortions and conflations of 112
  epistemologies of 139

INDEX

Euro-modern law school 145–7
experiences 133
jurisdiction in 139
law curriculum 137–40
micro-regulation of 64
praxis 137
research agendas and practices 140–4
structural hierarchisation of 43
visions of 130–6
SQE *see* Solicitors Qualifying Examination (SQE)
state law 47
state policy, legitimation of 67
status quo 151
structural racism 81
structural violence 9
subjectivity, articulations of 144
superiority, ideology of 5

T

teaching 140–1
technologies of inclusion and exclusion 67–8
teleology 132
 of humanity 98
temporal ambiguity 54
temporal dislocation 113
temporality 108–9, 120–1
 contingent nature of 113
 of law 118
 time and 118
terra nullius 58
territorial colonisation 139–40
territorium nullius 58
Thomson, Alan 5
Thornton, Margaret 9
time
 concurrence of 111
 disparate allocations of 136
 Euro-modern linearity of 135
 ruins of 123–7
 and temporality 118
Todd, Zoe 46
trade
 in Africans 17
 in enslaved Africans 60
transdisciplinarity 131
transformation 62
transformational knowledge 150
transportation systems 112
transport goods, infrastructure to 61
Travis, Mitchell 86

Triangle trade 55
true justice 45

U

Ubuntu ways of living 103–4
UKHE, contemporary decolonisation discourse in 66
UK Slave Emancipation Act 56
uncertainty 55, 130–6
unfree labour 20, 27, 82, 97
universality 39, 45, 54
university 4–9, 148–9
 abolition of 152
 Euro-modern 150–3
 financialisation of 143
 in Global North 151
 neo-liberalisation of 150
 power for repair 153–4
 structure of 152
 version of 151–2

V

valuation of entity 56
value assignation, practices of 154
violence 2, 9, 86, 108–9, 119, 126–7
 of abstraction 52
 perquisite of 119
 ruins of time 123–7
 threats of 146
 waters of difficulty 109–23
von Linne, Carl 42
vulnerabilities, combination of 31

W

ways of knowing 154
white ignorance 43
Whiteness 6, 31, 104
white privilege 52
white racial non-disadvantage 52
white supremacy 78
WhyIsMyCurriculumWhite 33–4
Wilderson III, Frank B. 76, 84
Wilson, August 155
Wolfe, Patrick 25
Wynter, Sylvia 16, 89

Y

Yanagihara, Hanya 1
Yang, K. Wayne 105

www.ingramcontent.com/pod-product-compliance
Lightning Source LLC
Chambersburg PA
CBHW051546020426
42333CB00016B/2117